£ 20

Gilles Deleuze

Continuum Studies in Continental Philosophy

Series Editor: James Fieser, University of Tennessee at Martin, USA

Continuum Studies in Continental Philosophy is a major monograph series from Continuum. The series features first-class scholarly research monographs across the field of Continental philosophy. Each work makes a major contribution to the field of philosophical research.

Gilles Deleuze

The Intensive Reduction

Edited by
Constantin V. Boundas

continuum

Continuum International Publishing Group

The Tower Building	80 Maiden Lane
11 York Road	Suite 704
London SE1 7NX	New York NY 10038

www.continuumbooks.com

British Library Cataloguing-in-Publication Data
A catalogue record for this book is available from the British Library.

ISBN-10: HB: 1-8470-6517-1
ISBN-13: HB: 978-1-8470-6517-9

Library of Congress Cataloging-in-Publication Data
Gilles Deleuze : the intensive reduction / edited by Constantin Boundas.
  p. cm.
  Includes index.
  ISBN-13: 978-1-8470-6517-9 (HB)
  ISBN-10: 1-8470-6517-1 (HB)
  1. Deleuze, Gilles, 1925–1995. I. Boundas, Constantin V. II. Title.

B2430.D454G54 2009
194—dc22   2008036065

Typeset by Newgen Imaging Systems Pvt Ltd, Chennai, India
Printed and bound in Great Britain by the MPG Books Group

To Costis and Katerina Tsalas
και φιλων μεν οντων ουδεν δει δικαιοσυνης

Contents

Acknowledgments

The essays included in this volume were first presented in the 2004 Trent University international conference, 'Gilles Deleuze: Experimenting with Intensities.' My thanks go to all of those who answered the call to this fourth and final Trent University gathering for four memorable days of study, a robust exchange of ideas, and a renewal of friendships. Between 1992 and 2004, with the assistance of the Canada Council, I was able to maintain a niche for Deleuze studies in Ontario and to witness the blossoming of the Deleuze scholarship in North America. The kindness of colleagues who came from far away to rural Ontario in order to participate in our Deleuze days made me grateful. With their help, I understood the meaning of Deleuze's claim that encounters—fundamental encounters and the *philia* that they nurture—is what calls for thinking. The present volume is a tribute to all those who made these years possible. Finally, a special acknowledgment and my sincerest thanks go to Antonio Calcagno, editor of *Symposium: Canadian Journal of Continental Philosophy*, on the pages of which these essays first appeared.

Contributors

Darren Ambrose teaches philosophy at the University of Warwick. His work focuses on post-Kantian Continental philosophy, in particular recent continental ethical theory and aesthetics. His most recent writings include *The Persistence of Skepticism: Levinas,* forthcoming; ' "*Illeity*" and the Persistence of Skepticism' in *Pli: Warwick Journal of Philosophy*, 17, Summer 2006; 'Logic of Sensation'—Review of Gilles Deleuze's *Francis Bacon: The Logic of Sensation* in *Pli: Warwick Journal of Philosophy*, 14, Winter 2003; 'Gilles Deleuze'—entry in J. Vickery and D. Costello (eds) *Art: Key Contemporary Thinkers* (Oxford: Berg Publishers, 2006); 'Painting Time With Light: Deleuze, Guattari and Contemporary Filmwork'—forthcoming chapter in S. O'Sullivan and S. Zepke (eds) *Producing the New: Deleuze & Guattari and Contemporary Life* (Continuum, 2007).

Zsuzsa Baross is a cultural theorist currently teaching in the Cultural Studies Program at Trent University. Her current work in the area of cinema, memory, history turns to Godard and Deleuze for inspiration to rethink the cinema as a mnemic apparatus and a temporalizing machine. In her more recent writing, she intervenes in the Godard-Lanzmann debate on the filmability of the Shoah, reflects on the time of the archive, and turns to 'found footage' films as cinematic machines for projecting the 'memories of the future.' Her recent publications include a series of essays on the ethics of writing ('On the Ethics of Writing, after "Bosnia" '; 'The (False) Gifts of Writing,' 'Noli me tangere') and on memory ('Remember to remember the future' and 'the Intolerable').

Bruce Baugh is Professor of Philosophy at Thompson Rivers University (Camloops, BC, Canada). Most recent publications: *French Hegel: From Surrealism to Postmodernism* (Routledge, 2003); 'Sartre, Derrida and Commitment: The Case of Algeria' (*Sartre Studies International* 9, 2003); 'The Influence of German Thought' in C. J. Murray (ed.) *Encyclopedia of Modern French Thought* (Fitzroy Dearborn, 2004); 'Temps, durée et mort chez Spinoza' (*Philosophiques* 29, 2002).

Alain Beaulieu has a PhD in philosophy from the Université de Paris VIII with a thesis on *Gilles Deleuze et la phénoménologie* (Sils Maria/Vrin, 2004).

He has edited the following works: *Gilles Deleuze. Héritage philosophique* (PUF, 2005), *Michel Foucault et le contrôle social* (Presses de l'Université Laval, 2005) and *Michel Foucault and Power Today. International Multidisciplinary Studies in the History of Our Present* (coedited with D. Gabbard, Lexington Books, 2005). He is Professor of Philosophy at the Université de Sudbury (Canada).

Véronique Bergen was born in Brussels in 1962, and has a PhD from the University of Paris (8). She has published a book on Jean Genet (*Jean Genet. Entre mythe et réalité*, preface by M. Surya, De Boeck-Université, 1993); a book on Deleuze (*L'ontologie de Gilles Deleuze*, L'Harmattan, 2001); many articles on Deleuze, Sartre, Badiou, Nietzsche and Bataille; four poetry books (*Brûler le père quand l'enfant dort*; *Encres*; *L'obsidienne rêve l'obscur*; *Habiter l'enfui*); and a novel, *Rhapsodies pour l'ange bleu* (CdM, 2003).

Ronald Bogue is Professor of Comparative Literature at the University of Georgia. He is the author of *Deleuze and Guattari* (1989); *Deleuze on Cinema* (2003); *Deleuze on Literature* (2003); *Deleuze on Music, Painting, and the Arts* (2003), all published by Routledge; and *Deleuze's Wake: Tributes and Tributaries* (2004), published by SUNY Press. He is also the coeditor (with Mihai I. Spariosu) of *The Play of the Self* (1994) and (with Marcel Cornis-Pope) of *Violence and Mediation in Contemporary Culture* (1995), both published by SUNY Press.

Constantin V. Boundas is one of the first translators and commentators of Gilles Deleuze in North America; the editor of *The Deleuze Reader* (New York: Columbia University Press, 1993); with Dorothea Olkowski, of *The Theater of Philosophy: Critical Essays on Gilles Deleuze* (New York: Routledge, 1994) and of *Deleuze and Philosophy* (Edinburgh: Edinburgh University Press, 2006). His translations include (with Mark Lester and Charles Stivale) Gilles Deleuze's *The Logic of Sense* (New York: Columbia University Press, 1990), and Gilles Deleuze's *Empiricism and Subjectivity: An Essay in Human Nature* (New York: Columbia University Press, 1991). Constantin Boundas has published essays on Nietzsche, Gadamer, Deleuze, and Guattari and he is on the editorial board of *Symposium: Canadian Journal for Hermeneutics and Postmodern Thought* and of *Angelaki: Journal of the Theoretical Humanities*. He has been the guest editor of two special issues on Deleuze (*The Journal of the British Society for Phenomenology* 24(1) [Jan. 1993] and *Man and World* 29(3) [July 1996]); the guest editor of a special issue on Rhizomatics, Genealogy and Deconstruction (*Angelaki* 5(3), Summer 2000), and of a special issue on Gift, Theft, Apology (*Angelaki* 6(2), August 2001). He is the Editor of *The Edinburgh Companion to the 20th Century Philosophies*.

Rosi Braidotti is Distinguished Professor in the Humanities at Utrecht University in the Netherlands. She has published extensively in feminist philosophy, epistemology, poststructuralism, and psychoanalysis. Her books include *Patterns of Dissonance* (Polity Press, 1991); *Nomadic Subjects: Embodiment and Sexual Difference in Contemporary Feminist Theory* (Columbia University Press, 1994); *Metamorphoses: Towards a Materialist Theory of Becoming* (Polity Press, 2002). She has co-edited the following: *Women, the Environment, and Sustainable Development. Towards a Theoretical Synthesis* (with E. Charkiewicz, S. Hausler and S. Wieringa) (Zed Books, 1994); *Between Monsters, Goddesses and Cyborgs* (with Nina Lykke) (Zed Books, 1996); *Thinking Differently. A European Women's Studies Reader* (with Gabriele Griffin) (Zed Books, 2002); and numerous essays and chapters in various texts. Her latest book is *Transpositions on Nomadic Ethics* (Polity Press, forthcoming).

Andrew Cutrofello is Associate Professor and Graduate Program Director in the Department of Philosophy at Loyola University, Chicago. He has written several books, including *Continental Philosophy: Contemporary Introduction* (New York: Routledge).

Eugene W. Holland is the author of *Baudelaire and Schizoanalysis: The Socio-poetics of Modernism* (Cambridge, 1993) and *Deleuze & Guattari's Anti-Oedipus: Introduction to Schizoanalysis* (Routledge, 1999). Recent and forthcoming essays include 'Nomad Citizenship and Global Democracy,' forthcoming in *Gilles Deleuze and the Social: Toward a New Social Analytic*; 'Death-State Citizenship,' forthcoming in *Deleuze and the Contemporary World*; 'Studies in Applied Nomadology: Jazz Improvisation and Postcapitalist Markets,' in *Deleuze and Music* (Edinburgh, 2004); 'Optimism of the Intellect . . .,' *Strategies* (2003); 'Representation and Misrepresentation in Postcolonial Literature and Theory,' *Research in African Literatures* (2003); 'On Some Implications of Schizoanalysis,' *Strategies* (2002); 'Nizan's Diagnosis of Existentialism and the Perversion of Death' in *Deleuze and Literature* (Edinburgh, 2000); and 'Infinite Subjective Representation and the Perversion of Death,' *Angelaki: Journal of the Theoretical Humanities* (2000). His new book on *Nomadic Politics* is forthcoming.

Philippe Mengue is teaching in the Collège International de Philosophie in Paris. He is the author of *La Philosophie au piège de l'histoire* (la Différence, 2004); *Deleuze et la question de la démocratie* (l'Harmattan, 2003); *L'ordre sadien* (Kime, 1996); *Deleuze et le système du multiple* (Kime, 1995); 'Les intellectuels et la critique' (*Revue Esprit*, May 2005); and 'The Absent People and the Void of Democracy' (*Contemporary Political Theory*).

Paul Patton is Professor of Philosophy at the University of New South Wales in Sydney, Australia. He is the author of *Deleuze and the Political* (Routledge, 2000), translator of Deleuze's *Difference and Repetition* (Columbia, 1994), and editor of *Nietzsche, Feminism and Political Theory* (Routledge, 1993), and *Deleuze: A Critical*

Reader (Blackwell, 1996). He co-edited (with John Protevi) *Between Deleuze and Derrida* (Continuum, 2003). He was one of the organizers of a major international conference in Canberra in 1997, papers from which have been published as D. Ivison, P. Patton, W. Sanders (eds) *Political Theory and the Rights of Indigenous Peoples* (Cambridge University Press, 2000).

Keith Robinson is Associate Professor of Philosophy at the University of South Dakota. He has interests in post-Kantian philosophy and has published works on Foucault, Deleuze and Whitehead. His most recent book, an edited collection of papers, titled *Deleuze, Whitehead, Bergson: Rhizomatic Connections*, is forthcoming from Palgrave MacMillan (2008).

Daniel W. Smith teaches in the Department of Philosophy at Purdue University. He has translated Deleuze's *Essays Critical and Clinical* (with Michael A. Greco) (University of Minnesota Press, 1997) and *Francis Bacon: The Logic of Sensation* (University of Minnesota Press, 2004). He has also published numerous essays on Deleuze's philosophy and is presently completing a book on Deleuze.

Henry Somers-Hall studied in the philosophy department at the University of Warwick and earned his PhD in July 2008. His research focuses on the criticisms which Deleuze and Hegel raise against 'representation.' He also has a strong interest in the French phenomenological movement, in particular, Merleau-Ponty's later philosophy of difference, and the philosophy of Sartre. His publications include 'Deleuze and Merleau-Ponty: Aesthetics of Difference,' *Symposium, The Canadian Journal of Philosophy* 10(1), Spring 2006; 'Sartre and the Virtual: A Deleuzian Interpretation of The Transcendence of the Ego' *Philosophy Today*, 2006 Supplementary Volume; and 'The Politics of Creation: Peter Hallward and The Philosophy of Creation,' *Pli: The Warwick Journal of Philosophy*, 18, 2007.

Arnaud Villani, docteur ès-lettres in philosophy, is a professor at the lycée Masséna in Nice and teaches at the University of Nice-Sophia Antipolis. He is the author of *La Guêpe et l'Orchidée. Essai sur Deleuze* (Belin, 1999) and General Editor (with Robert Sasso) of *Vocabulaire de Gilles Deleuze* (*Les Cahiers de Noesis* 3, Spring 2003). He has published numerous essays on Gilles Deleuze, including 'La modernité' (*La pensée philosophique française, revue de l'enseignement philosophique* 2, Dec. 1982–Jan. 1983); 'Deleuze et la philosophie microphysique' (*Philosophie Contemporaine, Annales de la Faculté des Lettres et Sciences Humaines de Nice* 49, 1985); 'Géographie physique de Mille Plateaux' (*Critique* 455, April 1985); 'Méthode et théorie dans l'oeuvre de Gilles Deleuze' (*Les Temps Modernes* 585, Jan.–Feb. 1996); 'Gilles Deleuze et les lignes de vie' (*Chimères*, Jan. 1996); 'Deleuze et Whitehead' (*Revue de Métaphysique et Morale*, June 1996); and 'Une généalogie de la philosophie deleuzienne: Empirisme et subjectivité' (*Concepts*, *hors série Gilles Deleuze*, Sils-Maria, 2002). He has also published poems and translations of poems in various journals.

Shannon Winnubst is Associate Professor of Philosophy at Southwestern University. She works at the intersections of twentieth-century French philosophy and feminist, queer, and race theory. She has published, *Queer Freedom: The Limits of Whiteness* (Columbia, 2005), and edited an anthology, *Reading Bataille Now.* She has also published in journals such as *Hypatia* and *Philosophy and Social Criticism.*

Introduction

Constantin V. Boundas

The present collection of essays wants to address some of the outstanding issues in Deleuzian scholarship and to be one more tribute to the 'stutterer,' whose rasping voice and rhizomatic writings do not, despite the passage of time, show signs of loosening their hold on our philosophical imagination. I am sure that I express the sentiments of everyone who has contributed to this volume as I acknowledge here our shared intellectual debt: *'Deleuze a été notre maître.'* While some of us will remember that these are the words Deleuze used once to express his own debt to Sartre, I feel even more comfortable in appropriating them as I begin to see how much the relationship that my colleagues and I have maintained with Deleuze resembles the one he had maintained with Sartre: our intellectual debt to him does not make us his disciples, any more than his debt made him a Sartrean. Never was it more pertinent than it is today to reiterate this thought. There are no Deleuzians; there are only people using Deleuze-blocs and Deleuze diagonal lines of transformation for the sake of creating concepts in philosophy, sensations in the arts, and modes of living in ethics and politics that are not necessarily (and sometimes not at all) Deleuze's.

Gilles Deleuze taught us that philosophy is the creation of concepts aiming, in a precarious manner, to impose, consistency upon a chaos that he himself preferred to see as the seething *apeiron* of Empedocles—rather than as a void and a naught. He placed plenty of demands on the creating philosopher: he asked her to face her canvas, and, like an artist, to begin by wiping away the clichés and the ready-mades of the *doxa* that stand in the way of her creation; to suspend the chattiness that the dominant ideology of communication encourages, and to opt for the desert of thinking and writing—a desert always populated by packs and tribes. The result of this condition, he promised, is not a dreaded *aphasia*, but rather the creative *glossolalia* of indirect discourse. As for the veracity of this *glossolalia*, Deleuze dares us to find it in the interesting and remarkable concepts that would punctuate and sustain it—in other words, in their ability to offer solutions to their parent problems or—perhaps the same thing—in their ability to make existing problems resonate together. *Est enim verum index sui. Salut donc à un maître Spinoziste.*

To create, rather than to represent or to recognize! The artist does not represent or recognize forms; she captures forces. Deleuze allowed this passion for creation to guide his search for an ethical stance that would be in constant experimentation with modes of living and sociability, transcending the moralities of the transcendent ought, the judgment of God, and the omnivorous Self. Such an experimentation, he thought, would locate its own *phronesis* in the wisdom of bodies discovering that, in assemblage with other bodies and in compossibility (in the extension of sympathy, as Hume liked to say), their *vis existendi* is magnified (intensified), and joyful passions point out the directions to adequate ideas. The same passion for creation shows up in Deleuze's politics, the subversive tendencies of which cannot be overlooked: temples are being destroyed as others are being constructed. But these subversive tendencies are framed by the leitmotif that says resistance cannot be a substitute for creation. One escapes exclusive disjunctions by creating something new, not by embracing one of the horns nor by playing the divine game of sublation. To reterritorialize in new institutions, to extend and transform existing jurisprudence, to diagrammatize so that hereto distinct problems begin to resonate together—these are signs of creative praxis. *Salut donc à un maître subversif et pervers.*

Deleuze also taught us to be deeply suspicious of the traditional image of thought, with its postulates of representation and recognition, good sense and common sense, and its preference for solutions and immutable knowledge. In his irreverent moments to attempt to reverse Platonism, he permitted himself this humorous designation of the traditional image: 'good day Theaetetus!' and offered us instead his preference for the chain reaction made possible by what he called 'fundamental encounters,'—one capable of transmitting intensities from one gerund to another (*sentiendum—imaginandum—loquendum—cogitandum*), and capable also of sustaining a new thought of difference that would no longer function as the old prop for identity—the thought of difference in itself. He spoke of *concordia discordata* between faculties, displacing the harmonious dovetailing of all faculties, which subtends the Kantian legacy and the lived body of a certain phenomenological tradition; he stressed the primacy of problems and apprenticeship, instead of solutions and knowledge. *Salut donc à un maître Nietzschéen.*

He fought a good fight against the compromises of psychoanalysis with the ambivalence of the dialectics of the Enlightenment, succeeding in creating the articulation of a new image of the unconscious as a factory of social forces under constant construction, rather than a theater of familial shadows that has to be witnessed and interpreted. He made us see that bodies function at their best when they are no longer, or not yet, organisms but rather surfaces of loosely assembled larval selves (one for the eye, another for the ear, a third for the liver). He launched a theory of impassive and untimely sense—sense best stated through verbal infinitive modes, in the place of phenomenological and hermeneutic meaning, being always expressed in the dative case. He cemented all this with a theory of time that bifurcates into the virtual *Aion* of the event and the actual *Chronos* of matters of fact and states of bodies—seeing the latter as the actualization of the former, and the former as the mobile reference point of all counter-actualizations, without which creative imagination and act would not be possible. *Salut donc à un maître Besgsonien.*

None of these claims could hold water, without Deleuze's transcendental empiricism (the quest for the conditions of actual experience) resting on the bold decision to open up a new domain of philosophical reflection in the new space that is exposed after the performance of an intensive reduction. If becoming is a force field that gives rise to the metastable figures of the same—if, in other words, becoming is the eternal different/ciation of a field of forces (as Deleuze, following Nietzsche, assumes)—the genesis of what comes to be and passes away has to be accounted for in terms of the intensities of forces (their differences and degrees) and in terms of the relations they establish with one other in concrete assemblages. Seizing intensities and calibrating their function demands that we go beyond the given (extended entities), toward that which causes the given to be given, that is, intensity. Without this 'going beyond,' without this intensive reduction, Deleuze's philosophy would make no sense. 'Reduction' of course, in this context, does not mean elimination of something epiphenomenal for the sake of whatever is deemed genealogically fundamental. The world of extended beings, with their provisional identities, is not an illusion. But to the extent that its constitution has to be accounted for, nothing is accomplished by postulating a transcendental foundation conceived in the image and the resemblance of the empirical and the ontic. The Deleuzian intensive reduction safeguards the reality of the actual (the actually given) but strives to account for it through the continuous interaction between the extended actual/real and the intensive virtual/real. In this case, the intensive reduction opens a transcendental field that is not the idealized reflection of the empirical. Virtual intensities raise problems and questions; the actual constitutes solutions and responses; and solutions do not resemble or copy the parent problems. *Salut donc à un maître non-phenomenologue.*

Finally, this tribute would not be complete without acknowledging the charm intrinsic to Deleuze's writings that captivates his readers. This charm is captured in the tension between his sober (some said 'dry') style and the playfulness of his aphorisms. Speaking of Spinoza'a *Ethics*, Deleuze liked to remind us that in Spinoza there are two *Ethics*: that of the axioms, the propositions, and the theorems, where things move slowly and methodically, and that of the scholia: 'Having another style, almost another language . . . herald[ing] the sign or condition of the new man who has sufficiently augmented his power in order to form concepts and convert his affects into actions.' Deleuze's writings may not have marked the distinction between scholia and demonstrations the way that Spinoza has in his *Ethics*, but they do not fail to have their own slow and methodical exposition and argumentation alongside 'the breath of fresh air coming from the backyard.' After a long and involved discussion of repetition and the place that repetition occupies in Freud's psychoanalysis, who among us can ever forget the delight we experienced the first time that we came across the haiku-like verse, 'Je ne répète pas parce que je refoule. Je refoule parce que je répète, j'oublie parce que je répète.'? Who among us escaped the call of the shortest and surest way to displace both a widespread mythology of the unconscious and the sovereign claims of consciousness that is present in what follows: 'Ce n'est pas l' inconscient que fait pression sur la conscience, c'est la conscience qui fait pression et garrot, pour l' empêcher de fuir.' Or again, how can we not feel the fatigue of us moderns that weighs on his speech: 'Le corps grec est une matière informée par une belle forme; il est le corps du savoir et de la croyance. Mais pour les modernes, il y a du temps dans le corps. Le nôtre, c'est un corps fragile, toujours fatigué. Mettre dans le corps la fatigue, l' attente, c'est ça le corps qu' incorpore le temps' (Seminar, November 20, 1984). *Salut donc à un maître styliste bègue.*

Part I

Deleuze and Philosophy

Chapter 1

Deleuze and the Question of Ontology*

Véronique Bergen

From among the many Deleuzes folded into the philosophical arrangement that Deleuze himself produced, how many would you say could be released, or set free as a bundle of conceptual personages capable of mobilizing the kind of perspectivism his work promised? How many representations of Deleuze could be made on the basis of the singular problem we uncover and the means by which we access it? For me, it is enough to say that Deleuze's philosophy is diffracted into as many senses as there are forces taking hold of it, and so I choose to approach his philosophy by following the lit fuse of ontology.

As I trace the construction of Deleuzian thought, I will follow that axis which treats the question of ontology as its golden thread—one that runs through the assemblage of this thought, all the while avoiding becoming the object of a treatment that would abolish the very thing it investigates. Of course, it is not possible to assess the question of ontology unless we inscribe it to the onto-logical montage that Deleuze refined, and thereby come to grips with the full measure by which it breaks free from the Kantian critique. Before I address the first point, however, I will deal with the second.

Transcendental Linkage/Ontology

The transcendental direction that Kant established was a bulwark against ontology: in demanding the conditions for the possibility of knowledge in order to define the zones of its validity, Kant turns the critical horizon into precisely that which derails every move toward Being—every possible access to Being. Inside the disjunction between the transcendental question and ontology—and, as a result, inside the exclusive connection between the crit-ical gesture (basking in its legitimacy) and the ontological ascent (struck by an interdiction)—the discovery of the limits of knowledge reveals the irre-ducible human finitude that characterizes the field of knowledge. Objectivity is accounted for on the strength of the bond between the categories of the understanding and the a priori forms of intuition. Knowledge is knowledge of experience and ceases to exist any longer at the point where an object escapes the conditions of appearance of all objects, that is, spatio-temporality.

Now, the transcendental question in Deleuze breaks away from Kant where, according to Deleuze, transcendental excavation and ontological ascent go hand in hand. At the stage where critique functions as a filter prohibiting intuitions of Being from entering, all the while separating the phenomenal from the noumenal fields, Deleuze brings about the coalescence of critique and ontology within a strict immanentism that detonates the Kantian dualism which sits between phenomenon and noumenon. There is no conflict, nor is there any tension to smoothen out between 'two modes of access that are, at first sight, incompatible.'[1] The ascent to the transcendental field of experience—to that by means of which the given is given—is to grasp Being as Event. Nietzsche is the lever that allows the critique to arc toward genealogy—as a genetic concern, free from judiciary proceedings and legislative worries. Bergson is the one who authorizes Deleuze to articulate the transcendental and the empirical in terms of the virtual and the actual, without deriving the transcendental from empirical forms. In opposition to the conjuring trick and the vicious circle that he attributes to the Kantian derivation of the transcendental from the empirical forms of the subject grounding the object, Deleuze posits a pure transcendental field, itself animated by intensive differences. This transcendental field is not of the order of the meta-empirical; it emerges only when a degree of discombobulation shatters the peaceful concordance of the faculties.[2]

This is why, for Deleuze, the adventure of thought begins where Kant's kingdom of knowledge ends. It is where, having been destabilized by the unthought or by an intense crisis that breaks the happy circularity of subject and object, thought must now reinvent itself through the mobilization of a transcendent and superior use of faculties. Kant's a priori ontic fit between subject and object has as its counterpart the exclusion of all and any adequation between the forms of knowing and the forms of being. On the other hand, in the failure of the ontic concordance and in the disjunctive synthesis of beings, Deleuze finds the other side of a possible harmony at the ontological level. Kant's validation that underwrites the circularity of the supreme principle of all a priori synthetic judgments ('the conditions of the possibility of experience are, at the same time, the conditions of the possibility of the object of experience') imposes a limit on knowledge, and exacts the price of consigning being to the unknowable. Deleuze, on the other hand, detects the mobilization of thought in places where experience, pushed to its limits, exceeds itself and releases quasi-phenomena, no longer disciplined by the linkage of categories and intuitions and therefore incapable of being schematized. For Deleuze, the limit is no longer an insurmountable border, but rather a threshold that can always be transcended and released to a continuous variation twisting it beyond itself. As a result, assailed by a problem that cannot be smoothed out through recognition, thought is conquered whenever it succeeds in rising up to the level of being: what is interesting surges up whenever the activity of judgment is undone; the given is no longer attuned to the forms of knowledge; and the failure of the ontic correspondence between subject and object is replaced by the union of thought and being. With Kant, the diverse is accommodated a priori to the unity of apperception and the advent of a differential being removed from the joint action of concepts and forms of intuitions (like the cinnabar that at times could be red and other times black) would be denied entry.

With Deleuze, on the other hand, thought posits itself when the adjustment of an object to the forms of knowledge breaks down. Only when the certitude of its provenance and the necessity of its destination are denied, when its presumption that it will always remain in its native land and its ability to prejudge what it is going to find are shaken up—only then is thought in a position to engender itself. Only when an ontological problem, a breath of being, or an unthinkable force overturn the coordination of the forms of being that are regulated in advance, is thought capable of liberating itself.

Deleuze's new image of thought, placed under the sign of immanence, ripostes to the intrusion of an outside, which, despite the crisis of the intentional relation at the ontic level, is grafted onto Being. Far from confining himself to a critical mooring that would have barred every route to being, Deleuze rolls the two movements together in one wave—the one that makes thought the fold of being. For Deleuze, the formal nature (the forms of intuition) and the categorical nature (the categories of understanding) of the Kantian transcendental reveal that the (formal and categorical) conditioned has been retrojected to the conditions. To this pseudo-conditioning field, he opposes a non-categorical and non-formal transcendental, which is composed exclusively of forces, intensive differences, and sensible variations.

The modulations that Deleuze produces throughout his work and that affect the nomination of Being—duration, event, univocity, plane of immanence, virtual, life—testify to the fact that Being abides as the unthought, forcing thought to convert itself into what is thinkable. Being is what persists as a problem. The untimely surge of an ontological problem that obliges thought to riposte has as little to do with the Heideggerean modality of appearing and veiling, of presenting and retreating, or of crossing over being, as it has to do with its destiny to disappear from the profit of relations and alliances.

Undoing the links of what, for Deleuze, exists only as interlinked—on the one hand, ontology and the transcendental, on the other, ontology and univocity—François Zourabichvili, ignores the heterodox inflection that Deleuze imposes on Kant, and reestablishes the differences of nature in the very places where Deleuze has managed to dissolve them. Zourabichvili's efforts to undo what he takes to be mixtures, gives the impression that it is less important to disabuse the disoriented commentators than to tear Deleuze himself away from the coup de force that he authorized: his compelling 'identification of ontology with one of its theses' univocity. In other words, one must prevent Deleuze from becoming the victim of the ontological confusion that he himself orchestrated. Zourabichvili arrives at a breathless, deflated, and extenuated being because of a logic of relations that establishes its impertinence and overthrows the plan, and he does so by separating that which finds consistency, so long as it is entangled, and by raising one dimension against another. As he continues with his separation of elements, which for Deleuze tumble together in one and the same wave, he cuts Being off from Event. By the same token, as if in a mirror or by means of an inverse gesture, he curiously joins together things that derive from two heterogeneous planes—Being and knowledge— the kind of knowledge under whose jurisdiction Being would abide.[3] This is what authorizes him to play univocity against ontology, Event against Being, and belief against knowledge.

Ontological Montage

Deleuze's unfolding of the ontological montage sheds light on the site reserved for the question of Being. The ontological montage he proposes links essentially diagrammatic traits coming from Kant (breakthroughs of the pure form of time and the sublime) to traits coming from Spinoza and Nietzsche (univocity of Being—ontological intuition—in the case of the former, and ontology of becoming for the latter).[4] The transcendental turn spurred on by Kant brings the question of time to ontology. Henceforth, thought will be separated from its being through the form of the internal sense of time. A certain distance—a certain crack—is interposed between the determination of the 'I think' and the indetermination of the 'I am,' through the temporal form of determinability. In short, time as a pure and empty form, not subjugated to the circular movement, separates the 'I think' from the 'I am,' shattering the Cartesian identity of the thinking substance. In criticism, this is the first opening that Deleuze finds that would permit thought to escape the empire of recognition. To this breach (time that breaks the coincidence of thought with itself), the breach of the sublime is added, which disorganizes the harmony of faculties. The sublime, in Deleuze's system, is presented as the intrusion of an unthought that, in making the schematization stutter, plunges the faculties (sensibility, memory, reason, thought) into powerlessness and provokes them into leaping onto a superior exercise. No longer assisting each other, each faculty, saturated by its lack of power, ignites another faculty, which in turn, as it deals with its own problem, continues to ricochet off toward yet another faculty. In this process, what each faculty cannot grasp will be revealed only after the fact, as one faculty leans toward one of its sisters.

In the ontological montage, Deleuze grafts these two Kantian diagrammatic traits (thereby tearing off the umbrella that protects them from chaos) onto the two champions of Being's univocity—Spinoza and Nietzsche. The affirmation of a being said in one and the same sense of all beings that names and expresses it, gives immanence its rights: the immanence of being in relation to itself; of thought in relation to itself; and of the one in relation to the other. 'All that Spinozism needed to do for the univocal to become an object of pure affirmation was to make substance turn around the modes—*in other words, to realise univocity in the form of repetition in the eternal return.*'[5] For Being to be said in one and the same sense of all beings, Spinozism must extend the dependence of modes on substance, making substance revolve around its modes. Spinoza, 'the prince of philosophers,' proposed a diagram of the real in terms of forces—degrees of speed and slowness, as well as affects—that would dismiss given identities and pre-existing forms to the advantage of a modulation of the entire world and in the guise of being and thought. This diagram then shifts toward a Nietzschean affirmation of an ontology of becoming and chance.

Following his practice of nuptials against nature, Deleuze links Kantian lines of flight (pure form of time and sublime) to traits drawn from Spinoza and Nietzsche (grafting thought onto the univocal being and ontology of becoming, the one being fecundated by the other). In this frame of paradoxical alliance another image of thought—and therefore of Being—finds its consistency: it lodges thought precisely where the phenomenological agreement of the subject and the object becomes unhinged, enabling power to be installed in the depths of being. With being reduced to passivity, thanks to the intrusion of a paradox, thought is always capable of lifting its limits and coming to reside in the depths of being.

War Machine of the 'and'

Thanks to the distance it takes from the profile that it acquired throughout the history of philosophy, an ontology woven around univocity and immanence is established. It finds its consistency by taking as its foil an ontology of equivocity and analogy, of being as foundation and transcendence. This is why it is important to take the exact measure of the points where Deleuze plays the logic of relations and the logic of the 'and' against ontology. The order-word—'establish a logic of the AND, overthrow ontology, do away with foundations'[6]—that circulates from *Dialogues* to *A Thousand Plateaus* is inscribed in the operations of a war machine intended to radicalize the opposition between the partisans of connective alliances and those faithful to the verb 'to be.' To the apostles of an ontology of equivocity, in which being is used in many senses, mistaken as it is for a principle and a prejudicial transcendental identity, we must oppose the fluidity of the 'and'—the speed of an empiricist war machine—in order to leap outside the representative orientation that led the history of Being 'to attribute to the Same, or the Identical . . . an ontological sense.'[7] The 'is (*est*)' that the 'and (*et*)' must dynamite and dynamize is the equivocal being, established as a foundation.[8] The thought of being's equivocity, insisting on a categorical carving of the real, subsumes the forces of what is transcendental in experience under the grid of originary forms. Through the oblivion of this specious maneuver, of this subreption that does not know itself as such, it propels back into the transcendental field whatever it draws from it. Only the deployment of a thought of univocity will permit us to investigate the common genesis of being and thought as we ascend to a transcendental site, stripped, unmediated, and without the empirical concretions that come to inhabit it in an ad hoc manner. The convocation of a thought-rhizome—spreading through alliances, becomings, transversal linkages, and heterogenesis—dislodges the arborescent thought acquired through filiation and the dogmatic image of thought indexed upon Being taken as a foundation. In other words, the song of immanence carried on the wings of nomadism and the deterritorialization of the 'and' joins the song carried by the univocal being. It seems that a double clearing was needed in order to enact a thought that would risk wrestling with the chaos from which it comes. Connective logic, together with disjunctive synthesis, offers itself as the instrument of guerilla warfare at the service of an ontology of immanence—and not as a weapon aiming at the extinction of the entire ontological continent that was taken.[9]

> To philosophize, for Deleuze, is to be held above the ontological intensive craters that bubble beneath categories and organisms. In other words, it is to take hold of all that occurs in its genetic process, instead of receiving, at the level of sense, 'already made qualities and already constituted extensities' or being satisfied, at the level of bodies, with the laws that Oedipus imposes on the organism.[10]

Deleuze's affirmation that forces compose the truth of forms and the intensive investments of Being sounds like a vulgar acceptance of ontology—of 'a metaphysical discourse that would have told us in the last instance the story with reality'[11]—if one overlooks the movement through which Deleuze focuses on the intensive criterion and extends it into a cognitive one. Schizoid thought grasps the presentation of Being and thought beyond their mediated representations and is capable of deploying their genesis without being content with the reverberation of their empirical concretions, only because, in positing itself by itself, it increases the powers of life and works out fertile connections. This energetic hierarchy and this pragmatic valorization overflow and translate themselves into a cognitive hierarchy, in the context of which the ontology of immanence issues appropriately its decrees on the condition of the real. It is well enough to dissociate oneself from the inflection of a cognitive criterion in the direction of a cognitive hierarchy (see below), but this requires that one recognize at least the stirrings of this inflection in the Deleuzian system.

That an ontology of radical immanence is something hybrid and hetero-dox in relation to the majoritarian ontology, which itself is full of transcend-ence, does not mean that ontology fritters away—that it voids itself and gives way to absence. Unless we withhold the ontological label from everything that deviates from an ontology lost in the vapors of transcendence, a proposition travels, without luggage or a signposted destination, through the arrange-ment of Deleuzian thought: that of an ontology of the virtual, becoming, and immanence.[12]

Open Questions

Over and beyond an all-too-peripheral analysis of the readings that Deleuze generates, over and beyond the confrontation of the points of view that have been brought to bear on his corpus, perhaps this is the right moment to ques-tion a few of the metaphysical theses that he proposed. My examination will be directed at the following three points: (1) the nature and sense of the ascent to Being; (2) the X-ray of a transcendental field composed of forces; and (3) the establishment of an intensive hierarchy.

1. Nature and sense of the ascent to Being   Deleuze has never changed his mind on this point: the importance of the interesting and the remarkable comes from the encounter of a crisis that undoes the organization of an ontic coherence (faculties, organism). There is no thought (or Body without Organs coming from desire) except where it succeeds in installing itself in the depths of the great 'clamor of Being' in the grips of an ontological problem. It is only when the sensori-motor schema breaks down that time presents itself in person 'off its hinges' and is given directly, without any subordination to movement. When the chain stimulus-reflex, perception-reaction, is curbed, a pure optic and sonorous image arises, which is reminiscent of the entrance to the light that accompanies the third kind of knowledge in Spinoza. It is in the very ruination of the intentional relation—whichever face it adopts—that an ascent is produced within the virtual reserve of Being, in the Outside, and yet most intimate, of thought. It is in the very failure of recognition that an intuition of 'the powerful inorganic Life that clasps the world' can rise. The hollow of a figurative and optic catastrophe is what enables Bacon to present forces and bend the invisible to the visible. It is in the failure of Logos—that is, a failure of the intelligence, which, in being ahead of itself will always be on the side of that to which it applies—that Proust is in a position to make time in person visible. We could multiply cases of this sort to infinity.

Deleuze praises Plato for having the intuition of a superior exercise of thought provoked by the rise of signs that cannot be integrated into the order of recognition; but he deplores the fact that Plato immediately betrayed the logic of the paradox under the reassuring hold of representation. By blocking the rise of faculties toward the gerund (the being of the sensible, the being of the memorable, the being of the thinkable), by lowering it to an ontic perspective (harmony of the sensed, remembered, and thought being), he bent the powers of thought as he integrated them into the tropism toward the true, and he restored a familiarity, a *philia*, between the object and the faculties of knowledge.[13] According to Deleuze, the history of philosophy testifies to this securitarian reflex that impels it to code thought by conferring to it a destinal necessity (truth) and occluding its risky and methodless movement of engenderment.

Let us review the requisites of the Deleuzian image of thought. For thought to exist, it is necessary for it to recognize the means by which the given is given—namely, intensive force—and for it to accede to the transcendental field as a condition of the possibility of real experience. But for this to happen, thought must be pushed *past* its limits—to the limits that separate it from non-thought—in short, it has to enter the zones of its powerlessness. Inverting the Copernican revolution according to which the object is transposed with the subject, it is thought now that overturns its compelling ontological problem. Put simply, there is no thought, unless it grafts itself on Being, after having freed itself from every intentional correlate. At the center of Deleuze's vitalism, which in its enveloping immanence prohibits all breaks and any distances between thought and world, thought is nothing but a fold, an inflection of Being, a self-modulation of Being in the Ideas, as if Being rises to its own translation as thought. At this point, a host of questions emerge, causing from inside the Deleuzian apparatus to move as the ontological unison of impersonal thought and the plane of Being—of thought and Life. Perhaps somewhere Deleuze's Idiot speaks through these questions, having picked up the scent of naïvity.

It seems to me that the problem raised by the ontological intuition resides in the indetermination of its proper consistency. Indeed, this intuition proves to be indirect and hollow because it essentially depends on its ability to offer itself as a double contingency that is never won ahead of time, being the possible follow up of a crisis of the intentional relation. In short, with reference to the dialectical operator (the negation of opposition), the ontological intuition seems to be defined by that which it is not: namely, the ontic element with its peaceful correlation, subject-object. Thus, a negative definition presents itself in a way that beckons toward a non-orthodox form of negative theology at the very moment that it is situated in an atheist pantheism. The failure at the level of harmony among ontic forms promises nothing by itself with respect to the construction of a thought having taken hold of Being or in search of Being. There are no signposted leads from one to the other, although the ascent to Being seems to be affirmed by the reversal of the sign that marks the failure of the empirical exercise of the faculties. And this renews the status of the event: nothing happened from the perspective of actualized history, yet everything has changed at the level of becoming and the virtual.[14] Nothing happened at the ontic level, except, of course, the undoing of forms, yet everything has changed at the ontological stage—thought has been installed in the intuition of Being. It is this 'nothing happened, yet everything has changed' that we find in the ascent to Being, the cosmos, the dehumanization of Tournier's Robinson, in the molecular and imperceptible becomings of Bartleby, in the telephonist of Henry James's *In the Cage*, and in the incestuous nuptials—beyond persons—of Pierre and Isabelle de Melville.

One way to discern what is at stake in this 'bonus' at the level of Being—and not to be satisfied to see in it only the contingent counterpart of a 'minus' at the level of beings—is to focus on the equivalence that Deleuze posits between the ontological/ontic, transcendental/empirical, virtual/actual, and molecular/molar. The installation of thought in Being comes to mean that it overcame the ordinary register of recognition and that it re-established contact with the transcendental field, the virtual plane, and the molecular field from which everything is derived. Thought is then of the order of a Clairvoyance,[15] a kind of epiphany, where, thanks to the shock of an encounter or the violence of a problem, it unlimits its powers and enters into an agreement and an adequation with the plane of Being. The freedom of thought is not due to its distance from the world, or its rupture from it, but rather to being encompassed by Being, of which thought is only a cutout, a modulation.

We can, of course, first bring out the fragility of an ascent to Being that affirms itself in an inversion of the sign: an inversion that turns an ontic failure into an ontological success. The intuition of Being is not that of essences, nor that of sense, but rather that of an intensive difference. Inclined to promote a 'moderate, truncated, and mutilated Spinozism,' that would remain at the level of the second kind of knowledge, without the need to reach the third kind where grasping essences takes place,[16] Deleuze makes the ontological intuition a 'pure, patient passivity,' as Blanchot used to say, and, at the same time, a construction: a creative conquest loyal to the transcendental force that engendered it. However, to the question 'what is it that testifies to thought's connection with the great wave of Being, in other words, to the ontological "leap"?' the only possible response seems to be the transmutation of the negative sign, borne by the ontic fiasco, to a sign beyond all signs: a univocal expression that makes thought feel, in the manner *index sui*, that it has been reunited with the being from which it comes.

On the other hand, it is possible to ask whether Deleuze does not lead the poietic part of the understanding to a dead end by placing all mental operations (relevant to the knowledge of the given) under the general banner of recognition, representation, or the dogmatic, orthodox, and moral image of thought. In short, it is possible to ask whether his suspicion toward *doxa* and his disdain for recognition do not oblige him to caricature them in the form of 'good day Theaetetus,' 'this is a triangle,' 'the time is three and a half,' thereby overlooking what has been constructed—and not merely observed—in the arc, stimulus-reflex. In the natural tendency of recognition (in contrast with the forced engendering, which is the source of all thought), the faculties do not apply a priori forms to the object in a blind manner following a pre-given prescription. On the contrary, they have to make them appear in order to construct them. Schizoid thought is the creation of a powerlessness that deposits itself on to the impersonal side and is extirpated after a fierce battle from chaos. Although recognition can never play for such stakes, this could not prevent it from being the enactment of procedures that have been worked out and not mechanically applied (and this is true for their first occurrence and also for those that come after) without being the creation of a totally novel gesture. Inside recognition, which of course can collapse into an idle repetition of a 'refried' evidence, there remains an operatory dimension that Deleuze passes over in silence—a dimension that helps recognition navigate beyond the waters of truth and error.[17]

2. X-raying the transcendental field Following the movement of what is engendered in the order of thought and the order of Being, transcendental empiricism tries to take the pure conditions of real experience to a groundlessness that would be heterogeneous to the empirical concretions that it generates. And whereas, according to Deleuze, the Kantian or Husserlian transcendental deduces its *de jure* from what is *de facto* and copies its conditions from empirical figures, the empiricism that Deleuze calls transcendental or superior does not hypostatize the molar forms of the subject and the object at the level of the virtual as if through a kind of retrospective illusion. The transcendental plane, from which derive the processes of individuation, must no longer be composed of forms (consciousness, object, matter) or of the extensive differences that people the empirical plane. It does not contain any a priori that would characterize the register of the actual but is rather heterogeneous to the latter. For this reason it will be declined according to forces, materials, and events; it will be, in short, a molecular field agitated by intensive differences. Nothing given at the empirical level ought to be presupposed and retrojected; conditions may not be used against that which they engender. Taking into account differences of nature between conditions and the conditioned permits the elimination of a retrospective fiction generated by a representation that takes the engendered for engendering, the explicated for the implicated, and the effect for a genetic agent.

Eliminating the hylomorphism, where the matter of phenomena acquires sense to the extent that it is disciplined by means of a priori forms that are brought to bear on it, transcendental empiricism aims at defusing all subreptions that erase the process of engendering Being and thought for results that are unduly taken to be the main engine of conditioning. Hence the substitution of the possible-real scheme (the vicious circle of a possible drawn *post facto* from a real derived from it through imitation) with the virtual-actual scheme (where the actual bears no resemblance to the virtual from which it is derived).

In order to x-ray that which makes the given be, the ascent toward the genetic 'basement' must traverse the world of representation so that it can reach a pure, non-mediated presentation. At this point, it seems that the problem affecting the intuition of Being reappears: what is it that shows from within that we have reached a site purified of all empirical leftovers apart from the leap beyond the molar forms in the direction of their genetic forge, apart from this kind of epokhē (which is not intended to bracket the world in order to return the object to its essence, but is rather an involuntary and forced transport of the perception of actual forms towards their virtual site)? Once again, lifting the focus from the actual does not *ipso facto* bring about a new focus on the virtual—the one does not at all guarantee the other. Nevertheless, it does discredit empirical signals in favor of a new belief: the belief of having regained the transcendental field. The topology of thought follows the topology of a Moebius strip without breaks as it slides across one and the same plane, and is capable of bifurcating from one regime to the other. From the fact that the actual circuit malfunctioned, it is as if it can be deemed that the apprehension of a large virtual circuit upstream imposed itself, in an enigmatic conversion of loss into gain, in an inversion of valences. It is as if, when the ontic regime fails and is invalidated, an ontological region swells to the very states of affairs, as a constant understudy that persists on the plane of empirical crystallizations. It is because the virtual does not cease to insist in actual productions that the cracking of the latter, without promising the achievement of the former, generates the intuition of having reestablished contact with it. The rise of pure presentation, the opening unto the time of the event that doubles the present, erupts only at the crises of representation, despite the fact that it does not unfailingly derive from the latter. Without being the automatic counterpart of the deregulation of the empirical, the addition of thought to the transcendental is witnessed where forms are deterritorialized and decoded: in other words, in the course of de-subjectivation and de-objectivation.

3. Establishing an intensive hierarchy To the extent that thought is a fold of life, every orientation of thought is a witness to a mode of existing. That schizoid thought succeeds in overcoming the representative mediations, and in espousing its own genesis as the genesis of Being, is observed by one functionalist and pragmatic criterion: it liberates and increases the powers of life. The genealogist sizes up ideas according to their vital forces and their connections. The idea is evaluated according to the effects, trajectories, connections, and the widening field of experience that it generates, and not on the basis of its correspondence with a pre-existing model. The 'interesting' is measured on the basis of the intensification of the life that it brings into being. Representation, on the contrary, testifies to a vile and low truth, to the extent that it extinguishes and lessens the powers of life and decomposes vital relations. Being afraid of life, representation atrophies and muffles forces and, by clinging to the figure of 'the man who wants to perish,' condemns itself to auto-consumption.[18]

It is within the context of this ethological hierarchy of a Spinozist and Nietzschean provenance that Deleuze works out a transposition—one that Spinoza realized but Nietzsche rejected: the derivation of a cognitive criterion from an energetic one. In its manifestation of weakening the powers of life, representation displays the illusion within which it is taken; namely, its spoiling of the transcendental level. In its consonance with the *amor fati* and its exacerbation of vital powers, schizoid thought attests to the fact that its grasp of a transcendental field, agitated by intensive differences presents itself squarely as an ontological assertion. The evaluation of thoughts according to their vitalist consequences makes the difference between reactive and transcendent and immanent assemblages of thought. It is the adoption of an intensive, vitalist typology, one that is immediately doubled by means of a cognitive hierarchy that testifies to the fact that reading the real in terms of ontological univocity yields a presentation of being and thought beyond all representation.

Insisting on 'there are no facts, only interpretations,' Nietzsche blocked every derivation of a cognitive hierarchy from entering an energetic typology: the people of fictions that thought liberates are distinguished only through their link to life—reactive and sick thought, that condemns and etiolates life, or the thought that affirms life. Evaluating conceptual productions through the powers to exist and their approach to life, Nietzsche refers philosophical, scientific, religious, or moral utterances to the one who proffers them—in other words, he interprets systems of value by a life criterion. But a montage of thinking, which increases the powers of life, is not indexed on the cognitive superiority of the one who has traversed the phenomenal level and grasped the essence of Being. Exacerbation of the forces of existence does not testify to a rise to the third genre of knowledge; it is not a sign that Being has been reached, beyond the crossing of masks. On the other hand, it is a Spinozist gesture that permits Deleuze to infer a cognitive hierarchy from an intensive one and to ratify their equivalence.

The problem inhabits this sliding, this translation which is not at all painless, and the consequences it implies. Without further ado, I will contentedly state the problem as follows: ex-communicating every judicative position that would separate the heroes of truth from the inmates of error, Deleuze introduces, from the vantage point of a vitalist typology, a cognitive scission between a thought that goes beyond what it can and a thought that prohibits itself from going to the limits of its possibilities. Even if, to a great extent, the stumbling blocks that were removed and the elucidations that Deleuze proposes do not agree with those that the 'history of philosophy' in its dominant version has established,[19] still, a line of demarcation separates the thought that has conquered itself from one that is entangled inside doxa and transcendence.

The latter, with inverse motives, repeats a scene of exclusion and prejudicial disqualification.[20] With this exportation of an instrument of intensive measurement to a cognitive register, the interesting is taken from the rear by the category of the true. Whereas Nietzsche was referring the true to the language of life, once again Deleuze catapults the criterion of life within the walls of truth.

It suffices to say that the three 'problems of problems' outlined here do not come from meta-problems overhanging those of which they speak; rather, once again they propose to expose that which would otherwise doze off inside the comfortable sedimentations. It is not that we must subject Deleuze to the treatment that he had reserved for the gallery of philosophers (make them a child from behind), but rather we must expose his conceptual machines to games that he himself had not tried, with the intention of introducing them to problems that he put aside or assigned to a secondary rank.

'One can conceive of . . . how to reduce or minorize (*minorer*—a term used by mathematicians), how to impose a minor or minimizing treatment in order to extricate becomings from history, lives from culture, thoughts from doctrine, grace or disgrace from dogma.'[21] We must question each of the pieces of the Deleuzian machine, their presuppositions, logic, utopia, and limits, if we want to prevent their preference for bifurcating roads from turning into its contrary. We must allow for many strong winds to blow through in order for a laugh, a shooting star or a perplexing point to become predisposed to creating an event—or for Deleuze's thought, in all its folded texture, to collide with those gusts that made up his element.

Intra-philosophical post-script: The philosophical domain is not, in my eyes, a domain of *polemos*, of combat,[22] but rather a field where thought reverberates according to points of inflection from which it is summoned. It is, therefore, in the context of this ignition of one thought by another that I conceived that which, somewhere earlier in this chapter, was offered as a response to theses posited by François Zourabichvili. From this point of view, we can speak of modalities that diverge within the folding Deleuzian assemblage—a folding that rejects the pertinence of the ontological plane and another which uses the witch's broom to cement the brick wall that shapes Deleuze's philosophy.

Notes

*Translated by Constantin V. Boundas and Susan Dyrkton

1   'The question that every reader of Deleuze must confront [. . .] is how this thinker could coordinate two positions, which, at first blush, look incompatible: the transcendental and the ontological.' François Zourabichvili, *Une philosophie de l' événement*, in François Zourabichvili, Anne Sauvagnargues, Paola Marrati, *La philosophie de Deleuze* (Paris: Presses Universitaires de France, 2004), 8.

² I am not going to question here the Deleuzian reading of Kant, the cut outs and the shifts that it produces, the axes that it privileges, the parts of the system that it leaves in the shadows, nor am I going to evaluate the maneuvers, and the interpretive operations by means of which, having confined Kant inside a comfortable vulgata, Deleuze succeeds in distinguishing his own position from the position of the critique. For a thoughtful grasp of the Kantian system that wakes Kant up from the *doxa* into which he has for a long time been immersed, see Frank Pierobon, *Kant et la fondation architectonique de la métaphysique* (Grenoble: J. Millon, 1990) and his *Système et réprésentation. Études sur la déduction trsanscendantale des catégories* (Grenoble: J. Millon, 1993).

³ François Zourabichvili, Deleuze. *Une philosophie de l' événement*, 11.

⁴ In addition to this metamorphic repetition of a double arrangement, elements coming from Leibniz (continuity between sensible and intelligible, integration of *petites perceptions*), from Bergson (virtual-actual, typology of multiplicities), or from Simondon (modulation of thought instead of molding, process of individuation) compose the Deleuzian montage of Being.

⁵ Gilles Deleuze, *Difference and Repetition*, trans. P. Patton (New York, Columbia University Press), 304.

⁶ Gilles Deleuze and Félix Guattari (1987) *A Thousand Plateaus, Capitalism and Schizophrenia*, trans. B. Massumi (Minneapolis: University of Minnesota Press), 25.

⁷ Deleuze, *Difference and Repetition*, 301.

⁸ One could say that the reversal of the 'is' (*est*) and the 'and' (*et*) is the reversal of 'Founding' (*Fondement*) and 'Building' (*Bâtiment*). 'The French are like landowners whose source of income is the cogito. They are always reterritorialized on consciousness. Germany [. . .] wants to reconquer the Greek plane of immanence [. . .] It must also constantly clear and consolidate this ground, that is to say, it must lay foundations. A mania for founding, for conquering, inspires this philosophy; what the Greeks possessed autochthonously, German philosophy would have through conquest and foundation, so that it would make immanence immanent *to* something, to its own Act of philosophizing, to its own philosophizing subjectivity (the cogito therefore takes on a different meaning since it conquers and lays down the ground). [. . .] The English are precisely these nomads who treat the plane of immanence as a movable and moving ground, a field of radical experience, an archipelagian world where they are happy to pitch their tents from island to island and over the sea. [. . .] In the Trinity Founding-Building- Inhabiting, the French build and the Germans lay foundations, but the English inhabit. For them, a tent is all that is needed.' Gilles Deleuze and Félix Guattari, *What Is Philosophy?* trans. H. Tomlinson and G. Burchell (New York: Columbia University Press), 104, 105.

⁹ "If there is an orientation of the philosophy of Deleuze, this is it: extinction of the name of 'being' and therefore of ontology [. . .] Deleuze spoke clearly and literally, time and again, of his programme: substitution of 'is' (*est*) by means of 'and' (*et*) or, therefore, substitution of being by becoming [. . .] Contemporary philosophy—Foucault, Derrida, to say nothing of the Anglo-Saxons—has abandoned or overcome ontology. What happiness, ingenious or perfidious, to want by all means to find one in Deleuze!" François Zourabichvili, *Deleuze. Une philosophie de l' événement*, p. 7.

10 Juliette Simont, 'Gilles Deleuze, à la rencontre de l'intensité,' *Les Temps Modernes*, n. 629 (Nov. 2004–Feb. 2005), p. 68.

11 François Zourabichvili, Deleuze. *Une philosophie de l'événement*, p. 6.

12 Monique David-Ménard's book, *Deleuze et la psychanalyse. L'Altercation* (Paris: Presses Universitaires de France, 2005) was published at the time that I finished writing my essay. I will be satisfied here with a few points of a dialogue showing our contrasting positions. Monique David-Ménard speaks sometimes of an 'ontology of life as affirmation' and sometimes of an 'ontology of affirmation of desiring machines'; nevertheless, she maintains, in the context of a subtle debate with Alain Badiou, that there is in Deleuze's work disjunction, incompatibility between contingent reason and ontology and marking the obsolescence of the term 'Being' in favor of a thought of becomings. Ontology is nothing but an illusory effect—the counterpart of a reason ignorant of its contingency and, therefore, returning as nature. But this forgets that the two faces of the plane of immanence—image of thought and matter of Being—imply that the infinite movements enveloping it go both ways. We are indeed faced with a shuttle that never stops moving—the 'return of one restarts the other right away,' so that the fold goes in both directions—from nature to thought and from thought to nature. David-Ménard's reading overlooks the fact that, when thought returns as nature, this nature is not its sole contingency; it is also its linkage with Being because the installation of philosophy in an infinite height (and its staying there for the purpose of giving consistency to chaos) indicates that the failure of forms can help us attain Being. Ontology is not a mere illusion that plays with thought anymore than thought would play with ontology. Nature is not what takes thought from behind but rather what composes the wave of Being that it then rejoins. One thing among others attests, I think, the perdurance of the ontological question across Deleuze's work: The definition of the plane of consistency as that which ought to be thought and yet it cannot be thought (*What is Philosophy?*) brings back the definition of the Idea in *Difference and Repetition*: the rise of an ontological problem and of an unthought, which is both the thing the most intimate to thought and also its absolute outside. In the last analysis, there is no disjunction at all between ontology and becomings because the fiber of becoming is made of a virtual thread and of an actual thread and there is no reason to substitute for this duality, which is of Stoic-Bergsonian inspiration, an impersonal arrangement and a reduction to the univocal.

13 Deleuze, *Difference and Repetition*, 142–3, 148–9.

14 Deleuze and Guattari, *A Thousand Plateaus*, 197.

15 'The sensori-motor break makes man a seer who finds himself struck by something intolerable in the world, and confronted by something unthinkable in thought. Between the two, thought undergoes a strange fossilization, which is as it were its powerlessness to function, to be, its dispossession of itself and the world [. . .] We should rather make use of this powerlessness to believe in life, and to discover the identity of thought and life.' Gilles Deleuze, *Cinema 2. The Time-Image*, trans. H. Tomlinson H. and R. Galeta, 169, 170.

16 See Deleuze's 1981 seminar on Spinoza: CD *Spinoza: Immortalité et éternité* (Paris: Gallimard, 2001).

17 *Difference and Repetition*, 129–67; Deleuze and Guattari, *What Is Philosophy?* 61–3.

[18] The evaluation proceeds in both senses: from thought to intensified life and from joyful affects to thought. 'There is asymmetry between joyful and sad affects: the joyful affects cause us to feel the increase of our power to act and to think. The sad affects, on the contrary, cause us to feel the decomposition of our complexion, of the aggregate of relations that we form with other bodies. And when, in suffering, hatred, anxiety, and regret we are being undone from the inside, this condition makes us, at the same time, unable to think. There is no true idea of the fact that we sense, in the sad passions, the destruction of ourselves' Monique David-Ménard, *Deleuze et la psychanalyse*, 142.

[19] I have analyzed the differences between the pitfalls of thought that the history of philosophy picked out, the orthopedic rectifications that it proposed and the 'nomad' pitfalls and stumbling blocs that Deleuze described in my *L' Ontologie de Gilles Deleuze* (Paris: L'Harmattan, 2001), 508–13.

[20] For the problematization of the Deleuzian separation of thought and *doxa* and the heroic fragrance surrounding the conquest of thought, see Isabelle Stengers, *Cosmopolotiques*, tome 7: *Pour en finir avec la tolerance* (Paris et Le Plessis-Robinson: La Decouverte/Les Empecheurs de penser en rond, 1997), 142–5; see also her *Penser avec Whitehead*. 'Un libre et sauvage création de concepts' (Paris: Seuil, 2002), 307–8. Whereas Deleuze and Guattari transform into a weapon against every 'philosophy of the subject that is called upon to accept its finitude' the schizophrenic, with his ignorance of disjunctions, exclusions, and renunciations imposed by logical alternatives that cannot be transcended, Whitehead, who intends not to fight against anything, to accept and to 'save' everything, endeavors to ignore effectively disjunctions, exclusions and dramatic alternatives. *Penser avec Whitehead*, 372.

[21] Gilles Deleuze, 'One Manifesto Less,' *The Deleuze Reader*, ed. Constantin V. Boundas (New York: Columbia University Press, 1993), 208.

[22] At least in the sense that Deleuze understands it in *Essays Critical and Clinical* where he spares the doctrine of judgment of combat and places battle under the prism of existence. See *Essays Critical and Clinical*, trans. Daniel W. Smith and John A. Greco (New York: Columbia University Press, 1997), 132–5.

Chapter 2

The 'Future' of Deleuze
An Unfinished Project

Zsuzsa Baross

1

I could begin by citing Godard, who in turn cites Brecht: 'J'examine avec soin mon plan: il est irréalisable.'[1] Or closer to my subject and plan, which will have to be aborted here or at least left incomplete, I could say with Deleuze, who himself repeats (ventriloquizes) the subject at the limit of its own impower (*impuissance*): 'it is too much for me.' Task or plan, effectuating a however minute difference—soliciting, in the old Latin sense of shaking up, the corpus of Deleuze, a colossus, opening up within it the line of a micro-fracture, a minor degree of difference: 'c'est trop grand, trop fort pour moi.' It will have to remain imagined; the future to which it corresponds, unrealized.

Ironically, the motivating question itself pertains to the future, or more accurately, the nature of the difference (of degree or of nature?) between the *new*—novelty, invention, creation, change, 'creative evolution,' becoming— and the *future* in the proper sense. Paradoxically, this sense or concept is characterized by a certain futurity: it is not given beforehand, as conceived or derived from another philosophy, from the other great thinkers of the future, Blanchot or Derrida; nor is it present, waiting to be discovered in the writing by interpretation, exegesis, or commentary. It is yet to be. . . . But what term should I use to nominate properly the *future* gesture and intervention responsible for it? Is it to be 'invented'? Or 'created' anew? Or would this sense have to be simultaneously extracted from and given back to the writing, meaning that the secret aim of solicitation would be to fecundate Deleuze, against his will (which is not the same as from behind) with a *proper* sense of the future— his own?

As we see, our choice of action is already implicated in the problematic: the future imagined, what shall it be? An extension and prolongation of the work? Or will it come only after an interruption and radical break, or itself constitute the abyssal hiatus of an interval? In *Difference and Repetition* Deleuze himself writes: 'Repetition is the thought of the future' (DR, 7).[2] I assume that the genitive in this simple proposition moves in both directions and concerns at

one and the same time the future of *thought* and the thought of the *future*.
Repetition—as concept and performative—is therefore not only the bearer of
the future of thought, or a future thought. It must also give us—lest the *future* of
thought be only something 'new'; the thought of the future a mere 'novelty'—a
wholly other sense of the future, or shall I rather say, a future concept of the
future? A concept that is proper or adequate to the thought of the future?

My plan was to turn to Deleuze's *Difference and Repetition*, that enigmatic,
often impenetrable book, which introduces three different orders of repetition and which itself repeats Bergson's two repetitions, habit and memory.
Or more modestly, I hoped to stay close to the few majestic, rhapsodic pages
of the third repetition, which have continued to profoundly move me since I
first read them. On those dramatic, pathetic pages, as if in testimony to the
introductory claim that 'repetition [is] . . . a power peculiar to language and
thought, a superior pathos and pathology' (DR, 5), the sun explodes, the figure of Empedocles leaping into the volcano is evoked, the ground of time is
overturned. It is here that Deleuze introduces a third and final repetition,
which, raising repetition to ever-higher powers, repeats the other two. And it
is on these same pages that—in the course of developing 'the absolutely new
itself' (DR, 90)—he introduces a wholly other concept of a 'future,' outside
the context of a theory of time, irreducible to a dimension of the present and
discontinuous with the past.

But here I am getting ahead of myself, forgetting that my plan is 'unrealiz-
able.' (Is it a symptom of obstinacy? A confirmation that the unconscious, as
says Derrida, is 'unwilling to give up anything'?) Or is it not just possible that
the 'impossible' facing me is structural, a condition imposed by the work and
not simply the result of (subjective) fatigue made manifest as the impower to
contract and repeat the whole of the work all at once? Does not Deleuze himself
place obstacles in the path of success, closing every opening for a future yet to
come (to overturn the past? To fecundate it with an incurable anachrony, with
a past that has never passed)? Does he not insist on a rigorous 'monism,' particularly in what I call here, for the sake of economy, his 'Bergsonisms,'[3] the collection of texts where he 'prolongs' the great philosopher's attempt? Or indeed,
repeats it? The term used in the original 'Postface' to the English edition of
Bergsonism is 'reprise' (Pf, 313); this more accurate rendering of Kierkegaard's
'*Gjentagelse*,' meaning taking up again, already bears the imprints of the *future*
sense he is to give to repetition: 'a category of the future.' (Should not this *future*
sense then guide us toward the 'sense' of the future that we seek?)

2

Limiting myself to his 'Bergsonisms,' this would be then my guiding hypothesis: 'monism' has no proper sense of the future.

I recall the vertiginous proposition: 'there is not a difference in kind between the two halves of the division [between difference in degree and difference in nature]; the qualitative difference is entirely on one side' (B, 31). It arrives at the beginning of *Bergsonism*, where it is parenthetically, almost casually, made; not before we reach the end of the work will we see the world it brings into disequilibrium right itself. The sentence itself forms part of one of several moves—turns, reversals, substitutions, conversions—that, pursuant a series of dualisms in Bergson (two tendencies, two movements, quality and quantity), restate (*reprise*) each division in other terms, on another plane. Still incomplete, the conversion in question concerns the 'principal division'—between duration and space—which, as the nomination already indicates, substituted itself for all the others ('all other dualisms involve it, derive from it, or result in it' [B, 31]). At this point in the text, the latest incarnation of the dualism is transposed and repeated on another plane as the division (difference) between differences in nature and differences of degree: 'When we divide something according to its natural articulations . . . we have: on the one hand, the aspect of space by which the thing can only differ in degree from other things *and from itself*; and on the other hand, the aspect of duration by which the thing differs in nature from all others and from itself' (emphases in the original, translation altered, 31). The troubling statement I have cited above in fact precedes this double proposition, but remains unaffected by it. It continues to dislocate and to unbalance (itself), even after we restore it to its proper context.

What, then, is . . . the source of our vertigo? Is it that the *principal* difference—between differences in nature and difference in degree—is not included in the 'right' half of the division? (But how could it be, since it is that which performs the cut, inaugurates the disjunction that cuts the whole into two halves.) Or is it the case that the privilege granted to the one half, which eventually leads to the assignation of *all* the difference to this one side ('Les degrés . . . sont déjà compris d'une certain façon dans les différences de nature' [B2, 46]), seriously destabilizes dualism as such, or at least disturbs the symmetry of the two slopes along which, in Bergson's scenario, being manifests itself as two kinds of multiplicities—one spatial, the other temporal; one discrete or discontinuous, the other continuous and heterogeneous? The principal division is thus not only dislodged from its place (at the origin); the difference that structures it is suspended with regards to its proper nature, as difference, without the promise of resolution. For the formula admits neither a third kind of difference nor a third place (vantage point on the outside, exterior to the division), starting from which a third order of difference could impose itself, bringing under the order of its 'nature' the other two, or rather, their difference. There will be no dialectical solution (overcoming) for this impasse; it will have to be left behind (*dépassé*) with the dualism itself.

In fact, as restated by the formula ('there is not a difference in kind between the two halves of the division') the principal division is included nowhere.

The difference between the difference of nature and of degree is not included among the differences of nature. Presumably, indeed a fortiori, the same holds true for the other side, for the lesser differences of degrees—which leaves the principal difference uncomprehended by the divided whole; suspended in no-space; hovering above the caesura of the disjunction that divides difference itself is this one (uncomprehended) difference. Our experience of an *aporia*, of a paralyzing obstacle, corresponds to this 'suspense.'

But this is only the first move ('Il faut aller plus loin' [B1, 35]). Next comes the mobilization of that which has been dislodged and suspended. Tilting the balance between the two sides in favor of one brings the whole into a disequilibrium: 'only one of the two tendencies is pure or simple'; there is always a 'right' half ('l'une des deux [tendances] seule est pure, ou simple'; 'il y a toujours une moitié droite' [B1, 35]). This right half always leads to durée, which in turn 'tends' for its part to take on or bear *all* the differences in kind (B, 31, emphasis added). But this colonization of one kind of difference by the right half could still leave us with a pure albeit uneven division, were it not that the privileged side also holds the 'secret' of the other ('car s'il y a une moitié privilégiée dans la division, il fait que cette moitié contienne en soi le secret de l'autre' [B1, 35]).This holding of the secret in turn places all the differences in the domain of one side, with the consequence that the one difference also comprehends its difference with the other, *and*—in a certain manner—the other difference, or its possibility, as well (B1, 35).

But one can—indeed, must—go still further, until the last nuance ('Il faudra aller plus loin, jusqu'au bout, jusqu'à voir . . . une dernière nuance' ([B2, 52]). One last substitution is left to make. In this final move, the principal difference—division and disjunction between differences themselves, between difference of nature and of degree—is taken up and repeated by the new category: degrees of difference itself. This last comprises the whole nature of difference: between duration (memory, spirit), which is difference in kind in itself and for itself and matter (space), which is difference in degree outside itself and for us, 'there are all the *degrees of difference*, in other words, the whole *nature of difference*' (B, 93, emphases in the original). Now, the most significant 'difference' accomplished by this last turn—which completes a whole series of bedazzling, almost diabolical turns, repetitions, and reversals on the part of Deleuze, who repeats the whole of Bergson ('si l'on considère toutes les définitions, les descriptions, et les *caractères*'; 'tout ce que Bergson en dit revient toujours à ceci' (B, 51, emphases added) and who, in repeating, transforms the whole of Bergson (but perhaps his own 'fold' would be a better term: as if in the baker's repeatedly folding of the dough, we recognize the old division but always in a new place and on a different plane)—the significance of this eminently philosophical thaumaturgy is that now the whole of difference is both heterogeneous and continuous. Difference (being or difference (self)differenciating) is now indivisible, without the cut of a caesura, the violent interruption of a disjunction, the hiatus of an abyssal interval—in short, without a future. The principal cut and discontinuity on one plane is now taken up on another plane as one extreme point in the continuous, incessant oscillation of two inverse tendencies—contraction and relaxation: there is no longer a dualism between nature and degrees. 'Duration is only the most contracted degree of matter, and matter is the most relaxed state of duration' (DR, 93). In other words, the whole is the play of Difference.

It is not difficult to see how this ontology immediately translates, without mediation or intervention by concept or concepts, to a 'theory of time.' This translation is given in the text in a series of equations: 'L'être est altération, l'altération est substance. Et c'est bien que Bergson appelle la durée . . . la durée est ce qui diffère ou ce qui change de nature, la qualité, l'hétérogénéité, ce qui diffère avec soi' (B1, 33–4). All this does not come as a surprise. Bergsonism has placed difference, and the concept with it, in time, says Deleuze (B2, 61); the 'plan' of Bergsonisms, repeated with and after and according to Bergson, is to continue to substitute temporal differences for spatial ones, or as given in an earlier formulation, to pose questions as the function of time rather than of space (B1, 29). According to the schema of this temporalizing ontology, being expresses itself as the function of three aspects of difference: difference with itself (*durée*), degrees of difference (*mémoire*), and differenciation of difference (a virtual actualizing). In other words, being *is* the 'stuff' of time. Time itself has three dimensions, or more precisely, there are three different times corresponding with being as the stuff of time: past, present, and duration. The past and the present are different times ('*se distinguent en nature*') that coexist in the same *durée*, forming one world; *durée* is that which differs, which changes in nature, changes quality and heterogeneity; it is that which differs from and by itself (B1, 34); in other words, durée is the temporal *reality* of a virtual (whole) actualizing itself in and through inventing itself. Formulating the relation on the horizontal plane, of 'chronology' or temporal succession, being is the past ('l'être est le passé, l'être était' [B1, 31]), while the present—which is never pure, which is at once the most contracted point of the past and the point where the past launches itself toward the future—defines itself as that which changes, the 'forever new.'

At long last, my divergent excursus turns to lead me back to the motivating concern: the nature of the difference between the new and the future. And while my account, which despite its indulgent divergence remains telegraphic, cannot but do injustice to this new (or is it a 'future'?) ontology (of duration), it may be sufficient to serve to indicate how this latter has no (need of the) future: it is the *past* that launches itself toward the future; it is the *present* that 'defines itself as that which changes in nature, is the forever new, the eternity of life' (B2, 41). The eternity of the *forever* new, however, does not need or depend on the future; the *imprévisible* event does not arrive from the direction of or lie in the future. Its inexhaustible source is the *reality* of time—as productive *delay*, as that which separates events, spreads out being in time as becoming: 'que tout ne soit pas donné, c'est la réalité du temps' (B1, 41). The *imprévisible* does not *arrive*. It *is*. It is a self-actualizing virtual inventing itself as absolutely new rather than resemblance. And if 'becoming' is not after an image already given, then the virtual does not 'have' a future, is not in a (virtual) future; it gives itself a future, or rather, in the course of inventing itself, breaches open a future proper to it, its own proper future. If the source of the *imprévisible* is duration, then its time is (in) the present. If the future can be thought or said to be as a dimension of the present at all, it is because the new is always in the present, emerges as it were at the tip of the living present, where the past launches itself toward the future. For there to be a 'future,' rather than an ever present 'eternity,' if the present is to continue to define itself as the forever new—what is needed is the *reality* of time—duration and not a future *to come*.

3

In truth, the future is but a minor concern of Deleuze. From behind the mask of Bergson, he sings 'in honor' of the new, the invention, the imprevisible (B1, 41), but '*futur*' and '*avenir*' are words that seldom appear in his writing, unless with reference to a theory of time. Even then, the future is assigned only a minor role to play as a dimension of time but not a different time. This tendency to devalue appears at first to prevail even in *Difference and Repetition*—a work already 'in color' (in contrast with the philosophical portraits in monochrome 'potato-brown'), and which, more importantly, deploys the category of the future: repetition. Yet not until we reach the prodigious pages of the third repetition do we encounter, indeed, experience, a future powerful enough to overturn the past, including this tendency to dispense with the future.

   In the first repetition by the passive synthesis of habit, the future is once again apprehended—and its futurity instantly effaced—as a dimension or element *of* the present (DR, 71, 81), on the one hand, and on the other hand, in its reflected state, as that which announces itself—as expectation, anticipation, prediction or need—*in* the present. Then in the second repetition, by the passive synthesis of the imagination, the future is taken up on another plane as a dimension of the *past*: 'the past far from being a dimension of time is the synthesis of all time, of which the present and the *future are only* dimensions' (DR, 82). In contrast, the past and the present are privileged as distinct times, reciprocally constituting different times, which together make up and provide for a time that passes (in time). For if the first repetition by habit constitutes the foundation of time, 'the moving soil occupied by the passing present,' the second synthesis, which is memory, is that which grounds time. We recall the poetic language, the vertiginous metaphors of soil and sky, each facing and reflecting (but also uprooting) the other in its own mirror: 'The foundation, concerns the soil . . . whereas the ground comes rather from the sky, it goes from the summit to the foundations, and measures the possessor and the soil against one another according to a title of ownership. . . . Habitus and Mnemosyne, the alliance of the sky and the ground' (DR, 79–80). The first and original synthesis constitutes the *life* of the passing present. The second and fundamental synthesis constitutes the *being* of the past into which the present passes.

Still, the poetic pathos of this language should not allow us to forget to notice the absence of the future; the schema of chronogenesis makes time pass without making it pass through the future and without recourse to a future in the proper sense. (This 'sense,' as one may begin to see, lies not in the direction of a rupture in time but in the uprooting of the schema itself.) Just as importantly we should not fail to observe a unique feature of this apparatus: making time pass, it imparts a new direction, it reverses the flow of the common-sense conception of time, but also of messianic and historical time, the time that remains and the time of the disaster, the time of the 'now' (*Jetztzeit*) and the time of the other . . . Albeit in irreducibly very different manners, the latter all project the threshold of an interval, insert a caesura in time, so as to posit the awaited *imprévisible*, the incalculable event to come, on the other side, in a future *time* to come. For they expect not a future but a future *time* to come (*à venir*). All this shows the novelty of Deleuze's chronogenetic schema (or is it rather a future which is in preparation?): as time's arrow 'goes from the past to the future in the present' (DR, 71), it is the past that gnaws at the future, presses against it, grows with every passing moment. Yet this 'moment' bears no relation to a future powerful enough to haunt the present and to overturn the past, to throw time off its hinges or to overturn its ground.

It is not, however, that this future time, on the *verge* of arriving, soliciting the present from behind a threshold, is simply absent or missing. Rather its very place has fallen away, so that no future to come could come to compose with or be grafted on this time, which passes between sky and soil. The future, if there is to be a future, will not be an addition or a supplement to the originary and the fundamental; it will have to subordinate both, the present and the past, the 'life' and the 'being.' With the backward move of an '*après coup*,' it will have to come first, be the first repetition that retroactively repeats all the others.

It is for this reason that the third repetition is so extraordinary, that it deserves, indeed, awaits a reflection far more profound, a solicitation of greater force than what I am capable of (here and perhaps elsewhere). Deleuze mobilizes the powerful examples of a Hamlet and an Oedipus, figures who (do) become equal to a task greater than the 'I' ('Oh, that the impossible should be asked of me!'). One cannot but tremble before this 'image of a unique and a tremendous event,' itself torn into two unequal parts, and whose symbols are 'to throw time out of joint,' 'to make the sun explode,' 'to leap into the volcano' . . . The writing on these rhapsodic pages is difficult to follow, but I believe it points us in the direction of a wholly other, an *imprévisible* sense, of the future: A future that leaps away from the past, following an act that cuts a caesura, ordains the before and the after. Oedipus at Colonus; the reign of Fortinbras, or on a rather different scale (and this may not have been an example for Deleuze): the future (Christianity) that appears when the son is sacrificed, in a repetition of another scene and thus for the second time, by God himself; and which sacrifice requires the son (and not the father, Abraham) to become equal to it, and who (unlike the father) is shattered by it. (The difference between the first and its repetition is a function of the future: the substitution of the ram for Isaac is to save the future of the present, not to tear it away from it.)

The rest is speculation. For what does it mean to 'leap away from the past?' True, the future is a synthesis, but like all repetitions, it is structured by a series of cuts on the interior (there is a first, a second, and a third time); one of these is the caesura that corresponds with the experience of death, marks the destruction, the shattering of the agent of repetition. The latter, like a Moses or Bataille ('the future I desire to be for others . . . requires that I cease to be,'[4]) is barred from entering the future. But what is this 'bar' (which also bars me from going to the very end, until the last nuance), if not the sign of an abyssal hiatus that will not be contracted and which also corresponds with the leap, meaning that the future that has just opened up is not a virtual actualized. How could it be, if the act breaching it equals the totality of time?

The future, says Deleuze, is that which is repeated, which is nothing but repetition, and which creates the 'possibility of a temporal series.' Could this 'possibility' be the sign of a future proper to Deleuze? A *future* concept of the future? But what is the meaning of this *syntagme*, as Derrida would say? What condition must this future concept satisfy, so as to be irreducible to the new, to invention, novelty, creative evolution? Does it need to create a future? Or only its place, the place for the repetition—eternal return—that is the machine (in the sense of Bergson, who calls the universe a machine)—not for the creation of (new) gods but of futures in the proper sense?

Notes

[1] Godard, J.-L. (1998), 'Interview with Serge Daney,' in *Histoire's du cinéma*, vol. 2 (Paris: Galimard-Gaumont), 161.

[2] Deleuze, G., (1994), *Difference and Repetition*, trans. Paul Patton (New York: University of Columbia Press), 5. Cited in the text as DR.

[3] The following texts are included under the heading of 'Bergsonisms': 'Postface pour l'édition américaine: Un retour à Bergson,' in *Deux Régimes de Fous, Textes et Entretiens 1975–1995* (Paris: Edition Minuit, 2003), cited in the text as Pf; 'Bergson, 1859–1941,' cited in the text as B1, and 'La conception de la différence chez Bergson,' cited in the text as B2, both in *L'Île déserte et autres textes* (Paris: Édition Minuit, 2002); and *Bergsonism*, trans. Hugh Tomlinson and Barbara Habberjam (New York: Zone Books, 1988), cited in the text as B.

[4] 'The Reasons for Writing a Book . . .' *Literature and the Ethical Question*, [*Yale French Studies* 79 (1991)], 11.

Chapter 3

The New Harmony

Ronald Bogue

In a 1988 interview, Deleuze remarks that philosophy has need 'not only of a philosophical comprehension, through concepts, but of a non-philosophical comprehension, one that operates through percepts and affects. Both are necessary. Philosophy has an essential and positive relation with non-philosophy: it addresses itself directly to non-philosophers.'[1] Deleuze views the arts as the domain that 'operates primarily through percepts and affects,' and hence as one that affords a particularly vital non-philosophical comprehension of philosophy. Philosophy's primary goal is the invention of concepts, he says, but the concept 'includes two other dimensions, those of the percept and the affect.' For this reason, 'the affect, the percept and the concept are three inseparable powers [*puissances*], which go from art to philosophy and back again' (*Negotiations* 187/137). In *What Is Philosophy?* (1991), Deleuze and Guattari speak at length of philosophy's relationship to the arts, but perhaps the best examples of this relationship, as Deleuze understands it, are to be found in *The Fold: Leibniz and the Baroque* (1988).[2] *What Is Philosophy?* is filled with references to various philosophers and artists, but it provides no detailed analyses of any single philosopher's relationship to the arts. *The Fold*, by contrast, offers an extended reading of Leibniz's thought as a philosophical counterpart of the Baroque sensibility expressed in the arts of the late-seventeenth and early eighteenth century. An especially intriguing and instructive instance of the philosophy–arts parallels established in *The Fold* is that which Deleuze draws between Leibniz's concept of harmony and the harmonic practices of Baroque composers. In Deleuze's presentation of Leibniz's 'new harmony,' one can see clearly how Deleuze envisions philosophy's relationship to the arts. And perhaps as importantly, one can see from this example what Deleuze regards as the role the history of philosophy and its encounter with the arts should play in contemporary philosophical and aesthetic endeavors.

In *The Fold*, Deleuze draws on several of the arts to characterize the Baroque and establish Leibniz as a philosopher responding to the aesthetic concerns of his age. Chief among those arts are architecture and painting. Deleuze likens Leibniz's differentiation of monads and bodies, for example, to a two-story Baroque building, the upper story representing the domain of monads, the lower that of bodies. The upper story is an essentially interior space, a monastic cell or *camera obscura*, like the monads, 'without doors or windows.' The lower story, by contrast, is an exterior façade, horizontally organized in the rhythms of its components (doors, windows, columns, pediments) but with no meaningful relationship between those components and the interior space (just as bodies constitute a causally interconnected domain without being linked in any simple or direct way to the domain of monads). Deleuze finds that opposition of lower corporeality and upper monadic spirituality in Baroque painting, and he argues that the motif that organizes both levels and allows for their intercommunication is that of the fold. In Baroque still lifes, the folds of draperies and tablecloths communicate with the whorls of wood grains and marble veins, the curves of goblets, plates, medallions, and armor, the flowing contours of fruit, wild game, and flowers. In El Greco, twisting bodies pulsate within undulating landscapes, earthly figures intertwining and often ascending into unearthly realms of vertical spirituality. The Baroque fold is one that 'goes to infinity' (*Fold* 164/121), just as Leibniz's bodies and monads form infinite series, bodies folded within bodies, monads within monads, each monad enfolding the infinite cosmos, each body unfolding a specific constituent of the infinite whole, the folds of bodies and folds of monads communicating through the additional mysterious folds of the *vinculum substantiale*.

Clearly, Deleuze's conception of the Baroque is predominantly visual, with architecture, painting, and to a lesser extent sculpture providing him with models of the period's aesthetic. Yet Deleuze does note that Leibniz makes regular use of the musical metaphor of harmony, and unlike most commentators, Deleuze regards this as more than a casual figure of speech.[3] It would be a mistake to look in Leibniz's thought 'for a direct transposition of musical chords [*accords*, the French word *accord* capable of denoting both a musical chord and the general notions of agreement, harmony, linkage, or entente] as they are developed in the Baroque,' Deleuze observes, 'and yet one also would be mistaken to conclude that Leibniz is indifferent to the musical model: rather, it is a matter of analogy, once it is added that Leibniz never stopped trying to bring the analogy to a new rigor' (*Fold* 179/131). That new rigor depends on a deep sensitivity to the new harmonic practices of Baroque composers.

Deleuze's primary guide to baroque music is Manfred Bukofzer, whose *Music in the Baroque Era* (1947) is one of the pioneering modern works in the field.[4] Bukofzer differentiates Renaissance from Baroque music first by observing the emergence of a plurality of styles in the Baroque. Unlike other transitions in music history, in which one period's style is replaced by another, at the beginning of the Baroque 'the old style was not cast aside, but deliberately preserved as a second language, known as the *stile antico* of church music' (Bukofzer 3). Theorists of the late sixteenth- and early seventeenth century frequently opposed the *stile antico* to the *stile moderno*, framing the opposition as well in terms of a *stylus gravis* versus a *stylus luxurians*, or a *prima prattica* versus a *seconda prattica*. Later in the seventeenth century, another classificatory scheme became common, one dividing the field into church, chamber, and theater music (*musica ecclesiastica, cubicularis, theatralis*), the *stile antico* roughly (but not entirely) coinciding with that of *musica ecclesiastica*. This rather confusing discourse of two practices and/or three styles, argues Bukofzer, was a sign that the Renaissance unity of style had been lost and that with the Baroque development of a plurality of styles had come a heightened consciousness of style *per se*.

For many seventeenth-century theorists, the *prima prattica* and *seconda prattica* could be differentiated primarily by their handling of music and word, the first practice giving precedence to music, the second to text. Advocates of the second practice often claimed that they alone represented the emotions in their settings of texts, but as Bukofzer points out, neither Renaissance nor Baroque composers attempted a direct, psychological representation of emotions, instead relying on a conventional ensemble of coded figures to render fixed emotional effects. What set the two practices apart was a Renaissance predilection for 'the affections of restraint and noble simplicity' and a Baroque love of 'the extreme affections, ranging from violent pain to exuberant joy' (Bukofzer 5). Renaissance settings also often muted emotional effects by allowing multiple voices to sing different words simultaneously, a tendency early *seconda prattica* composers deliberately countered through the development of the recitative, the rhythmically free, declamatory solo component of opera, which from its inception was intended to render extremes of pathos and affective violence by following the inflections of natural speech. Indeed, Bukofzer argues, that impulse to render powerful emotions was the primary motivation for the Baroque's creation of opera, not (as is often claimed) a vague desire to 'imitate the Ancients,' something Renaissance and Baroque musicians both professed. Although Baroque representations of emotions tended to adhere to conventional musical codes, the recitative's adoption of oratory as a guide to the handling of speech opened music to extra-musical elements (much to the dismay of *prima prattica* composers). Hence, concludes Bukofzer, 'renaissance and early baroque concepts of music stand, at this point, clearly opposed. The renaissance artist saw in music a self-contained autonomous art, subject only to its own laws. The baroque artist saw in music a heteronomous art, subordinated to words and serving only as musical means to a dramatic end that transcended music' (Bukofzer 8).

In strictly musical terms, Renaissance and Baroque compositions may be differentiated in several interrelated ways. In the Renaissance, dissonance occurred only on the weak beat or as a suspension of the strong beat. Harmony was conceived of as a concordant sounding of individual voices on strong beats, the voices maintaining an equal and relatively autonomous role. In the Baroque, harmony was thought of as a sequence of vertical chords, and as a result, dissonance on the strong beat became possible as long as the chord was clearly delineated. The Renaissance's equality among the voices gave way to a dominance of the outer voices, the bass line supplying the foundation for the chord, the melody providing an expressive ornamentation of the harmonic structure. The prominence of the bass line and melody was especially evident in the convention of the thorough-bass, or *basso continuo*, a convention virtually coextensive with the Baroque era. According to this common practice, the *continuo* keyboardist accompanying a violin soloist, for example, was simply given a bass line with a sequence of numerical figures accompanying each note, the numbers merely indicating the chord to be played but not the specific notes of the chord. In such a composition, while the bass line and melody were written out by the composer, the subordinate inner voices of the chord were improvised by the keyboardist.

Of course, Renaissance compositions also had bass lines, but the Baroque bass voice, while still a line with a horizontal continuity, was constructed to emphasize a system of tonal chordal relations. Unlike Renaissance harmonies, which were primarily modal, Baroque harmonies were tonal, that is, organized around the attraction of a tonal center. In Renaissance intervallic harmony, individual voices were coordinated so that concords sounded on strong beats, but with no pressing concern about the sequence of chords from one strong beat to the next. In Baroque tonal harmony, by contrast, the progression of chords was regulated by a system of relations between chords, the tonic (the C triad in the key of C major) providing maximum stability, the dominant (G major triad in C), the subdominant (F major triad in C), and various other chords having degrees of instability that required resolution according to fixed sequential movements from one chord to the next. This tonal foundation of chord sequences made possible a much greater freedom in the treatment of the melody, both harmonically and rhythmically. Not only was the Renaissance dictum that all dissonance be resolved by downward movement no longer observed in the melody, but dissonance occurred on strong beats and melodies made use of a wider range of intervals, most notably chromatic steps and intervals corresponding to augmented and diminished progressions. That increased chromaticism in melodic construction had as its corollary a greater harmonic chromaticism, Baroque composers significantly expanding the Renaissance palette of triads and sixth chords by introducing unprepared seventh chords, augmented triads, and diminished chords. The heightened freedom of the melodic line was manifest especially in the Baroque system of ornamentation, whereby melodies were embellished with various grace notes (mordants, trills, turns, appoggiaturas, etc.), those additional melodic notes either indicated by signs above the melody or simply improvised by the performer without any explicit instructions from the composer.

Rhythmic innovations also informed Baroque practices. Renaissance compositions typically were organized by the *tactus*, an even flow of beats maintained throughout a given section of music. A strict system of mathematical proportions governed the rhythms of individual voices, and all voices were coordinated by the unifying *tactus*, yet the autonomy and equality of the voices tended to weaken the sense of a dominant, emphatic measure controlling all voices. Duration rather than dynamic stress was the primary technique for creating melodic syncopation or accent. Baroque composers, by contrast, exploited the rhythmic extremes of a freely pulsed, expressive lyricism and a heavily stressed, insistently repetitive dynamism. The first extreme was on display in the opera recitative, which followed the fluid cadences of spoken speech, at times entirely without any regular pulse. The other extreme was manifest especially in the dance forms (allemande, courante, sarabande, gigue, gavotte, minuet) that so intrigued Baroque composers. Like their Renaissance predecessors, Baroque composers exploited a full range of contrapuntal techniques, but they handled the individual voices in such a way that the overall metrical organization of the composition was seldom obscured.

The Baroque saw as well the introduction of idiomatic writing, whereby composers exploited the features peculiar to a given voice or instrument, or a group of voices and instruments. Renaissance music typically was conceived in terms of a single part-writing practice common to vocal and instrumental music. Choral compositions generally could be performed a cappella or with instrumental doubling of the lines, or they could be performed by instruments alone. Conversely, instrumental compositions often bore the inscription, 'to be played or sung.' With the invention of opera, Baroque composers explored the lyrical possibilities specific to solo voices. In their church music, they exploited a cappella sonorities that would be compromised by instrumental accompaniment. They developed differentiated vocalic and instrumental practices in operas, oratorios, and cantatas. And they gradually formulated distinct styles for various families of instruments, especially strings and keyboards. Such idiomatic writing made possible as well an exchange of idioms, a violin line adopting a vocalic idiom, a lute ornament appearing in a harpsichord composition. These exchanges and interpenetrations could also take place at the level of entire compositions, the idiom of an organ prelude shaping a choral work, the recitative idiom dominating an instrumental piece. Finally, idiomatic writing informed the widespread practices of the Baroque 'concertant style,' in which groups of instruments were opposed to one another as contrasting compositional blocks (that contrast of groups frequently taking the form of an opposition of homophonic chord blocks that stressed vertical harmonic relations).

We may say in general, then, that Baroque music displayed an increased heterogeneity and heteronomy in comparison with Renaissance music. Baroque composers developed three separate styles and two distinct practices. They made use of the rhythmic extremes of unpulsed recitatives and heavily stressed dance forms. They expanded the Renaissance harmonic vocabulary to include various altered chords. Melodic composition gained a new freedom, chromatic variation and ornamental elaboration providing options for linear construction unavailable to Renaissance composers. The development of idiomatic writing complemented the Baroque's increased sensitivity to stylistic differences, the Renaissance's single part-writing technique giving way to divergent techniques suitable for individual voices, instruments, and ensembles. The Baroque's fascination with emotional extremes in early opera was gradually communicated throughout a number of other forms, and opera's openness to textual, extra-musical influences gave evidence of an increased sensitivity to extra-musical affectivity in general. What made all this possible was a new harmonic system, one based on tonality and a chordal conception of harmony, with a privileging of the outer voices of a foundational bass and an expressive, ornamental melody. This harmonic system was the force designed to bring unity to the multiple styles and idioms, the extremes of rhythm, intervallic movement and harmonic palette, and the centrifugal influence of extra-musical concerns.

In this opposition of Renaissance and Baroque conceptions of musical harmony Deleuze sees a parallel to the opposition of Malebranche's occasionalism and Leibniz's pre-established harmony.[5] In Malebranche, the occasion of God's constant intervention ensures a harmonious relationship between bodies and souls. The occasion, says Deleuze, 'plays the role of a sort of counterpoint that still belongs to a melodic or polyphonic conception of music' (*Fold* 175/128). In other words, Malebranche thinks of bodies and souls as equal and autonomous melodic voices brought into regular harmonic relations through a single unifying force, as in Renaissance musical practice. Leibniz's pre-established harmony, by contrast, is a harmony of accords, one that is analogous to Baroque musical harmony in its emphasis on vertical relations and the production of unity within a pervasive heterogeneity.

Like many before him, Leibniz finds inspiration in the Pythagorean conjunction of music and mathematics when articulating his notions of harmony. In Deleuze's analysis, the controlling metaphor in Leibniz's conception of pre-established harmony is that of the relationship among inverse, or reciprocal, numbers (e.g., $5/1$ is the inverse, or reciprocal, of $1/5$). Pre-established harmony 'is a numeric harmony, in that it envelops a multiplicity' (*Fold* 175/128). The one of God envelops the multiplicity of monads. Each monad is an unfolding of the one, and each monad expresses the entirety of the one from a specific point of view. God is the infinite one, and God envelops an infinity of monads; each of the infinite monads, though only an infinitely small entity, expresses the infinite one from its individual point of view. Hence, if $God = \infty/1$, the individual monad is the inverse of God, or $1/\infty$. According to Leibniz's principle of indiscernibles, however, no two monads are exactly alike, and thus we must insist as well that each monad has a specific value, say $1/3$ or $1/7$, even though the number of monads is infinite, each monad is infinitely small, and each expresses the entirety of the infinite one. Leibniz reconciles this dual nature of the monad by asserting that 'each monad expresses the world (1/∞), but clearly expresses only a particular zone of the world (1/n, *n* having in each case a specific value)' (*Fold* 178/130). Each monad is like the singular point at which a curve meets a tangent straight line. The straight line and the curve are made up of an infinity of points, the line and curve converging at the singular point, the distance between the line and curve decreasing by infinite gradations as the two near the singular point. The singular point may be said to integrate the differentials of this particular relation between tangent and curve, and it is in this sense that each monad's zone of clarity may be characterized by the convergent series of differentials it is capable of integrating. From this analogy, Deleuze concludes that 'each monad, in its portion of the world or in its clear zone, *thus presents accords*, inasmuch as one calls 'accord' the relation of a state with its differentials, that is, with the differential relations between infinitely small elements that are integrated into that state' (*Fold* 178/130).

Pre-established harmony, then, is a harmony of accords. The accords produced in the individual monad are of three basic types, which Deleuze sees as analogous to the basic chords (again, in French *accords* = musical chords) of the tonal harmonic system—major chords, minor chords, and dissonant chords. Each monad is a point of view on the world, and as such, it has perceptions and affections specific to its point of view. Each monad perceives and senses the entire world in a confused way, but only a small portion of the world in a clear fashion. That clear perception is like the sound of waves at the shore (a favorite example of Leibniz's). That sound is an integration of unconscious, differential micro-perceptions of the infinite sounds of individual waves, individual drops of water, individual molecules, and so on. The monad's zone of clarity is its clear perception of the sound of the sea, but its perception extends confusedly to include an infinity of vague and decreasingly distinguishable micro-perceptions. Likewise, a monad's specific affection is like a moment of hunger, a conscious feeling that integrates a differential series of moments passing by infinite gradation from unconscious appetitive inclination, to vague gastric unrest, to full-fledged hunger. Major accords are those integrations that allow the monad to expand its zone of clarity, to continue its pleasures in proliferating accords. Minor accords are those integrations that are unstable and temporary, 'simple pleasures that are inverted into their contrary, unless they are attracted by a perfect [i.e., major] accord' (*Fold* 179/131). And dissonant accords are those integrations that interrelate negative and positive series, such that dissonance is, according to standard Baroque musical practice, either prepared or resolved. When a dog enjoying a juicy bone seems to be abruptly sent into pain by a blow from a stick, it actually has already been sustaining a watchful alertness to possible danger, has had a vague sense of some approaching movement, an unconscious awareness of the scent of a human, and so on, and in this regard its has been preparing itself for the dissonant blow, thereby integrating the series of its eating pleasure into the series of corporal pain.

Conversely, the martyr at the stake resolves the dissonance of rising flames by integrating her torments into the prospect of an imminent eternal glory.

The accords of monads are constantly forming and unforming, tending 'toward a resolution or a modulation' (*Fold* 180/132). Although each monad's accords express the entire world, and hence extend through all other monads, its accords arise from within, for each monad is without doors or windows, a self-enjoying, self-contained locus of unfolding. And though that unfolding occurs as a temporal process of constant transformation, through major and minor integrations of differential series, through preparations for and resolutions of dissonance, the accords of each monad trace a trajectory of instants that exist in a co-present, virtual simultaneity. In each moment of a monad's unfolding, the entire history of the world is implicit, as is the future course of the world. The course of each monad's unfolding has been inscribed in it from its creation, that course like a musical score that the soloist monad performs without promptings from its sonic surroundings. The monad's unfolding, then, though manifested in a horizontal temporality, exists vertically as a virtual score, the total history of the monad's changing accords already written in its soloist part. In the simplest terms, one may say that the monad's accords are like arpeggios, melodies made up of the notes of a chord, temporal unfoldings of simultaneous, virtual forms. In that each monad integrates multiple series, however, we must imagine its solo score as one made up not solely of monodic arpeggios but also of multi-voiced chordal progressions (perhaps the score of a truly grand piano).

Each monad acts spontaneously, without prompting from without, and hence its accords constitute a harmony of spontaneity. Yet in addition to spontaneity, there is a harmonious arrangement of all monads among one another, a harmony Deleuze calls 'concertation' (a harmony, he suggests, that may be seen as the analog of Baroque music's 'concertant style'). Although each monad plays its individual part without regard to other monads, all the monads belong to a single world and perform the music of that world together as a harmoniously coordinated orchestra. Concertation is 'an accord of spontaneities themselves, an accord among accords' (*Fold* 181/132). The cosmos is God's great orchestral score, each monad a separate part in the score, the whole composition a manifestation of an unfolding pre-established harmony. Deleuze insists, however, that Leibniz's God does not so much create the individual monads as he creates the world within which the monads unfold, that world incapable of existing outside the monads that express it. The harmonies of spontaneity and concertation are mutually implicated, then, in that God's orchestral composition is a total world, selected from all possible worlds, a world already replete with its monads, which are the necessary expressions of that world.

The harmony specific to concertation is one of clarity and obscurity, of pre-established mutual adjustments of relations among monads. Each monad is characterized by its zone of clarity, no two monads possessing precisely the same range and degree of clarity. As a given monad expands its zone of clarity, necessarily somewhere else another monad's zone contracts. All monads express the same world, but in a given event that which expresses it with greater clarity is a cause, and that which expresses it with less clarity is an effect. The causality among monads is not like mechanical causality, since each monad is an autonomous entity and hence unaffected by any other monad. Rather, it is an ideal causality, the causality of mutually coordinated harmonious relations that constitute the unified world created by God. Ideal causality always proceeds from clarity to obscurity, or from the more-clear to the less-clear. Concertation, then, may be defined as 'the ensemble of ideal relations of causality.' Ideal causality 'is concertation itself, and thus it is in perfect agreement with spontaneity: ideal causality goes from the more-clear to the less-clear, but that which is more-clear in a substance is produced by that substance by virtue of its proper spontaneity, and that which is less-clear in the other is likewise produced by virtue of its own spontaneity' (*Fold* 183/134).

In addition to spontaneity and concertation, Deleuze proposes the existence of a third element of Leibnizian harmony, one that parallels the *basso continuo* of Baroque music: the *vinculum substantiale*, or substantial link (*vinculum*, literally 'fetter,' 'chain').[6] Late in his life, Leibniz addressed the question of transubstantiation in a series of letters to Father Des Bosses, and in the process took up the question of the identity of bodies as they change through time. We humans have bodies that are more than aggregates of particles (such as buckets of sand). Our bodies are organisms, collectively organized entities, and yet they also include various organs, themselves more than aggregates. And while the components of our bodies function together as unified entities, they are routinely replaced (skin is shed and regrown; blood is lost but then replenished). The body, as Leibniz frequently expresses it, is like Theseus' ship, patched and repaired piece by piece such that the ship that docks is entirely different from the ship that set out at the voyage's beginning, and yet it is the same ship. Every monad has a body, and that body's formal unity comes from its related monad. The human body's organs are also bodies, and hence bodies with their own corresponding monads (a heart monad, a liver monad, a blood cell monad, a bile cell monad). The monad of an individual human body is a dominant monad, the monads of its component are dominated monads, and that which puts the dominant and dominated monads in relation to one another is the dominant monad's *vinculum substantiale*. Itself not a monad, the *vinculum* is a pure relation, created by God, one that produces a cooperative cohesiveness among monads, while also allowing for periodic reassemblages of monads, as some dominated monads break away from the *vinculum* and other, new monads fall under its sway. What the *vinculum* adds to Leibnizian harmony is an element of flux and variation. The *vinculum* is like the Baroque *basso continuo*, the anchoring harmonic foundation that supplies a solid tonality, yet that also makes possible a new freedom in the melodic line. The *continuo*'s subordination of inner voices secures the piece's chordal harmonic structure, thereby ensuring that the wide-ranging chromatic, intervallic, rhythmic, and ornamental variations of the melody do not compromise the work's tonal logic. In a similar fashion, the *vinculum* of a given body establishes its dominant tonality, while allowing its assemblages of dominated monads to form, partially dissolve, and reform again in a flux of changing combinations.

Yet the *vinculum* effects more than links among monads. Though it is itself neither monad nor material body, and though it only links monads to monads, in its linking of a dominant monad to its dominated monads it induces a 'back-and-forth from the soul [of the dominant monad] to the body [that belongs to the dominant monad], and from bodies [that belong to the dominated monads] to souls [of the dominated monads]' (*Fold* 162/120). Monads actualize the virtual, whereas bodies realize the possible, and the domain of actualized monads remains separate from that of realized bodies. Leibniz generally explains the alignment of monads and bodies as the result of God's pre-established harmony, but in his speculations about the *vinculum* Deleuze sees an additional principle at work, one that connects monads and bodies in a new way. The back-and-forth induced by the vinculum suggests that it serves an intermediary role, one that presides over the incarnation of monads. Bodies realize the possible, but that which makes them real is their animation by their attendant monads. Bodies become real as that which is actual in the monad (a given perception or affection) is realized in those bodies. 'One does not realize the body, one realizes in the body that which is actually perceived in the soul. The reality of the body is the realization of phenomena in the body. That which realizes is the fold between the two stories [i.e., the two domains of monads and bodies], the *vinculum* itself' (*Fold* 163/120). This mysterious passage from monads to bodies, this realization of the actual within bodies, is the principle of incarnation and creation in general, a divine principle beyond human comprehension. By interfolding monads and bodies, the *vinculum* animates matter, creating a harmony that is characteristically Baroque in its simultaneous spirituality and insistent sensuality. Because of the *vinculum*, in Leibniz 'there is not only harmony within harmony [i.e., spontaneous harmony within the harmony of concertation], but harmony between the harmony and the melody. It is in this sense that harmony goes from the soul to the body, from the intelligible to the sensible, and continues within the sensible. . . . It is in the melody that the harmony realizes itself' (*Fold* 185–6/135).

Deleuze sees many parallels between the new harmony of Baroque music and the Leibnizian harmony of spontaneity, concertation, and the *vinculum substantiale*, but that analogy, though brought by Leibniz 'to a new rigor' (*Fold* 179/131), by no means provides the program for a mechanical or rigid construction of philosophical concepts. The Baroque harmonic system has an internal coherence as well as a specifically musical relationship of continuity with, development of, and departure from Renaissance contrapuntal practices.

Likewise, Leibniz's harmony is part of a philosophical system, with its own inner coherence and a strictly philosophical relationship to the systems of his contemporaries and predecessors. The Baroque's musical harmony of chords, tonality, and *basso continuo*, its heterogeneity of styles and extremes of rhythm, its idiomatic handling of instruments and concertant-style contrast of ensembles, its free-flowing chromatic and intervallic ornamentation of melodic lines, its heteronomous, oratorical approach to the setting of texts, and its pervasive expressive sensuality—all may have their counterparts in Leibniz's thought, but the relationship among the elements differs from the musical to the philosophical system, and there is no way one could predict what role the *basso continuo* might play once one had established the role of accords/chords in the Leibnizian system. Nor could one predict what form Leibniz's thought would take based on an identification of occasionalism with Renaissance harmony, for Leibniz's response to occasionalism, though principled and systematic, is an inventive and unforeseeable transformation of the questions and terms informing occasionalism, just as Baroque tonality represents a creative and unpredictable metamorphosis of Renaissance polyphonic counterpoint.

Yet there remains a common concern in Leibniz and Baroque music, an effort to conceive of the One and the Many in a new way, to develop a model that stresses heterogeneity and differences among components, that provides for cohesiveness while admitting flux and variation, and that allows for both centripetal and centrifugal forces, thereby ensuring the internal structural integrity of the One while making possible its expansive engagement with new elements. Leibniz's philosophical response to the non-philosophy of Baroque music remains philosophical, yet his concept of harmony reverberates with the new harmony of the music of his age, especially with that music's percepts and affects, its expressiveness, its delight in extremes, its play with contrast and variation, and its incessant effort to engage the spiritual within the sensual. Leibniz and the composers of his era pursue their separate ends, but they all inhabit the world and attempt to engage that world through thought, Leibniz via a thought in concepts, the composers via a thought in sonic percepts and affects. And Leibniz's thought in concepts and the composers' thought in sonic percepts and affects meet in a permeable membrane that forms the outside of each thought, one that affords passages from concepts to percepts and affects and back again.

Deleuze regards Leibniz's system as a last, valiant effort to sustain theological order in a rapidly disintegrating world, and in Voltaire's critique of 'the best of all possible worlds' he sees evidence of the system's demise.[7] Yet Deleuze finds much in Leibniz that is of more than historical interest. *The Fold* is not a mere exercise in the history of philosophy, for while Leibniz's system may have collapsed, its component concepts have a potential for exploitation that goes beyond his times, an 'untimely' potential that Deleuze is intent on exploring. In a parallel fashion, Deleuze discovers in the contemporary arts certain tendencies that echo Baroque artistic practices, such that he can speak of a 'new Baroque, neo-Leibnizianism' (*Fold* 187/136) in modern aesthetic practice. Those contemporary tendencies in the arts and his own philosophical explorations have in common the practice and concept of the fold within a new harmony, a harmony that is Leibnizian, but with a difference. Leibniz's world of infinite folds-within-folds, of monadic minds/spirits interfolded with matter and topological folds of reversible insides and outsides, remains a potent model, but the harmony of that world can no longer be conceived of as a unity, since our interfolded universe is not circumscribed and complete. Leibnizian monads are subject to two interrelated conditions, 'closure and selection' (*Fold* 188/137). Each monad is without doors or windows, entirely closed in upon itself, spontaneously expressing the entire world. Its spontaneous harmonic interrelationships with other monads arise from God's selection of the best world from among the infinite number of possible worlds. In our neo-Leibnizian cosmos, by contrast, the principle of selection no longer holds. Multiple possible worlds coexist, worlds that are incompossible and yet co-present. Each monad expresses a world, but not necessarily the same world, nor does a given monad express the same world from moment to moment. Hence, with the demise of the principle of selection, the principle of closure also falls away, as the monad opens onto the various divergent, incompossible worlds with which it is attuned. 'To the extent that the world is now made up of divergent series (chaosmos), or that the throw of the dice has replaced the game of Plenitude, the monad can no longer include the entire world as if it were in a closed circle that can be modified by projection. Instead, the monad now opens itself on a trajectory or an expanding spiral that moves further and further from a center' (*Fold* 188/137).

In *The Fold*, Deleuze offers an extended example of the ways in which a given philosopher may respond to the arts. Leibniz's pre-established harmony is analogous to the new harmony of Baroque music in many respects, but the musical analogs take on different functions in their philosophical milieu, and their transfer from the aesthetic to the conceptual sphere obeys no simple transformation rule or procedure. For Deleuze, philosophy has an internal integrity and rigor, and its thought in concepts is incommensurable with other modes of thought. Yet it also opens itself to the non-philosophical, finding counterparts to artists' thought in percepts and affects within its own conceptual field. The new harmony of the Baroque is Leibnizian, in part because Baroque composers and Leibniz operate within a similar world, attempting to think the One and the Many in new ways. Yet their musical and philosophical innovations possess an untimely potential as well, their practices and concepts capable of assuming unexpected configurations and functions in other contexts. For this reason, the history of philosophy is a vital component of contemporary philosophy, just as the history of the arts supplies invaluable inspiration for modern artistic practice. And if philosophy bears an essential relationship to the non-philosophy of the arts, that relationship is not restricted to one with the contemporary arts. The new harmony of the Baroque is as much a contributing element of Deleuze's thought as is the new harmony of Cage, Berlioz, Stockhausen, and Berio. In philosophy and in the arts, a continuing co-presence of untimely elements from both domains prevails, each with its own mode of thought, but each open to the movements of the other. Hence, at the conclusion of *The Fold*, Deleuze can say of both philosophy and the arts, 'we remain Leibnizians, even though accords are not what express our world or our text. We discover new ways of folding, like new kinds of envelopment, but we remain Leibnizians, because it's always a matter of folding, unfolding, refolding' (*Fold* 189/137).

Notes

[1] Deleuze, G. (1990), *Pourparlers* (Paris: Minuit), 191; *Negotiations*, trans. Joughin, M. (1995), (New York: Columbia University Press), 139–40. All translations from Deleuze are my own. Citations include page numbers of the original French edition followed by page numbers of the corresponding passages in the published English translation.

[2] Deleuze, G. and Guattari, F. (1991), *What is Philosophy?*, trans. Hugh Tomlinson and Graham Burchell (Columbia: Columbia University Press, 1994); *Le pli: Leibniz et le baroque* (Paris: Minuit, 1988); *The Fold: Leibniz and the Baroque*, trans. Tom Conley (Minneapolis: University of Minnesota Press, 1993).

[3] Christiane Frémont, for example, in *L'Être et la relation* (Paris: Vrin, 1981) says of Leibniz's use of the word 'harmony' and other musical terms that he 'makes use of these musical notions without worrying too much about their technical sense or the difficulties that they imply' (p. 32).

[4] Bukofzer, M. F. (1947), *Music in the Baroque Era: From Monteverdi to Bach* (New York: Norton).

[5] At another point in *The Fold*, Deleuze proposes a tri-partite parallel between philosophical approaches to the soul–body problem and musical conceptions of harmony. 'Leibniz likes to compare diverse concepts of the soul-body to modes of correspondence between two clocks: either influx [the soul directs the body through a direct influence], or occasion [occasionalism], or harmony (which Leibniz judged to be superior). These are the three 'ages' of music: monodic, or unison [Medieval music], polyphonic or counterpoint [Renaissance music], harmonic, in chords—that is, baroque' (*Fold* 187/136). This periodization is unfortunately obscured in the English translation of *The Fold*.

[6] Deleuze bases his reading of the *vinculum substantiale* on the analyses of Frémont in *L'Être et la relation*, 31–42, and Belaval, Y. (1962), *Leibniz: initiation à sa philosophie* (Paris: Vrin), 240–53.

[7] Deleuze does not offer this historical reading of Leibniz in *The Fold*, but in an interview about *The Fold* Deleuze comments: 'What takes place from Leibniz to Voltaire is a fundamental moment in the history of thought. With Voltaire, we are in the Enlightenment, that is, precisely a regime of light, of matter and of life,

of Reason, completely different from the Baroque regime, even if Leibniz prepared the way for this new age: theological reason had crumbled and become
purely and simply human. But the Baroque already marks a crisis in theological
reason: it was a final attempt to reconstruct a world in the process of disintegrating' (*Negotiations* 221/161).

Chapter 4

The 'New Whitehead'
An Ontology of the 'Virtual' in Whitehead's Metaphysics

Keith Robinson

Introduction

A good deal of recent work on Deleuze has focused on his importance as a philosopher of the 'virtual' and the intensive processes that emerge from it. That Deleuze finds the ontological and metaphysical expression of these virtual processes in the work of Nietzsche, Spinoza, and Bergson is perhaps now well known. The 'trinity' of Deleuzian thought—with Spinoza as the 'Christ' of philosophers—is now established in the commentaries. However, one task that remains open for Deleuze scholarship is to retrieve those often marginal figures and multiple voices that populate Deleuze's texts since these figures often provide the conceptual innovations that inform Deleuze's readings of the Nietzsche-Bergson-Spinoza trinity, underpinning his unique trajectories and novel routes through disciplines, knowledges and traditions.[1] The immense promise of this research into the margins of the Deleuzian text is that it offers the potential to not only 'counter-actualize' or 'deterritorialize' the now perhaps received views of Deleuze's thought but it also opens up possibilities to re-energize and transform long forgotten concepts, to revalue and experiment with ignored or neglected traditions of thought and release under-appreciated thinkers for new becomings and futures. Perhaps above all, outside of the 'official' blocs of philosophy, this research offers the opportunity for thought to once again 'diagnose our actual becomings' (WP, 56).

In this respect, and still widely underappreciated, at least in the Anglo-American reception of Deleuze, is the extent to which Deleuze returns with a difference to the inestimable—yet abandoned (intriguingly, Deleuze says 'assassinated'[2])—work of Alfred North Whitehead in order precisely to experiment with the virtual logic of becoming and difference and to continue the work of creating transformative and transversal relations in between science and philosophy. In relation to this task a few Anglo-American readers of Deleuze have, albeit very briefly and indirectly, alluded to the presence of Whitehead in Deleuze's thought.[3] However, perhaps the most sustained and serious engagement with the Deleuze-Whitehead nexus is now taking place in the Francophone world. In a context already informed by Bergson, Ruyer, Simondon, Serres, Latour, and so on, thinkers like Eric Alliez and Isabelle Stengers are exploring the possibilities that a Deleuze-Whitehead conjunction offers for rethinking some of the most important problems of contemporary philosophical, aesthetic and scientific thought. In his *The Signature of the World* (Continuum 2004), for example, Alliez had already worked through some of these possibilities by showing how Deleuze and Whitehead together provide conceptual resources for conceiving a truly 'speculative empiricism' and a 'superior ethology' that would move us closer toward a 'theory of thought capable of diagnosing in our becomings the ontological conditions for the real experience of thought' (xxiii). In her most recent book *Penser Avec Whitehead* (Editions de Seuil 2002), Isabelle Stengers deploys Whitehead's concepts as a 'free and wild creation' of the Deleuzian type, as nomadic 'empirico-ideal notions' that set up camp where they are, luring us toward new feelings and novel forms of experience.

Perhaps the most important aspect of both Alliez's and Stengers' approach to highlight here is that such new concepts and methods operate in accordance with a carefully defined principle of *constructivism*. This constructivist stance enables Stengers to pursue her Deleuzian inspired 'thinking with' Whitehead in relation to some of the most important abstractions of philosophical and scientific thought just as it enables Alliez to find in Deleuze-Whitehead a new transcendental philosophy (a 'transcendental materialism') that counter-effectuates the Copernican Revolution in the ontological production and auto-constitution of the new.

By developing some of the leads of the authors mentioned above—especially in relation to the role that this kind of constructivism plays in Whitehead's ontology—I would like to draw out a more detailed resonance between certain elements of the metaphysical framework developed in Whitehead's later works, particularly *Process and Reality* and *Adventure of Ideas*, and Deleuze's own virtual philosophy, especially in *Difference and Repetition*. Here I am trying only to establish a firmer basis in Whitehead's texts from which further work could proceed. It is hoped that this will not only open up new perspectives on Deleuze's thought but it will also show the extent to which Whitehead's work is ready for what one commentator calls 'rehabilitation,'[4] opening a space in which Whitehead's philosophy becomes once again a living and creative possibility for thought.

It is well known that with his 'untimely' practice of philosophy Deleuze invents for himself a tradition of his own, a tradition of 'immanent' philosophy within which he would think with and alongside his 'nomads,' creatively transforming and releasing a thinker for new becomings. I want to demonstrate that Deleuze's work offers us this possibility with Whitehead, but also I want to encourage others to develop this power in conjunction with other neglected Anglo-American thinkers. For example, Samuel Alexander, who Deleuze describes as a 'very, very great philosopher,' surely deserves to be read carefully by Deleuzians, especially those working on questions relating to the virtual and intensive magnitudes. Indeed, at many points Deleuze's philosophy of immanence connects up with the submerged tradition of 'process' philosophy, reconfiguring it in important ways. Placing Whitehead in resonance with Deleuze makes visible a range of marginalized philosophical resources, helping to retrieve process metaphysics and Anglo-American speculative philosophy as vitally relevant and still important but ignored traditions of philosophical modernity.

Thus the objectives of this chapter are several. Retrieving and beginning the work of developing these connections will enable us to see not only the extent to which Whitehead is one of Deleuze's 'mediators,' it will also allow us to contribute to a 'new Whitehead,' placing his thought before us once again as a philosophical 'event' worthy of attention. As Whitehead says, 'philosophy never reverts to its old position after the shock of a great philosopher' (PR, 11). Whitehead helped to place philosophy in a new position but we need the contrast of Deleuze, I argue, to help us feel this 'shock to thought.'

On the Deleuze side many have enjoyed Deleuze's appeal to getting 'behind' the authors he loves and, as we have mentioned, Deleuze recognized that a number of authors were already 'behind' him in this sense. To that group, then, I wish to add Whitehead as another that Deleuze loved and entered into 'encounters' with. But, apart from two or three brief, often very brief, discussions, this love is perhaps more 'secret,' operating internally, virtually and intensively as a kind of profound 'repetition' at the heart of Deleuze's texts. What this repetition and encounter show, I would argue, is the extent to which Deleuze could be read fruitfully as a process philosopher, a philosopher 'of' nature and a speculative metaphysical thinker of a deeply 'Whiteheadian' stripe. Thus, against the all too facile Anglo-American assimilation of Deleuze to 'postmodernism'—with which he has little in common (in fact more a deep antipathy) we posit a different image of Deleuze's thought, in connection with traditions and temporalities that still remain undeveloped and distant to its initial and continuing Anglo-American reception. Placing Deleuze's thought within these contexts opens the texts once again to the possibility of unforeseen and novel becomings.

The Actual and the Potential

Although there is much one could say about Whitehead's and Deleuze's shared conception of philosophy, their creative relation to the metaphysical tradition, and their understanding of the relation between philosophy and science, I will focus on how something like an ontology of the virtual operates inside the conceptual structure of Whitehead's later texts, especially *Process and Reality* and *Adventure of Ideas*. The key context for understanding the development of this ontology in Whitehead, which I can only very briefly sketch here, but will refer to again later, is to refuse to read Whitehead as simply a pre-Kantian metaphysical realist.[5] If Whitehead is read as exclusively pre-Kantian then he is an anachronism and the Anglo-American philosophical tradition's treatment of Whitehead is vindicated. Rather, Whitehead's pre-Kantianism plays much the same role in his thought as it does in Deleuze: a way of approaching and confronting the aporias of Kantianism as preparation for the laying out of an essentially post-Kantian philosophy of creativity and becoming. Whitehead is a deeply post-Kantian philosopher in much the same way that Deleuze is post-Kantian. We could say, crudely, that Whitehead's ontology is a fusion of pre-Kantian metaphysics with post-Kantian 'constructivism.' The concept that Whitehead returns to again and again to articulate this fusion or transformed relation to the tradition is '*inversion*': Whitehead inverts the pre-Kantians toward a principle of constructive or synthetic activity just as he inverts Kant's epistemic conditions toward a principle of ontological conditioning. Thus, although Whitehead's constructivism is dependent in part upon a Kantian principle of synthetic activity, his 'pre-Kantianism' nevertheless steps over any mere cognitive constitution toward a transcendental principle of ontological constitution. Whitehead still wants to explain the conditions of knowledge-being in terms of an a priori, but an 'ontological a priori' that is not grounded universally in human cognition but emerges and changes with the processual conditions of the world. Thus, Whitehead develops his own distinctively modified yet non-anthropological form of the transcendental where 'experience' is a given whose genetic conditions must be found in the ontological apriori. Rather than beginning with the subject and deducing its universal and ahistorical conditions of possibility, Whitehead begins with the objects of real experience and 'deduces' their genetic processes and ontological conditions. It is this ontological constructivism or *speculative empiricism* that Deleuze will take up in the name of 'transcendental empiricism' and turn completely in the direction of immanence.

In *Process and Reality* Whitehead's ontological constructivism is developed in terms of a distinction between the actual and the potential that resembles the Deleuzian distinction between the actual and the virtual and parallels the division of the given into extensive and intensive, space and duration, atomic/discrete and continuous, differen*c*iated and differen*t*iated. Whitehead's 'virtual' has two components: creativity and eternal objects and both have the virtual ontological status that Deleuze gives to the term: they are 'real without being actual, ideal without being abstract' (DR, 208). These components parallel Deleuze's own notions of 'difference' and 'Ideas.' Both are real potentialities but only creativity actualizes or differentiates itself. As with difference-in-itself only creativity is active, a univocal activity that is expressed, as Whitehead says, through 'two kinds of fluency.' Creativity is at once an activity 'conditioned by the objective immortality of the actual world' (PR, 31) and the creative advance into novelty. Whitehead's virtual and the actual enter into a relation of reciprocal determination and mutual presupposition such that each mode of process and each actual occasion is the general activity of creativity individualized by the imposed conditions. Creativity creates its own creatures and, apart from these 'accidents,' Whitehead says, creativity is 'devoid of actuality.' However, apart from the conditions imposed by these accidents there would be no novelty. It is what Whitehead calls the 'real potentiality' providing both the objects for a new occasion and the 'factor of activity' (AI, 179) for the initial phase of the new occasion. Creativity thus serves as the virtual or 'transcendental' principle behind the becoming and internal genesis of actuality as well as the principle of movement or extrinsic conditioning between actualities. If, in Deleuze, the virtual must be actualized along lines of difference, in Whitehead the virtual must be actualized through processes of creativity: 'creativity is the actualization of potentiality, and the process of actualization is an occasion of experiencing' (AI, 179).

In one of its manifestations of fluency, creativity actualizes potentials through eternal objects. Eternal objects form a 'reservoir' of 'pure potentials' (MT, 128). Eternal objects are indeterminate, passive, ideal structures 'devoid of becomingness and extension,' as Whitehead says, that undergo various modes of 'ingression' or 'incarnation' into the actual. This is what Deleuze, following Whitehead, calls the 'adventure of Ideas' (DR, 181). The adventures of eternal objects are double: on the one hand they involve both their realization or differen*c*iation into actual occasions where their 'individual essence' remains unique or 'isolated' ('eternal objects of the subjective species') and, on the other hand, the adventures of potentials concern the determination or differen*t*iation of their 'relational essence' with other eternal objects whereby patterns of connection and consistency between them are established ('eternal objects of the objective species'). Thus eternal objects form a fully determinate consistency or pattern of connection to each other but are indeterminate in relation to actuality. As Deleuze would say, every occasion or event is double with one part implicated in the fully determinate content of the virtual and the other explicated and receiving actual determination without either half resembling the other. This is no less the case with Whitehead: as 'eternal' the objects are 'pure potentials' in relation to the actual; as 'realized' the objects are to be considered as 'real possibilities' in the creation of new actualities. As 'pure potentials' eternal objects are organized as a 'multiplicity' (Whitehead's term in PR that replaces 'realm' in SMW), what Deleuze, referring to the structure of Ideas, calls 'virtual multiplicities,' understood as 'an organization belonging to the many as such, which has no need whatsoever of unity to form a system' (DR, 182). The general system of relatedness among potentials is a multiplicity of interconnected elements, point and relations, an infinite system of incompossibilities held together in 'differentiated relevance' by the 'prim-ordial nature of God.' In relation to this divine element Deleuze comments 'even God. . . . becomes Process, a process that at once affirms incompossibili-ties and passes through them.'[6]

Like the virtual in Deleuze the reality of the Whiteheadian virtual may be characterized according to the order of the problem. Thus, Whitehead describes each actual occasion as the 'solution' of indetermination in deter-minateness (SMW, 160). Eternal objects are, like Deleuzian Ideas, multipli-cities that acquire the status of a virtual problem when differentia*t*ed and a determinate integration and solution in the actual when differen*c*iated. Thus, Whitehead's virtual components function together in a twofold role: first, they function as something like the continuing potentiality of actual multiplicities (what Deleuze calls 'centres of envelopment') to enter into and condition new processes of becoming or intensive multiplicities and, second, by conforming to the conditions laid down in the actual and synthesizing and unifying these conditions with potential objects ('conceptual prehensions'), the processes of virtual becoming acquire their own individualized subjective form that may potentially generate richer and more intense, implicated contrasts or complex forms of individuation. The drive to individuation and unification is the prod-uct of the two phases of creative process and brings together the other notions ('many,' 'one') that form, along with creativity, what Whitehead calls the 'cat-egory of the ultimate' (PR, 21). Thus the creative advance into novelty is the process whereby the many become one and are increased by one, but this one creative process of unification is split into the two 'multiplicities' of process.

The Two Multiplicities: Transition/Concrescence

For Whitehead, like Deleuze, if these creative processes or multiplicities are not properly articulated together we will be left with a series of 'fallacies' regarding the nature of experience ('the fallacy of misplaced concreteness,' 'the fallacy of simple location,' etc.) not unlike the 'illusions' that Deleuze diagnoses. Like Deleuzian 'transcendental empiricism' and Bergsonian 'intu-ition,' Whitehead's method of 'descriptive generalization' aims to overcome the spatializing fallacies of consciousness and the 'bare' repetitions of habit and memory in order to account for the creative 'temporalizing' or processual conditions of experience. To explore this notion of time and Whitehead's two multiplicities of process in a little more detail we can contrast Whitehead's pro-cedures with Kant, as Whitehead himself does, revealing the extent to which Whitehead inverts the Kantian transcendental.

As is well known, Kant shows in his first *Critique* how objects conform to the structure of finite reason and he locates that structure in an opposition between intuition and understanding. Intuition is the form of receptivity and is dependent on what is given. Space and time are the pure forms of receptivity that 'we' bring to the given. Space is the 'outer sense' through which we represent objects outside us and time is the 'inner sense' through which we receive inner sensations. Kant gives time primacy as that which conditions all our representations. Time for Kant is self-affection, the mode through which the self relates to itself as a continuous identity. Through this self-relation objectivity is possible: to be an object for us that object must relate to time in one of its phases as past, present or future. Kant's 'Copernican turn' is effectively a revolution in the conception of time—crudely, time is now 'in us' in the sense that time is the formal condition though which any experience is possible. However, spatio-temporal determinations on their own are famously 'blind.' To be an object of experience that which is received must be filtered though the concepts of the understanding. Understanding might be thought of as a kind of gridding or net through which lumps of intuition must pass to receive conceptual form and shape. For Kant, sensibility and understanding are completely irreducible components but are brought to unity by the synthesizing activity of the transcendental ego—the 'I think' that must be able to accompany all my representations. In other words, the disconnected and passively received data of intuition and the concepts of the understanding are shaped into meaningful experience by the synthesizing activity of the 'transcendental unity of apperception' mediated by the 'schema' of the imagination. This forms the very rough and basic outline of Kant's solution to Hume's skepticism in the first *Critique*.

Whitehead will seek to invert the Kantian solution since it 'assumes the radical disconnection of impressions *qua data*' (PR, 113) such that knowledge begins with the bare datum or percept affecting an essentially passive and simple receptivity of intuition. Thus, Kant 'conceives his "Transcendental Aesthetic" to be the mere description of a subjective process appropriating the data by orderliness of feeling' (PR, 113). This is a false beginning for Whitehead since the datum is already an interconnection and an activity of 'feeling' or synthesis of 'prehensions' already in process. Behind the receptiveness of the ego and its perceptions (what Whitehead calls 'perception in the mode of presentational immediacy') lies the 'causal efficacy' of the 'I' of the understanding to represent what is given there must be sub-representative or non-representative syntheses conditioning its activity, what Michel Foucault would call an 'unthought' element that conditions me and that I do not control. The 'other' lives in me or Rimbaud's formula: 'I is another.' The 'other' lives objectively for Whitehead through the 'transference of throbs of emotional energy' (PR, 116) passing through the 'vector' of time, an experience that Whitehead designates as 'the passage of nature.' In *Process and Reality* Whitehead names this mode of process 'transition' and describes it variously as the 'vehicle of the efficient cause,' the 'immortal past,' or the 'perpetual perishing' (PR, 29, 81, 210) in us. Traditional readings of Whitehead tend to downplay or just ignore the role

played by 'transition' in Whitehead, but it is the key to Whitehead's ontology of
the virtual. Without transition there would be no real creative or differential
'repetition' and, as Whitehead says, 'tear "repetition" out of "experience" and
there is nothing left' (PR, 206). For Whitehead 'what becomes involves repetition transformed into novel immediacy' (PR, 207) and this process of transforming the bare, naked, material repetition and clothing it with feelings of
novel immediacy is initiated in transition. Transition is, then, not just the handing over or 'picking up' of already completed occasions. It is both the 'perishing,' or better, the 'immortalizing' or 'becoming immortal' of the present but
also the power of repetition that originates a new present in conformity with
the past. It is the 'passing on' (PR, 213), as Whitehead calls it, of the creativity
into which the actual occasion will infuse its own particularity. This unthought
or unconscious creative element is, then, more properly understood as a *temporalizing* synthesis in conformation with the past or as Whitehead says, following
Bergson, the synthesis is 'unspatialized' (PR, 114). These non-conscious and
non-spatialized elements or 'feelings' exhibit a vector character transforming
the past into a merging with the present. As Whitehead says: 'The *how* of our
present experience must conform to the *what* of the past in us.' (SYM, 58).
Creativity here is the ever advancing reality of the world, 'the throbbing emotion of the past hurling itself into a new transcendent fact' (AI, 227). The
processes of transition from the past, then, include an 'active' factor of desire,
creativity or power, a 'living urge' which, at a critical stage, *changes in kind* and
intensifies forming *concrescences* or modes of intense becoming which precede
and enable the formation of things, individuals or organisms. Whitehead's
theory of 'objectifications' explains how, in its transitional phase, this activity
drives the processes whereby the completed occasions of the past are repeated
inside the concrescing occasion. Objectification involves 'decisions' that push
the datum to a critical or poised threshold, marking points at which the process of transition spontaneously changes its structure, breaks symmetry and
becomes self-organizing. Whitehead describes this self-actualizing nature of
concrescence in terms of how the nascent occasion 'feels' that datum given
in the transition, and makes its 'decision' with respect to what it has received,
'grafting,' feeling and incorporating the data as an increasingly unique individuated 'subjective aim.' The process of concrescence is, then, properly *causa
sui* or self-actualizing but it emerges out of the datum given in transition. If the
transition is the disjunctive datum stripped bare with creativity approaching
zero, yet still carrying a factor of activity or desire, concrescence is the inten-
sifying subjective form, including the 'ingression' of relevant eternal objects,
that conjunctively 'clothes' itself in its movement of becoming toward 'satisfaction': the subject becomes 'superject.' In any case, the product of transition
is the new occasion in its earliest stage and concrescence is the complex self-
directed unfolding, dissociation and differentiation of transitional components into intensive fields, dynamisms and interiorities progressively passing

through what Whitehead calls the 'diverse routes' and 'borders of chaos' (PR, 111) that eventually determine and compose the extensive organism. As Whitehead says, 'organism has two "meanings," interconnected but intellectually separable, namely, the microscopic meaning and the macroscopic meaning' (PR, 128–9). The microscopic process is 'the real internal constitution' of the organism, enabling its growth from the real to the actual by a complex process of condition conversion. The macroscopic process is the transitional movement from the actual to the real, the 'superjective' advance or thrust whereby 'the future is merely real without being actual' (PR, 214). The actual occasion can be understood as an indissoluble double process with two odd dissimilar and dysymmetrical 'halves' or multiplicities, what Whitehead calls a 'subject-superject,' a process-product, an organism and environment that are meaningful only with reference to one another.

Thus, both transition and concrescence are distinct yet continuous phases or multiplicities of creativity. Transition *from* concrescence is creativity that is other-caused and transition *to concrescence* is other-causing, yet concrescence itself is self-causing creativity. Transition is creativity *that affects and is affected by the other* and concrescence is creativity that *affects itself.* Transition is creativity of the product to enter into other processes and concrescence is creativity to enter into the product.[7] These modes of creativity together drive the processes of becoming that constitute the real and its individuation.

Conclusion: Whitehead's Virtual as the Inversion of the Kantian Transcendental

Although there is much more that we could add here, this constitutes the basic core of Whitehead's ontology of the virtual. Like Deleuze's, Whitehead's ontology is dependent on a reconfiguration or 'inversion' of the Kantian transcendental, what Whitehead calls a 'critique of pure feeling' (PR, 113), and essentially Whitehead reproaches Kant for laboring under a misapprehension generated 'by an inversion of the true constitution of experience' (PR, 173). Rather than appeal to the a priori structures of consciousness to explain how something can be given to the subject, Whitehead, like Deleuze, points to an ontological constructivism to describe how the subject is constituted in the given according to the multiplicities of process. Thus, for Whitehead, 'Kant's "Transcendental Aesthetic" becomes a distorted fragment of what should have been his main topic' (PR, 113).

Whitehead's thought here may be understood as detaching the power of synthesis and unification from the transcendental subject and transposing it onto the creative processes, multiplicities, and occasions of real experience rather than possible experience, refusing any externally transcendent and anthropocentric first principle, ground, or foundation. Thus Whitehead's ontology of the virtual as an 'inversion' of Kant includes a return to a 'pre-Kantian' sense of the transcendental as relevant to all the properties of being and not just its cognitive representation through concepts. However, Whitehead retains the Kantian development of the transcendental as a condition's analysis but the conditions are not 'universal' (in the Kantian sense) but 'concrete universals' since they are no broader than the conditioned and the relation of condition to conditioned is radically heterogeneous and yet 'causally efficacious.' In other words, although the transcendental pertains to all acts of existence and cannot be reduced to any anthropocentric principles, Whitehead's transcendentalism still includes the search for the antecedent and genetic conditions of all real acts of existence, but the conditions operate according to different 'laws' from the conditioned empiricities they govern. In effect, Whitehead's 'categoreals' as he calls them are the 'nomadic' conditions—or speculative constructions—of the self-differentiating or self-creating nature of what is. For Whitehead, Kant's positions in the first *Critique* require a transcendental, virtual, or 'ontological' account of their conditions, an account of their internal genesis, and this is in part what Whitehead's later texts, especially *Process and Reality*, provide. Deleuze himself recognizes this in *Difference and Repetition* when he declares that *Process and Reality* is 'one of the greatest books of modern philosophy' (DR, 284–5) on account of Whitehead's construction of 'empirico-ideal notions' that radically modify and reconfigure Kantian categories of representation. Whitehead's philosophical positions here are deeply and distinctively recognizable as *post–Kantian*, an effort to '*supersede*,' as Whitehead himself says, the Kantian philosophy (PR, 113). These strategies are taken up and repeated with a difference by Deleuze as part of the effort to continue, in a radically revised form, the Kantian critical project as an 'ontology of the virtual.'

Notes

[1] One thinks, for example, of Maimon and Cohen from the neo-Kantian tradition and their respective understandings of the concept of 'intensity'; Duns Scotus and the doctrine of univocity; Peguy and the 'aternal'; Deleuze's use of C. S. Pierce, etc.

[2] 'En ce sens j' accuse la philosophie analytique anglaise d'avoir tout détruit dans ce qui était riche dans la pensée, et j' accuse Wittgenstein d' avoir assassiner Whitehead, d' avoir réduit Russell, son maître, à une sorte d' essayiste n' osant plus parler de logique. Tout ça fut terrible et dure encore.' See Deleuze's course on Leibniz—cours Vincennes, St Denis: l' évènement, Whitehead, 10/03/1987 @www.webdeleuze.com.

[3] John Rajchman, for example, in a discussion of Deleuze's adherence to a 'radical empiricism,' mentions the importance to Deleuze of Whitehead's 'fallacy of misplaced concreteness' in the claim that the abstract does not explain but must

itself be explained. See his *The Deleuze Connections* (MIT Press 2000). Most recently Brian Massumi, in his *Parables of the Virtual* (Routledge 2004), suggests that there is a 'close kinship' between Deleuze/Guattari and Whitehead, especially in relation to a shared commitment to an expanded empiricism. Although Manuel Delanda does not explicitly reference Whitehead, his own 'ontology of the virtual' is also, in my view, close to a certain understanding of Whitehead.

4   George Lucas (1989), *The Rehabilitation of Whitehead* (SUNY Press). I would like to think of my work here and elsewhere as a contribution to the project laid out in Lucas' outstanding work.

5   One of the notable exceptions here is the work of James Bradley who is one of the most original and important readers of Whitehead. See especially his 'Transcendentalism and Speculative Realism in Whitehead,' *Process Studies* 23(3) (Fall 1994).

6   Deleuze, *The Fold*, trans. Tom Conley (Minneapolis: University of Minnesota Press, 1993), p. 81. Deleuze, in his only extended discussion of Whitehead (*The Fold*, pp. 76–82), argues unequivocally for the pure immanence and openness of Whitehead's system as a 'chaosmos.' However, to what extent Whitehead's 'virtual' retains elements of transcendence is a very important topic. Eternal objects are arguably still too Platonic for Deleuze and although Whitehead's God may not prevent incompossibles from passing into existence, He would not affirm them. I do not have space here to do full justice to this topic.

7   In terms of Whitehead's work it is Jorge Luis Nobo who has argued the most persuasively for this distinction between transition and concrescence. See his *Whitehead's Metaphysics of Extension and Solidarity* (SUNY Press, 1986). The Spinozist distinction between the power to affect and be affected operates throughout Deleuze's work and is transposed into varying contexts and vocabularies. This distinction would form the basis for an analysis of the 'ethical' in Deleuze and Whitehead.

Works Cited

Deleuze, G. (1994), *Difference and Repetition*, trans. P. Patton (New York: Columbia University Press); cited in the text as DR.

Deleuze, G. and Guattari, F. (1994), *What is Philosophy?*, trans. G. Burchell and H. Tomlinson (New York: Columbia University Press); cited in the text as WP.

Whitehead, A. N. (1933/1967), *Adventure of Ideas* (The Free Press); cited in the text as AI.

—(1938/1966), *Modes of Thought* (The Free Press); cited in the text as MT.

—(1929/1978), *Process and Reality* (The Free Press); cited in the text as PR.

—(1925/1967), *Science and the Modern World* (The Free Press); cited in the text as SMW.

—(1927/1959), *Symbolism: Its Meaning and Effect* (Capricorn Books); cited in the text as SYM.

Part II

Schizoanalysis and Lacan

Chapter 5

On the Idea of a Critique of *Pure* Practical Reason in Kant, Lacan, and Deleuze

Andrew Cutrofello

Psychoanalytic reflections on Kant's account of the moral law tend to oscillate between two opposed hypotheses. On the one hand, Kantian ethics is said to be symptomatic of something—either obsessional neurosis or a perversion such as moral masochism—that psychoanalysis seeks to cure or mitigate. On the other hand, it is argued by some Lacanians that the stance of the Kantian moral agent who succeeds in sacrificing all pathological objects of inclination coincides with the ideal of separation at which the analytic cure itself aims. On this second view, Lacan's question 'Have you acted in conformity with the desire that is in you?' is itself an imperative to 'not give way on one's desire.'[1] The point of the comparison is that the Lacanian distinction between *desire* in its pure form and the *demand* which the subject directs toward imaginary objects is supposed to coincide with the Kantian distinction between an autonomous and a heteronomous will. Like Kant, psychoanalysis would direct the subject away from a eudaimonistic ethic to an ethic that is 'beyond the pleasure principle.' The problem with this second interpretation arises when the much-touted secret complicity between Kant and Sade is factored in. Lacan argues that from a strictly formal point of view, Sade's maxim to exercise 'the right to enjoy any other person whatsoever as the instrument of our pleasure' is just as universalizable as is any of the maxims that Kant takes to accord with the categorical imperative (S VII, 79). To accept this view is to face a choice: either to embrace an ethic that can manifest itself equally well through Kantian or Sadean maxims, or to go back to the initial interpretation of Kantian ethics according to which this ethic represents something to be worked through in analysis. Bataille sought a third solution, namely, to adopt a Sadean ethic thoroughly opposed to the Kantian. But Lacan suggests that Sade's disavowal of Kant—that is, his disavowal of the fact that diabolical evil is just another form of fidelity to the law—is no less naive than is Kant's disavowal of Sade, an insight which, had he accepted it, would have greatly depressed Bataille. Unlike Bataille, Lacan claims that if we are to sustain our status as *desiring* subjects, we must keep our distance from the Kantian–Sadean Thing, the too-intimate Good–Evil around which desire circulates (S VII,

73). In espousing this position, he seems to keep to the first interpretation of Kant—that is, the one according to which the Kantian experience of morality attests to a form of suffering that psychoanalysis promises to alleviate. But if this is so, what are we to make of the imperative not to give way on one's desire? Were it a question of not giving way on one's *demand*, we could read Lacan as saying that psychoanalysis frees us from the superegoic pangs of conscience by saying that it's OK to follow one's inclinations, to pursue not the Good but those pathological 'goods' that bring us pleasure. But in fact, Lacan explicitly argues that such a position—that of a eudaimonistic ethics based exclusively on the pleasure principle or 'the service of goods'—is untenable (S VII, 303). Not to give way on one's *desire* is, precisely, to give way on one's demands. Thus we find ourselves back with an ethic that seems close to that of Kant; whence the oscillation that I spoke of at the beginning. In what follows, I want to ask whether this oscillation is unavoidable, first by elaborating on the psychoanalytic critique of Kantian ethics, and then by considering Deleuze's attempt to radicalize it.

I

From a psychoanalytic point of view, it might seem as if Kant's principal mistake was to regard the sense of duty as an a priori fact of reason rather than as the a posteriori precipitate of the Oedipus complex. But Kant himself was perfectly willing to concede that we first become aware of the categorical imperative through education. Only if the *content* of this law turned out to be empirical would its a priori character be vitiated. Of course, the psychoanalyst might respond that the categorical imperative is in fact just an internalized version of the father's 'No,' from which it would follow that although the categorical imperative appears to command autonomy it remains a fundamentally heteronomous appeal. But such an analysis would already belong to the critical arsenal in terms of which Kant would have us distinguish between the moral law itself and its false impostors. Put otherwise, one cannot call attention to the fundamentally heteronomous character of the superego without implicitly making reference to the ideal of genuine autonomy—which is to say that if there were such a thing as the categorical imperative, it would carry within itself the basis for a critique of the pathological content of superegoic ethics.

Lacan pursues another line of argument. Instead of claiming that psychoanalysis reveals some supposedly hidden pathological content in the idea of the moral law, he suggests that Freud's account of the Oedipus complex explains how it is that we accede to the purity of the law, thereby learning to distinguish between (in Kantian terms) formal and material determining grounds of the will. On this view, psychoanalysis seeks to explain how it is that one becomes a subject with the capacity to bind one's will to maxims with determinate content, but this capacity remains that of pure, not empirical, practical reason. To the extent that psychoanalysis opens up the possibility for a critique of Kantian morality, it does so not by appealing to unconscious pathological incentives, but by calling attention to a paradoxically *non-pathological* symptom that emerges precisely when the subject *succeeds* in renouncing all such incentives (whether conscious or unconscious). Freud first detected such a symptom in his analysis of the Rat Man. Like Kant, the Rat Man feels compelled always to act as if he were obeying universalizable maxims, as when he tells himself 'You must pay back the 3.80 crowns to Lieutenant A.'[2] From a Kantian point of view, of course, the sense of being under an obligation to repay a debt is perfectly rational. But what about the Rat Man's conviction that he absolutely must count up to fifty between successive claps of thunder? (TCH, 32) He seems to treat this maxim as if it were a perfect or imperfect duty, that is, an obligation that follows directly from the categorical imperative itself. It might be argued that the Rat Man's moral reasoning is actually governed by an obscure *hypothetical* imperative, for he worries that if he fails to obey his maxims, something terrible will happen to a loved one. But this seems to be a way of giving his anxiety empirical content through a kind of secondary elaboration. Kant does something similar when he supposes that something terrible will happen to *us* if we fail to act on universalizable maxims, namely, when God apportions happiness and misery in accordance with moral desert. Thus it would seem that the only significant difference between Kant and the Rat Man lies in the specific duties which each purports to derive from the idea of a categorical imperative.

Kant thought that to carry out a critique of practical reason it was sufficient to show that there was such a thing as *pure* practical reason.[3] That is, he supposed that, unlike pure *speculative* reason, pure *practical* reason was immune to transcendental illusions. Such confidence encouraged him to think he could deduce a list of duties that were binding on *all* finite rational agents. Some of the duties that Kant puts forth in his *Metaphysics of Morals*—like the duty to repay the debts we have incurred—are acknowledged by a sufficiently large number of people that, provided we are 'normal' enough, they can seem to us to be genuinely universal. But others—such as the duties never to masturbate or engage in homosexual acts—are sufficiently controversial as to appear (at least to many of us) to be no less idiosyncratic than the Rat Man's rule about never failing to count to fifty between successive claps of thunder. This observation suggests that the moral systems of Kant and the Rat Man differ only in their respective degrees of idiosyncrasy. It also suggests that *any* attempt to deduce specific duties from the categorical imperative will be 'symptomatic' in some way. Freud claims that symptom formation in neurosis takes place not through repression per se, but through the peculiar way in which the repressed returns. Analogously, we could say that moral symptom formation takes place not in the *ascent* from inclination to respect for the law but in the subsequent

descent from consciousness of this law—which, insofar as it is pure, is empiric-
ally empty—to the formation of maxims with determinate content. The point
of the analogy is not that repression is *undone* in this descent, thereby enabling
the inclinations to play a direct, if hidden, role in maxim formation, but rather
that maxim formation allows the inclinations to reappear *as* repressed.

In the *Critique of Practical Reason*, Kant associates the subject's awareness of
the moral law with a sense of humiliation, a negative feeling that has as its
positive correlate the feeling of respect. This double feeling of humiliation
and respect is said to be unique in that it is not based on the principle of
self-love which governs the inclinations. On the contrary, it is occasioned by
the awareness of the categorical imperative, which gives rise to the feeling of
humiliation precisely insofar as it 'strikes down' this principle (CPrR, 63). The
fact that respect for the law is non-pathological is supposed to be a sufficient
guarantee of the non-idiosyncratic character of the subject's sense of what is
or is not a duty (CPrR, 64ff.). But what if this strange feeling of commingled
humiliation and respect—despite its genuinely non-pathological character—
attested to the influence of *another* heteronomous principle, one that was different in kind from the principle of self-love? This other principle is the one
that Freud identifies as the death drive, an impulse said to manifest itself in
its pure state only when all pathological incentives of the will have been put
aside, that is, when the death drive is no longer 'bound' to Eros. This is the
point that Lacan picks up on when he calls attention to the uncanny proximity between Kant and Sade. Lacan's point is not that Kant's system of morality
is just as pathologically motivated as Sade's, but that Sade's is just as pure as
Kant's. Obviously, Kant would have insisted that the statement 'Let us take as
the universal maxim of our conduct the right to enjoy any other person whatsoever as the instrument of our pleasure' (S VII, 79) violates the categorical
imperative, for no rational being could choose to live in a Sadean 'kingdom of
means.' But this is just to say, tautologically, that Sade is not a rational being.
Put otherwise, Kant can refute Sade only by purporting subjective universality
for the fact that he himself could not will to live in such a world, which is to say
that his argument rests on nothing more than his own *jouissance*, that is, on the
non-pathological feeling that arises when *he* renounces all material incentives
for his will[4] (S VII, 189).

The evident fact that Sade's *jouissance* was structured in a way diametrically
opposed to that of Kant suggests that it is possible to construct an antinomy of
pure practical reason in which Kantian maxims would be opposed by Sadean
maxims. Kant denied that there could be such an antinomy in part because he
thought that human beings, though radically evil in the sense that our maxims
are always informed by the principle of self-love, are incapable of diabolical
evil, that is, a principled rebellion against the moral law. But the problem goes
deeper than Kant thought. For even if we concede that the feeling of humiliation before the law has as its positive flip side the feeling of respect, how can

we rule out the possibility of a subject for whom respect is felt for the force that humiliates rather than for the force that elevates the will into the sublime realm of the kingdom of ends? Or, more radically, since the force of humiliation and the force of sublimation turn out to be but two aspects of one and the same law, what if one of the two could become an object of respect only insofar as the other did as well? Would it not follow that Kant could be Kant only by repressing his inner Sade, and that Sade could be Sade only by repressing his inner Kant?

Freud gave the name 'Rat Man' to one of his patients because of the peculiar way in which a torture involving rats figured in his symptoms. Someone had told him of a 'horrible punishment' in which rats were made to bore their way up the victim's anus (TCH, 12). Freud claims that when the Rat Man described this torture, the expression on his face suggested that what horrified him most was not the torture itself but the fact that, although he did not know it, the idea of inflicting such a torture on someone gave him great pleasure: 'his face took on a very strange, composite expression. I could only interpret it as one of *horror at pleasure of his own of which he himself was unaware*' (TCH, 13). Freud implies that the Rat Man is a Kantian desperately trying to repress his own Sadean impulses. But perhaps what horrifies the Rat Man most of all is the obscure awareness that his pleasure attests not merely to a sadistic inclination which respect for the moral law could combat, but to the non-pathological temptation of diabolical evil, a temptation that always necessarily accompanies respect for the law as its flip-side. On this interpretation, what the Rat Man shrinks back from is not just the fact that part of him is like Sade and part of him is like Kant, but rather the insight that he cannot be Kant without being Sade at the same time. Support for this reading can be found in a childhood anecdote which Freud recounts:

> When he was very small—it became possible to establish the date more exactly owing to its having coincided with the fatal illness of an elder sister—he had done something naughty, for which his father had given him a beating. The little boy had flown into a terrible rage and had hurled abuse at his father even while he was under his blows. But as he knew no bad language, he had called him all the names of common objects that he could think of, and had screamed: 'You lamp! You towel! You plate!' and so on. His father, shaken by such an outburst of elemental fury, had stopped beating him, and had declared, 'The child will be either a great man or a great criminal!' (TCH, 46)

This account is remarkable for a number of reasons. First, because it suggests that in his early childhood the Rat Man was confronted with an apparent either/or—a great man *or* a great criminal—that he secretly knows to be a both/and (one cannot be Kant without being Sade and vice versa). Second, because of the related ambiguity as to whether we are witnessing a good father beating a naughty child, a bad father beating a good child, an already-great-man-great-criminal-father beating a not-yet-great-man-great-criminal-child, etc., etc. Third, and especially, because of the truly fantastic speech act with which Freud credits the child: 'You lamp! You towel! You plate!' The idea that the child could know what cursing was without knowing any bad words seems improbable, and it ignores the question of what he might have *meant* (whether consciously or unconsciously) in calling his father these things. One possibility is suggested by an insult which Murellus hurls at the Roman citizens in Shakespeare's *The Tragedy of Julius Caesar*: 'You blocks, you stones, you worse than senseless things!' (I, I, 35). In comparing the Romans to inanimate objects, Murellus accuses them not only of stupidity, but of an *even greater* stupidity—'you *worse* than senseless things'—of which mere things are incapable, namely, *moral* stupidity: 'O you hard hearts, you cruel men of Rome' (I, I, 36). Similarly, in calling his father Lamp, Towel, and (worse than) Plate, the Rat Man—or, rather, the child destined to become *neither* a great man *nor* a great criminal but the Rat Man—seems to have accused his father of moral stupidity. The adult neither remembers the event (it was recounted to him by his mother) nor is consciously aware of the fact that he would very much like to shove a rat up his father's ass. Unable to confront the pleasure from which he continues to recoil in horror, the Rat Man remains caught within the double bind or antinomy of his father's either/or.

The idea that there is an antinomical relationship between Kantian and Sadean moral principles suggests that Kant's *Metaphysics of Morals* and Sade's *Philosophy in the Bedroom* both represent 'dogmatic' moral theories, and that the conflict between them necessitates a critique of *pure* practical reason. It is precisely such a critique that Lacan attempts to carry out in his seminar on the ethics of psychoanalysis. Following Lévi-Strauss, Lacan takes the prohibition of incest to represent the primordial 'You must!' the acknowledgment of which first introduces the subject into what analytic philosophers like to call 'the space of (moral) reasons.' But for Lacan, the lost maternal object which the subject must abandon only exists *as* lost. Like the Kantian 'transcendental object = X,' the lost object—*das Ding*, or the Thing—is different in kind from any empirical object that might appear within phenomenal, or imaginary, reality. As such it belongs to the order of the real, conceived not as a transcendent noumenal realm from which we are barred by our lack of intellectual intuition but as an impossible object that only 'exists' as a function of the law that prohibits access to it. By obviating the need for a distinction between appearances and things in themselves, Lacan is able to restrict the law to its immanent employment, the idea of the good functioning as a kind of *focus imaginarius*. Kant sought to determine this imaginary point of reference by transporting the subject into a kingdom of ends, and Sade did something analogous by describing his inverted ideal of a kingdom of means. But both solutions turn out to be 'false' in that they presuppose the existence of some transcendent object of a law-abiding will. Lacan resolves the antinomy of pure practical reason not by dissipating Kant and Sade's shared dialectical illusion but by simply calling attention to it. In this way he allows for a *critical* response to the categorical imperative, one that enables the subject to take on moral responsibilities by paradoxically *refusing* the commandment to love thy neighbor as oneself (S VII, 194). Herein lies the oscillation of which I spoke at the beginning of this paper.

II

Anti-Oedipus is usually read as repudiating the Lacanian theory of desire, but it is better read as radicalizing it. In 'How Do We Recognize Structuralism?' Deleuze had already claimed that in contrast to the unified and unifying Kantian subject, the Lacanian subject is essentially 'nomadic.'[5] In *Anti-Oedipus* he and Guattari praise Lacan for calling attention to the differential character of the unconscious and for resisting the normalizing tendencies of Oedipalization: 'he does not enclose the unconscious in an Oedipal structure. He shows on the contrary that Oedipus is imaginary, nothing but an image, a myth.'[6] Lacan is criticized on one ground only, namely, for putting forth a 'structural' rather than a 'machinic' account of desire, that is, for taking desire to manifest itself at the *symbolic* level of a logical combinatory' rather than at the *real* level of 'desiring-production' (AO, 53, 97, 109). Despite this criticism, Deleuze and Guattari credit Lacan with restoring desire to its strictly immanent employment. Like them, he recognized in desire 'the set of *passive syntheses* that engineer partial objects, flows, and bodies, and that function as units of production' (AO, 26). Unfortunately, a number of Lacan's followers *re-imposed* a 'transcendent' use on the syntheses of the unconscious by construing desire as lack (AO, 109). The aim of *Anti-Oedipus* is to complete the Copernican turn that Lacan made when he recognized that desire produces its own lost object. In carrying out their transcendental critique of the unconscious, Deleuze and Guattari seek to dispel a number of 'paralogisms of the unconscious,' thereby 'restoring the syntheses of the unconscious to their immanent use' (AO, 177, 112).

In *Difference and Repetition,* Deleuze carried out a similar operation with respect to thought. There it was a question of freeing the three time-constituting syntheses of Habitus, Mnemosyne, and the Eternal Return from the transcendent employments to which Kant's critique of speculative reason had delivered them.[7] In the practical register of *Anti-Oedipus,* the syntheses of Habitus, Mnemosyne, and the Eternal Return manifest themselves, respectively, as (1) the 'connective syntheses of production,' through which linear sequences of the form 'and then' are constituted, (2) the 'disjunctive syntheses of recording,' which have the form of 'either . . . or . . . or,' and (3) the 'conjunctive syntheses of consumption,' which take the form of a concluding 'so it's . . .' (AO, 12, 16). Deleuze and Guattari credit Kant with the discovery that desire is productive rather than privative, but they criticize him for reverting to the Platonic conception of desire as lack by reducing the object produced by desire to the status of a mere 'psychic reality' (AO, 25; cf. CPrR, 8n). They maintain that desire is productive not merely of representations but of the real itself (AO, 26). Desire is no longer a faculty belonging to a unified and unifying subject but a function of a differential manifold. Deleuze and Guattari characterize this manifold as a field of desiring machines each of which produces a flow that is siphoned off by another (AO, 1ff.). These linkages comprise the connective syntheses of the unconscious which collectively produce the so-called 'body without organs,' a virtual object that exists 'alongside' the series of connective syntheses (AO, 326). At the first level of synthesis, the body without organs stands opposed to its desiring-machines, repelling them in the manner of a 'paranoiac machine' (AO, 9). This can be thought of as the practical analogue of what Deleuze called in *Difference and Repetition* the 'pure present,' for the paranoiac machine immediately erases whatever appears on its surface so that something new can appear. Corresponding to the constitution of a 'pure past' are the disjunctive syntheses by which whatever is produced through the connective syntheses is recorded on the surface of the body without organs. Thus the body without organs also functions as a gigantic memory or 'miraculating machine,' attracting rather than repelling the desiring-machines that constitute or populate it (AO, 11). Finally, the conjunctive syntheses give rise to the 'celibate machine,' which, as the practical equivalent of the 'pure future,' unites the repulsive tendency of the paranoiac machine and the attractive tendency of the miraculating machine. The celibate machine is the locus of *jouissance* and affirmation (AO, 18, 84). In *Difference and Repetition* Deleuze characterized the intensive magnitudes which the celibate machine produces and consumes as 'differentials' whose reciprocal determination gave rise to manifest qualities. *Anti-Oedipus* suggests that the entire field of intensities is produced through desiring-production, the body without organs being its 'degree zero' locus (AO, 20).

According to Deleuze and Guattari, the desiring *subject* appears at the level of the third (conjunctive) synthesis, but only as 'a mere residuum alongside the desiring-machines'—a kind of surplus value that 'confuses' itself with the celibate machine (AO, 17). This misrecognition can be likened to the one that Lacan describes in his account of the mirror stage. The child's triumphal 'So it's *me*' is to be understood not as the self-recognition of a unitary subject but as a surface effect of desiring-production itself (AO, 20). Both Lacan and Deleuze treat the subject (as Sartre did in his essay 'The Transcendence of the Ego') as the precipitate of a network of fundamentally passive syntheses rather than as the instigator of active syntheses governed from the first by a principle of 'common sense.' Kant saw that the subject's pretension to intuit itself as a simple substance was a transcendental illusion, but he failed to recognize that his own conception of the 'original unity of apperception' was no less of an illusion. Oedipalization is the process whereby this illusion is generated. More precisely, Oedipalization can be understood as the process by which the three syntheses take on a transcendent as opposed to an immanent use. The connective synthesis of desiring-production, originally geared to 'partial' and 'non-specific' objects, is oriented toward parental figures and a system of conjugal rules. Desire is repressed, but in such a way as to give rise to the illusion that what had been desired all along is what is now explicitly prohibited by the conjugal rules themselves: 'Incest is only the retroactive effect of the repressing representation *on* the repressed representative: . . . it projects onto the representative, categories, rendered discernible, that it has itself established' (AO, 165). It is precisely through this 'paralogism of extrapolation' that desire comes to appear as lack (AO, 73, 110). In a similar way, the disjunctive synthesis, which had been inclusive ('either . . . or . . . or') now becomes exclusive ('eithr./or') as the subject is forced to think of differences in terms of rigid opr ositions (AO, 76). Here desire can only choose between subjecting itself to a transcendent law that directs it toward the symbolic order and retreating to an undifferentiated imaginary space—the choice between 'normality' and 'neurosis.' In either case, its 'real' nature as desiring-production is dissimulated. Deleuze and Guattari call this the 'paralogism of the double bind' (AO, 80). Finally, the conjunctive synthesis, whose immanent use had been 'nomadic and polyvocal,' becomes 'segregative and biunivocal' (AO, 110–11). This occurs when the third synthesis is subjected to a transcendent signifier which, as Lacan would say, 'represents' the subject in the symbolic order. Segregation involves the demarcation of a previously mobile field of intensities into series of determinable objects. Biunivocalization occurs when the mobile and immanent conjunctive synthesis 'so it's . . .' gives rise to the determinate and transcendent 'so *that* is what *this* meant.' (AO, 101). This corresponds to what Deleuze refers to in *Difference and Repetition* as 'the form of recognition'; Deleuze and Guattari call it 'the paralogism of application' (AO, 111). The problem with an Oedipalizing psychoanalysis—that is, one that succumbs to the dialectical illusion of transcendent uses of the syntheses of desire—is that instead of enabling subjects to free themselves from these paralogisms, it reinforces them by tying desiring-production to the capitalist machine. Deleuze and Guattari see Lacan as having tried to expose the paralogisms of Oedipus, but, again, 'certain disciples of Lacan have put forth "oedipalizing interpretations of Lacanism" which suggest that everyone—schizophrenics included—should be made to act like a neurotic subject caught within the Oedipal triad' (AO, 53, 73).

Earlier I suggested that the psychoanalytic critique of Kant does not undercut the distinction between pure and empirical practical reason but that it seeks to identify the antinomy to which pure practical reason succumbs at the moment when it renounces all pathological incentives of the will. Deleuze and Guattari do something similar, conceiving of Oedipus as the imaginary support of the transcendent exercises of the will. This suggests that the schizo represents a solution to the antinomy represented by Kant and Sade. However, the antinomy revealed in *Anti-Oedipus* concerns not the relationship between obsessional neurosis and perversion—that is, the difference between a Kantian desperately trying to repress a Sadean unconscious and a Sadean disavowing a Kantian unconscious—but between a 'normal' Kantian subject and a 'neurotic' Kantian subject. In *Coldness and Cruelty*, Deleuze asks: 'Is there no other solution besides the functional disturbance of neurosis and the spiritual outlet of sublimation? Could there not be a third alternative which would be related not to the functional independence of the ego and the superego, but to the structural split between them? And is not this the very alternative indicated by Freud under the name of perversion?'[8] In the face of this antinomy—the two horns of the Oedipal dilemma—the schizo finds a way out precisely through perversion. Whence the fact that for Deleuze—as for Blanchot and Bataille, but not for Lacan—Sade represents not one of the dead ends but rather a way out. Following Blanchot, Deleuze reads Sade as forging an alliance between the father and the daughter against the mother, and Masoch as staging an alliance between the son and a disavowed mother against the father, two different strategies for freeing desire from the Oedipal triangle (CAC, 60ff.). Sade subverts the law through irony; Masoch through humor, and so on (CAC, 86–8). Deleuze credits Bataille with identifying an authentic Sadean ethic, and for bringing out 'Sade's hatred of tyranny' (CAC, 17, 87). The question that would need to be posed is whether Deleuze's Sadean schizo remains Kant's inseparable twin when all is said and done. This is connected with another question that I can only touch on here, namely, whether it is possible to break decisively with Kantian morality once and for all, or whether the critique of pure practical reason must remain caught in its oscillation. What Lacan seems to be saying to Deleuze is that there is no purely immanent exercise of desire, not because there really is a transcendent object but because the production of the 'lost' object prevents desire from closing on itself. Not to give way on one's desire means *both* to resist the obsessional neurosis of Oedipus *and* to keep one's distance from the Thing. The point, in other words, is not to be *either* like Kant *or* like Sade, but to be *more* than a lamp, a towel, or a plate.

Notes

[1] Lacan, J. (1992), *The Seminar of Jacques Lacan Book VII: The Ethics of Psychoanalysis 1959–1960*, ed. Jacques-Alain Miller, trans. Dennis Porter (New York: W.W. Norton & Company), 314. Hereafter cited in the text as S VII.

[2] Freud, S. (1993), *Three Case Histories*, ed. Philip Rieff (New York: Simon & Schuster), 14. Hereafter cited in the text as TCH.

[3] Kant, I. (1997), *Critique of Practical Reason*, ed. and trans. Mary Gregor (New York: Cambridge University Press), 12. Hereafter cited in the text as CPrR.

[4] Here it would be necessary to elaborate on Kant's distinction between perfect and imperfect duties, and on the different ways in which we can tell if a maxim violates one or the other.

[5] Deleuze, G. (2004), 'How Do We Recognize Structuralism?' in *Desert Islands and Other Texts 1953–1974*, ed. David Lapoujade, trans. Michael Taormina (New York: Semiotext (e)), 190.

[6] Deleuze G. and Guattari, F. (1983), *Anti-Oedipus: Capitalism and Schizophrenia*, trans. Robert Hurley, Mark Seem, and Helen R. Lane (Minneapolis: University of Minnesota Press), 310. Hereafter cited in the text as AO.

[7] Deleuze, G. (1994), *Difference and Repetition*, trans. Paul Patton (New York: Columbia University Press), 70–91.

[8] Deleuze, G. (1991), *Coldness and Cruelty*, trans. Jean McNeil, in *Masochism* (New York: Zone Books), 117. Hereafter cited in the text as CAC.

Chapter 6

What if the Law is Written in a Porno Book?
Deterritorializing Lacan, De-Oedipalizing Deleuze and Guattari

Shannon Winnubst

Reading Lacan often feels like an exquisite practice in female masochism. It hurts, stuns, burns, resists—only to pull me further into its maze, seducing with the intensity of its pain. I identify all too easily with the indignant woman in Jacques-Alain Miller's introductory dialogue of *Television*, who refuses to submit to the label of 'idiot' that Lacanian discourse designates as her proper name. Reading Deleuze and Guattari, on the other hand, often feels like candy—both the high fructose kind that rots my teeth, and the 'candy' that euphemizes heroin, plunging me into hallucinations and bodily euphoria of the most pleasurable sort. To read these authors together thereby produces a most startling conflation of pain and pleasure, fertile ground upon which to explore the machinations of the law—that structure through which our ethics and politics are cathected.

Reading the law as this site of pain and pleasure, I pose the question: what if the law is written in a porno book? The phrase, lamentably, is not mine. It comes from Deleuze and Guattari's reading of that great scene from Kafka's *Trial*: Joseph K breaks into the inner sanctum of the law only to find several—not One—law books filled with bad porn, 'an indecent picture' (*Trial*, 52) of a nude man and woman. Crudely drawn images of pleasure displace the esoteric language of authority as the alleged site of justice. And all that hinges on the mechanisms of the law—identity, recognition, judgment, causality, temporality—shift with this unmooring of the law from its stable perch.

Deleuze and Guattari rail against the stupidity of those who would render Kafka's prose metaphorical. Distinguishing Kafka's texts as a 'minor literature,' they sever his language from systems of referentiality and representation: 'Kafka deliberately kills all metaphor, all symbolism, all signification, no less than all designation' (*Kafka*, 22). A deterritorializing rhizome, Kafka's texts resist the introduction 'of the enemy, the Signifier and those attempts to interpret a work that is actually only open to experimentation' (3). This severance from representational language is a political act, constituting politics as the dethroning of interpretation machines.

　　The line between interpretation and experimentation thereby becomes the boundary for good and bad readings—of Kafka, the world, oneself, and desire. And the conceptual fulcrum of that boundary is Oedipus. To enter Kafka's 'micropolitics of desire,' we must 'deterritorialize Oedipus into the world instead of reterritorializing everything in Oedipus and the family' (*Kafka*, 10). The charge against psychoanalysis is explicit, not only in their text on Kafka but across so many of Deleuze's and Deleuze and Guattari's texts: when psychoanalysis renders desire as a lack, it simultaneously renders politics as a matter of signification, a matter of the law as it is written in the Symbolic. This is what draws Deleuze and Guattari to Kafka: 'We believe only in a Kafka *politics* that is neither imaginary nor symbolic. We believe only in one or more Kafka *machines* that are neither structure nor phantasm. We believe only in a Kafka *experimentation* that is without interpretation or significance. . .' (7). While psychoanalysis would allegedly *interpret* Kafka, reducing his bizarre scenes of pleasure and pain before the law to unusual twists of signification that we can nonetheless decipher and judge, Deleuze and Guattari find *experimental* resistances to this latent fascism.

　　To read psychoanalysis as this reterritorializing force is to read its texts as the work of arborescent structures, just as Deleuze and Guattari insist across *Anti-Oedipus* and *A Thousand Plateaus*: 'Take psychoanalysis as an example: it subjects the unconscious to arborescent structures . . . central organs, the phallus, the phallus tree' (*A Thousand Plateaus*, 17). This arborescent reading reduces psychoanalysis to the singular conceptual figures of a Freudian Oedipus or Lacanian phallus. To think conceptually about the law and desire is to appeal to a transcendental structure that fully recognizes the subject in a manner which surpasses the capacity of the subject to grasp itself. This transcendental law renders the subject as lacking the capacity for self-consciousness and subsequently dependent upon the law for its own meaning, which it craves: recognition-lack-dependency-desire. It is an old story. And, for Deleuze and Guattari, it is the mechanism of interpretation-machines and their latent fascism—the political epistemology they bestow upon psychoanalysis.

　　But if we look more closely at the texts of both Deleuze and Guattari and Lacan, such a reading of psychoanalysis is not so easily found. In several texts, Deleuze and Guattari hold Lacan out as an exception that apparently proves the rule of dogmatism in psychoanalysis. For example, early in *Anti-Oedipus* amidst their condemnation of psychoanalysis' disastrous rendering of desire as lack, they note that 'Lacan's admirable theory of desire appears to us to have two poles: one related to 'the object small *a*' as a desiring-machine, which defines desire in terms of real production, thus going beyond both any idea of need and any idea of fantasy; and the other related to the 'great Other' as a signifier, which reintroduces a certain notion of lack' (*Anti-Oedipus*, 27). While we are left to lament the triumph of the latter pole, they indicate the possibility of Lacan conceiving of a productive desire through the *objet a*.[1]

We also find traces of experimentation and productive desire in Lacan's texts. In 'The direction of treatment and the principles of its power,' Lacan explains that the role of analysis is not to interpret a subject's behavior, but to confront and provoke the resistances that block particular pathways of desire, behavior, pleasure. He even appears to disavow the cardinal rule of Freudian Oedipal machines, demonstrating the insufficiencies of reading dreams as metaphorical. And, finally, he initiates us into a complicated tangle of causality and temporality when he shows how the final value of an interpretation emerges through what it provokes, not through what it explains: 'to confirm that an interpretation is well founded . . . will emerge as a result of the interpretation' (*Écrits*, 234). Interpretations are not referential for Lacan: they are productive.

To *experiment* with rather than interpret Lacan is therefore not only to read Lacan as Deleuze and Guattari read Kafka, but also to read Lacan as Lacan reads the world. It brings us into a world that may sound more Deleuze and Guattarian than Lacanian: mazes of temporality and causality where subjectivity and desire emerge as effects without causes, surfaces without depths, forces without intentions. Rather than the classic reading of desire as driven by an ontological lack, the following *experimentation* with Lacan approaches the question of the law and desire through this 'other pole' of Lacan's theory of desire—namely, through the Real and *objet a*.

This reading of the law in its relation to the Real will trace out Lacan's suggestion that interpretation is a problem of chronos—a matter of introducing something 'into the synchrony of the signifiers that compose [interpretation] . . . in order to decipher the diachrony of unconscious repetitions' (*Écrits*, 233). The process of introducing this 'something' into the synchrony of signifiers opens us onto a second 'cut' in discourse—namely, the asignifying effects of the Real that surface as *objet a* to cause our desire. Developing this different reading of desire as emergent from the asignifying Real, rather than the call of the Other into the Symbolic, I will trace how this leads Lacan to his infamous reading of Kant as initiating a purely formal law that is not cathected with pleasure or pain and, therefore, is not distinguishable from its Sadean counterpart. Drawing parallels between Lacan's 'Kant avec Sade' and the reading of Kant that Deleuze offers in *Coldness and Cruelty*, I suggest that Lacan may not be so different from Deleuze. For Lacan, we respond to the asignifying scene of the Real as Deleuze suggests we might best respond to the purely formal law: we can only laugh, that gleeful noise through which we subvert the law and its absurdity. It will be through this laughter that we will find final resonance between Deleuze and Guattari and Lacan. Having traced the similarities in their depictions of the purely formal law of modernity, I will return to Kafka and *experiment* with Lacan, listening for the distinctly Lacanian ring in the boisterous laughter over Joseph K's *mis*identification before the law. Reading the masochistic scene of The Whipper, we will find Lacan also laughing at that moment when K is asked by the Examining Magistrate: 'Well, then, you are a house painter?'

The Block of the Phallus

We must first work our way back through the construction of Lacan's texts as a conceptual machine. The dominant reading of Lacan in the Anglophone academy has focused on his transposition of Freudian schemas into the field of language. Most readings have focused on his development of the Symbolic as the register in which the law operates, specifically the submission to the phallic signifier through which all meaning must pass. While many theorists have deconstructed this model of subjectivity and its erasure of sexual difference, several have argued that this reading over-emphasizes the role of the Symbolic, at the expense of Lacan's later shifts toward the Real and *objet a*.[2]

In the dominant reading, desire is framed as the translation of need and demand into the Symbolic order. Grounded in the ontological break of the infant from the Mother, the phallic signifier intercedes in the mother–child dyad to introduce the law, completing the Oedipal triangle and granting entrance into language. Desire is thereby doomed to failure, haunted as it is by this ontological lack of demand and need. Furthermore, the law functions primarily through the rule of prohibitions, which locates subjectivity in a self-splitting double-bind: its entrance into language severs it from the plenitude of pre-linguistic/pre-Oedipal contiguity with the M/Other; and yet the phallic law of language prohibits any return to this romanticized realm of plenitude. Cast out of Eden, the subject can only desire that which the law will always prohibit. Moreover, the *méconnaissance* endemic to the field of signifiers will render the quest for one's identity only more and more dependent on this cruel prohibition of the law. It is a sadistic law that produces a masochistic subject who cannot resist its attraction. It is also the reading of desire that dominates Deleuze and Guattari's renderings of psychoanalysis as the phallic-tree-machine.

Lacan never disavows his early work on the field of language as a phallicized entrance into signification. Nor does he ever disavow the role of the 'barred S,' the impossibility of coming to any full or transparent recognition of a 'pure self' before the law. In keeping with these prior formulations, he is forced into particularly convoluted speech as he attempts to delineate the register of the Real. The most well-known formulation is the one he offers via double-negation, 'the lack of a lack,' indicating the impossibility of rendering the Real directly in speech. Desire stands in a different relation to the Real than that form through which we experience desire. *Experience* is always already mediated through the Symbolic, which renders desire as a lack that stands before the judgment of the prohibitive, phallicized law. But the Real, this 'lack of a lack,' is devoid of signifiers and does not submit to that law. Functioning as a limit to the Symbolic order, the Real stands in as a representation of that which cannot be represented. But rather than taking the Heideggerian, Derridean or Levinasian turn of rendering this 'unrepresentable' as that which cancels itself out upon articulation, Lacan struggles to trace the *effects* of the Real without positing some conceptual structure as the *cause* of those effects, a turn that looks more like strategies we associate with Deleuze and Guattari, as well as Foucault. To trace the effects of the Real in the register of desire therefore requires a sense of its relation to language, the site of our *experience* of desire and subsequent failure to experience—or render into language—the Real.

When Lacan tells us that 'the channel of desire flows . . . as a derivation of the signifying chain' (*Écrits*, 259), the vertiginous effects of the Saussurean play of signification on the subject emerges. '[T]the subject does not even know where to pretend to be [the] organizer' (*Écrits*, 259) of this signifying chain; the subject can only realize itself as an *effect* of a play of signification that has no anchoring cause in the signified. Contingent effects layer one upon another to produce a desiring subject that cannot understand the desire it is experiencing. To have even the possibility of recognizing this desire as 'his own,' the subject must assume the position of the Other, the site and *apparent* cause of desire—a move also known as analytic transference.

According to the dominant reading, we should understand this place of the Other through the phallic signifier: the Other functions as the site allowing entrance into the law and replaces the Mother as the child moves, in Freudian terms, into the Oedipal drama and, in Lacanian terms, into the field of signification. The Lacanian twist on the Hegelian struggle for recognition emerges as the desire not only to be recognized by the Other, but the desire to be the *cause* of desire in the Other. But if we emphasize the relation of the law to the Real, Lacan introduces yet another figure, the *objet a*, which he (annoyingly!) describes as 'the *cause* of desire' (*Television*, 82).

In 'The subversion of the subject and the dialectic of desire in the Freudian unconscious,' Lacan distinguishes Hegelian and Freudian notions of desire vis-à-vis the Real, and distances himself from his earlier Hegelian models. He argues that the Hegelian model of desire forecloses the Real in its claim to absorb it into the viable possibility of full self-consciousness. For Hegel, desire is fundamentally the desire to know; consequently, it unfolds in the time-space of the Symbolic and its desire (driven by lack) for self-consciousness, not fundamentally altering the Master–Slave dialectic.[3] To the contrary, Freud reads desire in the scene of the unconscious, rendering Hegelian self-consciousness impossible. Again placing us in a field of effects without causes, Lacan writes that 'in the Freudian field, . . . consciousness is a feature . . . inadequate to ground the unconscious in its negation . . ., since it is a service that has no holder' (*Écrits*, 297). The unconscious is not a suppliant to any dialectic of consciousness—neither as negation nor as cause. And desire, as unconscious and involving 'the real of the body' (*Écrits*, 302), is irreducible to demand and need. The unconscious is a service that has no holder, an effect with no cause, a surface with no depth. This is the other scene (*Écrits*, 297) that psychoanalysis opens.

In reading this scene through the relation of the law to the Real, we shed the Hegelian overtones of a self-Other dialectic. The analytic scene operates in 'the function of the cut in discourse' (*Écrits*, 299). Lacan acknowledges two cuts in language. One kind 'acts as a bar between the signifier and signified' (*Écrits*, 299) and he addresses it through the phallic signifier in the Symbolic. But the analytic scene opens onto another cut in the signifying chain, which 'verifies the structure of the subject as discontinuity in the real' (*Écrits*, 299). These are moments when discourse 'stumbles or is interrupted' (*Écrits*, 299)—for example, witticisms, slips of the tongue, jokes, perhaps laughter. The analytic scene opens onto 'holes' in signification that are not mere slippage between word and object, but effects of that strange time unconscious forces, which erupt into signifying relations.

The lack endemic to language thereby assumes another dimension—these 'holes' produced in the signifying chain by the eruption of asignifying forces. We can best map these holes through the breaks in synchronous temporality they initiate. In his 'Names-of-the-Father Seminar,' Lacan turns toward the function of the *objet a* to map those moments in which 'the subject is affected by the desire of the Other . . . in a nondialectizable manner' (*Television*, 82). That is, he turns to this figure of the *objet a* to outline the effects of the Real, which resists signification, in experience. He subsequently alters our orientation to the scene of desire by focusing on the *objet a*, rather than the call of the Other, as the cause of desire.

Awkwardly temporalizing a phenomenon that does not fit into chronological schemas, Lacan describes the *objet a* as a 'primal' falling away from the subject, through which the subject comes to desire. The Real is thereby interpellated by the Symbolic, producing the diversity of forms in which we experience desire. For example, whether we experience the object of our desire as oral, anal or genital depends on how 'its' fall is signified by the Symbolic mediation: 'The diversity of forms taken by that object of the fall ought to be related to the manner in which the desire of the Other is apprehended by the subject' (*Television*, 85). These experiences are already phallicized through the law of the Symbolic; but the *objet a* indicates the limits of such experiences and the subsequent 'obscurity into which the subject is plunged in relation to desire' (*Television*, 87). The subject comes to be constituted as a legible subject of desire through a cutting-away of *objet a*, through the resistance against signification that propels the subject into the phallicized signifying field. The 'lack of a lack' of the Real erupts into the signifying field through the *objet a*, which is mediated by the Symbolic into legible forms of desire, experienced through the lack endemic to signification. The *objet a* thereby 'causes' the desire of the subject through this 'primal' resistance of signification and cutting-away from the subject.

To trace the effect of the *objet a* requires a technique that will not render it a causal or conceptual structure: Lacan returns us to the voice of the Other in the scene of desire. In Seminar I, he developed the voice of the Other, which is critical to the analytic scene, as the essential site through which the ego is interpellated by the Symbolic. But in the 'Names-of-the-Father Seminar,' Lacan focuses on the phenomenality of the voice, rather than its issuance from the Other, as an '*objet a* as fallen from the Other' (*Television*, 87). Through this phenomenological approach to the structural function of the voice, Lacan attunes us to the asignifying quality of the voice *per se,* rather than its signifying speech. We hear the voice as sound, even as noise, not as signification: we are no longer in the scene of *experience* and the interpellation of the Symbolic. It is no longer a matter of meaningful speech calling us from the Other into subjectivity, but of a more 'primal' question about the emergence of voice at all: 'we can no longer elude the question: beyond he who speaks in the place of the Other, and who is the subject, *what is it* whose voice, each time he speaks, the subject takes?' (*Television*, 87)

Here Lacan confronts the convoluted schemas of temporality and causality. In following out this question of how a voice emerges at all, Lacan suggests we are not wholly 'animals at the mercy of language' (*Écrits*, 264). Because desire is experienced as an effect of the second cut in language, the Real functions as the impossible against which symbolization is constantly elaborated. But rather than reduce this to a matter of dialectical negation and submit the Real to the laws of signification, Lacan strives to maintain the Real as generative, as lacking the lack of the Symbolic. Ultimately, this will require a turn to geometrical topologies to map the temporality of a deferred, nonlinear chronology that does not assume the unfolding causality of time.[4] But we can already see that the Real *has no substance and can only be read via effects, which it produces out of excess and abundance that do not signify.*

So, what happened to the porno book? When Deleuze reflects on his work with Guattari on Kafka, he recognizes that he was attempting similar dynamics in his prior work on Sacher-Masoch, where he also found the law in a porno book, of sorts.[5] He describes Sacher-Masoch's texts as 'pornological literature[, which] is aimed above all at confronting language with its own limits, with what is in a sense a "nonlanguage"' (*Coldness*, 22). Sacher-Masoch's texts enact a law that is not Symbolic. As Deleuze elaborates the contours of this law, which emerges out of contracts and exemplifies the modern condition of law, we find inversions of temporality, causality, and identity that bear strange resemblances to those we have encountered with Lacan and his subsequent reformulation of the law through 'Kant avec Sade.'

Chastising psychoanalysis again, Deleuze focuses on the characteristic of masochism that psychoanalysis misses: the role of contracts. Reproducing two of Sacher-Masoch's contracts with his 'torturesses,' Deleuze shows how 'the function of the contract is to lay down the law, which, once established, becomes increasingly cruel and restrictive toward one of the parties' (*Coldness*, 76). The contract thereby generates a law and the terms of this law often 'over-step and contravene the conditions which made it possible' (*Coldness*, 77). Resembling the classic social contract, these masochist contracts generate a law that erases the consent which made the contract possible. But rather than guaranteeing security and protection, these masochist contracts guarantee wholesale submission to the whims and caprices of another, including expli-·citly those that cause suffering and pain.

Turning to Kant, Deleuze develops how the law in Sacher-Masoch's contracts exemplifies the condition of modern law. Kant inverts the classical Platonic-Christian relations between the law and the Good, thereby rendering the law a purely formal concept: 'Kant gave a rigorous formulation of a radically new conception, in which the law is no longer regarded as dependent on the Good, but on the contrary, the Good itself is made to depend on the law. This means that the law no longer has its foundation in some higher principle from which it would derive its authority, but that it is self-grounded and valid solely by virtue of its own form' (*Coldness*, 82).

Because the law is now defined by its pure form, its content is insignificant and indeterminate; consequently, we can never be edified in our adherence to the law. We cannot discern either our own motivations or the righteousness of our acts: we only know we are guilty. Constantly judged by the internalized, hyper-vigilant law, we are always guilty in advance of any action or desire: 'the law manifests itself in its absolute purity, and proves us guilty' (*Coldness*, 84).[6] This sounds strikingly similar to the reading of modern law Lacan offers us in his essay, 'Kant avec Sade.' This is where we also find the shift in the function of the law that follows from our re-orientation toward the Real and *objet a* as the cause of desire. For Lacan, Kant renders the moral law a purely formal structure, void of signification just as it is void of any object or pathological cathexis.[7] If *objet a* is the cause of our desire, rather than the call of the Other, the law is removed from the libidinal forces that it judges. We are no longer drawn to the law by our need for its (mis)recognition; rather, emerging through the cutting-away of the *objet a*, we come before the law without any possibility of signification. Coming before a purely formal entity that no longer judges us according to the specific content of our actions or intentions, we no longer attempt to justify ourselves before the law: signification has no place here. Beyond good and evil, in the asignifying scene of the Real, the purely formal law is absurd. Not only can we not distinguish between Kant's and Sade's imperatives, but we also begin to hear how we laugh—with Lacan and Deleuze and Guattari—at dear old Joseph K.

The Boisterous Laughter

In his reading of Kant in *Coldness and Cruelty*, Deleuze turns back to Kafka's world as a delineation of this 'dimension of the modern conception of the law' (84). And he seems to turn there because it is all so funny. As he tells us, 'Max Brod recalls when Kafka gave a reading of *The Trial*, everyone present, including Kafka himself, was overcome by laughter' (*Coldness*, 85). Laughter ushers us into the comic—not the tragic—as 'the only possible mode of conceiving the law' (*Coldness*, 86). Deleuze argues that irony and humor are how we are cathected to this modern law: they are the libidinal forces through which the law functions and, consequently, through which we respond. In the purely formal law of modernity that renders us all guilty in advance, the law does not heed or depend upon any transcendental Good to keep it in its bounds: unhinged from any determinate content, it becomes a potential seat of tyranny. We are thereby called upon to transcend or subvert the law, and irony and humor are the two modes through which we can do so.[8]

For Deleuze, the texts of Sacher-Masoch provide a humorous subversion of the law that twists its authority to such extremes that the absurdity of a law-without-content is exposed. The laughter in, at, and of Kafka thereby becomes crucial. When we laugh at and with Kafka, Deleuze hears the laughter of a masochist humor. When we laugh at and with Kafka, we have consented to a contract with a masochist: the pure formal law that judges Joseph K guilty without his consent is merely the agreement generated out of the masochist contract. And, yes, the contract is expressed in the images of bad porn—a very odd, and very funny, moment in K's Trial.

The humor that this masochism provokes in us exposes the absurdity of an empty, formal law that pre-emptively judges us guilty. The masochist humor subverts the law through a temporal reversal: 'A close examination of masochistic fantasies or rites reveals that while they bring into play the very strictest application of the law, the result in every case is the opposite of what might be expected (thus whipping, far from punishing or preventing an erection, provokes and ensures it)' (*Coldness*, 88). Rather than occurring after the forbidden act of pleasure, the punishment now becomes the necessary condition for the possibility of pleasure. And this subverts the law: 'What else but a demonstration of absurdity is aimed at, when the punishment for forbidden pleasure brings about this very same pleasure?' (*Coldness*, 89) The punishment does not cause the pleasure: it becomes the necessary condition for achieving pleasure. When we laugh at Joseph K's discovery that the law is filled with bad porn, are we not receiving pleasure on the condition of his ongoing torture for a crime he never committed by a law that is patently absurd?

Jospeh K is not a masochist: he never submits to the law. Moreover, he constantly identifies with the law, positioning himself as the one man who can see the Truth of what is happening. But Kafka has submitted to the purely formal law, and his bizarrely comic literature is the masochist contracts he offers us. If we can, in turn, submit to Kafka, we may then be under the spell of 'a logician of consequences' (*Coldness*, 89), a masochist who subverts the law through reversing its temporal and causal orders: Joseph K is harassed, tortured, haunted by, and ultimately killed as a consequence that has no cause. The purely formal law is a seat of tyranny, and we can only subvert it through laughing at its absurdity.

Does Lacan, then, laugh at Kafka as well?

The Whipper

Whipping is one of the most fetishized acts of sado-masochism. And it is also one of the funniest and kinkiest scenes of *The Trial*. Erupting seemingly from nowhere into the narrative, K cannot resist the scene: 'Seized by uncontrollable curiosity . . . he literally tore the door open' (83) and stumbles upon the two warders receiving a whipping—allegedly for having stolen K's undergarments. The scene is saturated with classic sado-masochistic details. Kafka immediately directs us to the whipper and his clothing, 'sheathed in a sort of dark leather garment which left his throat and a good deal of his chest and the whole of his arms bare' (84). Deleuze and Guattari point out that '(t)oday still, these are the clothes of American sado-masochists, dressed in leather or rubber, with folds, buckles, piping and so on' (*Kafka*, 68): we cannot avoid the erotically charged details of the scene, which lead to temporal and causal reversals that vertiginously threaten K's identity. From a Lacanian perspective, K opens onto 'that other scene' of the unconscious when he stumbles into the scene of the whipper—a scene of the Real, saturated with *objet a* and their stirring of desires we cannot understand.

Kafka teases us with an explicitly Oedipal interpretation that would wrap this into a neat package of the Symbolic law: the warders plea their innocence on the basis of familial and marital commitments, and the justice of the punishment centers on K's intentions. Moreover, in case we didn't really get it, the Whipper is literally beating these men with a phallus, a 'rod.' But the Whipper does not speak in ways that can be understood in the causal order of the law: 'the punishment is as just as it is inevitable' (84). And the role of the mouth, that organ of the Symbolic, is doubly desacralized: Willem's mouth eats rather than speaks, and it is smacked by the rod. No speech makes any sense here.

Upon entering the room (which hilariously resembles a closet), K persists with his assured self-identification as a moral super-hero out to fight the corruption of the law. He takes it as 'obviously his duty to intervene on this occasion' (88). But two events unhinge this self-identification: Franz's animal shriek, 'single and irrevocable' (87), and the exact repetition of the scene the next day—an asignifying voice and a temporal/causal impossibility. At this final moment, K spins vertiginously, slams the door, and beats it with his fists, ordering that the room be cleaned out: 'We're being smothered in dirt!' (90).

For Lacan, he may as well be the house-painter: can you hear him laughing?

Notes

[1] Deleuze and Deleuze & Guattari sprinkle other texts with similar suggestions regarding Lacan. For example, in *Dialogues*, Deleuze parenthetically remarks that, contrary to 'the dead look' and 'stiff necks' of psychoanalysts, 'only Lacan has kept a certain sense of laughter' (82). I will return to this central activity of laughter as a mode through which Lacan resists the arborescent structures of interpretation.

[2] Some of the most important feminist readings of Lacan include Irigaray, Grosz, and Braidotti. For the argument that widespread misreadings of Lacan have been circulated in Anglo-American contexts due to the influence of French feminism, which have centered readings of Lacanian psychoanalysis strictly on the dynamics of the phallic signifier and the enactment of the Law in the register of the Symbolic, see Dean. Dean also focuses on 'the later Lacan' of the 1960s and 1970s for greater emphases on the Real.

[3] For a provocative reading of this aspect of Hegelian desire as therefore 'unfolding in time' and an effort to exceed its grasp through a move into general economy, see Bataille, 202.

[4] Lacan attempts to capture this in his phrase, 'wo es war, soll Ich werden' (*Écrits*, 299), which inverts both the temporal chronology and the surface-depth spatiality of desire-as-lack-before-the-Law. As Lacan tells us, 'the idea that the surface is the level of the superficial is itself dangerous. Another topology is necessary if not to be misled as to the place of desire' (*Écrits*, 240).

[5] See *Dialogues*, 119.

[6] To continue down another corridor in this maze of mirrors, Deleuze recognizes Freud for capturing concisely when he shows in *Civilization and Its Discontents* that 'the more virtuous a man is, the more severe and distrustful' (*Coldness*, 84) is his conscience.

[7] For more on this dynamic, see Andrew Cutrofello's chapter in this volume.

[8] I focus on the masochist humor to subvert the law, but Deleuze also shows how Sade provides an ironic transcendence of the law into a non-place that undermines its authority.

Works Cited

Bataille, Georges (1993), *The Accursed Share*, vols 2 & 3, trans. Robert Hurley (New York: Zone Books).

Braidotti, Rosi (1991), *Patterns of Dissonance: A Study of Women in Contemporary Philosophy.* (New York: Routledge).

Dean, Timothy (2000), *Beyond Sexuality.* (Chicago: University of Chicago Press).

Deleuze, Gilles and Félix Guattari (1983), *Anti-Oedipus: Capitalism and Schizophrenia,* trans. Robert Hurley, Mark Seem and Helen R. Lane (Minneapolis: University of Minnesota Press).

—(1986), *Kafka: Toward a Minor Literature,* trans. Dana Polan (Minneapolis: University of Minnesota Press).

—(1987), *A Thousand Plateaus: Capitalism and Schizophrenia,* trans. Brian Massumi (Minneapolis: University of Minnesota Press).

Deleuze, Gilles (1991), *Masochism: Coldness and Cruelty,* trans. Jean McNiel (New York: Zone Books).

Deleuze, Gilles and Claire Parnet (1987), *Dialogues,* trans. Hugh Tomlinson and Barbara Habberjam (New York: Columbia University Press).

Grosz, Elizabeth (1990), *Jacques Lacan: A Feminist Introduction.* (New York: Routledge).

Irigaray, Luce (1985). *Speculum of the Other Woman,* trans. Gillian C. Gill (Ithaca: Cornell University Press).

Lacan, Jacques (1977), *Écrits: A Selection,* trans. Alan Sheridan (New York: Norton).

—(1989), 'Kant with Sade', trans. James B. Swenson, Jr. *October,* vol. 51, 55–75.

—(1990), *Television: A Challenge to the Psychoanalytic Establishment,* trans. Denis Hollier, Rosalind Krauss, and Annette Michelson (New York: W. W. Norton & Co.)

Kafka, Franz (1984), *The Trial,* trans. Willa and Edwin Muir (New York: Schocken).

Chapter 7

From the Surface to the Depths
On the Transition from *Logic of Sense* to *Anti-Oedipus*

Daniel W. Smith

In his 2004 book *Organs without Bodies: Deleuze and Consequences*, Slavoj Žižek curtly dismisses *Anti-Oedipus* (1972) as 'arguably Deleuze's worst book,' and instead elevates *Logic of Sense* (1969) to the status of Deleuze's pivotal work.[1] At the heart of *Logic of Sense*, Žižek claims, one finds a tension between two competing ontologies, which are in turn derived from two competing conceptions of sense: sense as the impassive *effect* of material causes, and sense as the principle of the *cause* or production of beings.[2] The former would be the logic of materialism, the latter the logic of idealism. Žižek's argument is that the conceptual edifice of Deleuze's entire philosophy oscillates between these two 'logics' of sense, which are, in the end, 'fundamentally incompatible' (OwB, 20). According to Žižek, however, the tension between these two ontologies is a necessary one, since it points to the fact that any genuine 'event' entails the emergence of something new that cannot simply be derived from corporeal causes, and which therefore has its own 'incorporeal' effects.[3] The problem with *Anti-Oedipus*, according to Žižek, is that it largely abandons the (Lacanian) presuppositions that govern *Logic of Sense*, and instead offers what Žižek takes to be the simplistic solution of a materialism of pure becoming. *Anti-Oedipus* was 'the result of escaping the full confrontation of the deadlock *via* a simplified "flat" solution,' and the thrust of Žižek's reading of Deleuze in *Organs without Bodies* is 'to confront again this deadlock' between the two ontologies (sense as effect and sense as cause) in order to retrieve the importance of *Logic of Sense* for an understanding of Deleuze's work (OwB, 21).

Žižek is certainly correct to see a shift in Deleuze's thought between *Logic of Sense* and *Anti-Oedipus*. The fact that such a shift exists is confirmed by Deleuze himself. 'The surface-depth problem [of *Logic of Sense*] no longer concerns me,' he remarked in a 1973 interview. 'What interests me now are the relations between a full body, a body without organs, and flows that migrate.'[4] And Žižek is also correct to perceive that this shift—from the surface-depth problem to the problem of the body without organs—is intimately linked to Deleuze's relation to and rereading of Lacan. It is perhaps inevitable that, to a Lacanian like Žižek, *Anti-Oedipus* could only be read as a regressive book, as a move away from Lacan's insights, whereas for Deleuze himself *Anti-Oedipus* was obviously a step forward, an exploration of problems that were left in abeyance in *Logic of Sense*. What the following reflections attempt to lay out, in a tentative manner, are the internal problematics of *Logic of Sense* that led Deleuze to reformulate his own position in *Anti-Oedipus*. After laying these out, we will be in a position to assess the relevance of Žižek's rather curt dismissal of *Anti-Oedipus*.

In the second half of *Logic of Sense*, Gilles Deleuze attempts to analyze what he calls the *dynamic genesis* of language, drawing in part on texts from developmental psychology and psychoanalysis. 'What renders language possible,' he writes, 'is that which separates sounds from bodies and organizes them into propositions, freeing them for the expressive function' (LS, 181). If a speaker before me suddenly relapsed into violent babbling and began to utter incomprehensible noises, one could say that the 'expressive function' of sound would have been lost, or at least fundamentally altered. This is the issue addressed of the dynamic genesis of language: it 'concerns the procedure that liberates sounds and makes them independent of bodies' (LS, 186). Deleuze distinguishes three different stages in the dynamic genesis, which at the same time constitute three distinguishable dimensions of language: the *primary* order of language, which is the dimension of noise produced in the depths of the body; the *tertiary* arrangement of language, which is found in the propositions of languages, and their various functions of denotation, manifestation, and signification; and finally, the *secondary* organization of language, which constitutes the surface of *sense* (and non-sense). The dimension of sense is the primary object of Deleuze's analyses in the *Logic of Sense*, since it conditions the movement from the primary order to the tertiary arrangement of language. I want to begin by considering each of these three stages briefly.

1. The Primary Order of Language The dynamic genesis begins with the dimension of *depth*, which constitutes what Deleuze calls *the primary order* of language. The paradigmatic example here is the newborn infant, and the clamorous, noisy depth of its body, with its gnashings, fartings, clappings, crackings, explosions, and cries. This dimension of Noise constitutes a first type of non-sense, and a first type of sonorous system. At this level of the body, 'everything is passion and action, everything is communication of bodies in depth, attack and defense' (LS, 192). Daniel N. Stern, one of the great specialists in child development, describes the world of the infant as a kind of human 'weatherscape,' made up entirely of sequences of risings and fallings of intensity—the jolting of a bright light or a sharp noise, the calming of a voice, or the explosive breakout of a storm of hunger, with its knot of agony and screams, and then the passing of the storm when the baby is fed, and the subsequent sense of pleasure and satisfaction.[5] This is what Deleuze calls the 'body without organs': a situation where the infant experiences no distinction between itself and the world, but only intensities-in-motion, with 'an entire geography and geometry of living dimensions' (LS, 188).

2. *The Tertiary Arrangement of Language (denotation, manifestation, signification)*
The second stage of the dynamic genesis then intervenes: in the midst of this world of intensities, there appears a particular noise, a transcendent Voice from on high, so to speak—the voices of the child's parents, or those of other adults. Long before the infant can understand words and sentences, it grasps language as something that pre-exists itself, as something always-already there: the familial voice that conveys tradition, or that affects the child as the bearer of a name. As opposed to the primary order of language (pure noise as the dimension of the body), the voice participates in what Deleuze calls the tertiary arrangement of language ('*langue*,' a fully formed language) which is made up of sentences or propositions.

In the important 'Third Series' of *Logic of Sense*, Deleuze identifies three dimensions of propositions that make up the tertiary arrangement of language: (1) *designation* or denotation, which is the relation of a proposition to an external state of affairs (theory of 'reference'); (2) *manifestation*, which marks the relation of the proposition to the beliefs and desires of the person who is speaking; and (3) *signification* or demonstration, which is the relation of the proposition to other propositions (the domain of logic, with its relations of implication or demonstration between propositions). In other words, in a language, propositions can be related either to the objects to which they refer, or to the subjects that utter them, or to each other. Each of these dimensions of the proposition identified by Deleuze can be said to be grounded in a specific Kantian principle: the World, and its states of affairs, is the principle of reference or denotation; the Subject is the principle of manifestation; and God, as the locus of abstract predicates, is the principle of demonstration. These are the three transcendent Ideas that Kant identified as the three great terminal points of metaphysics in the 'Transcendental Dialectic' of the *Critique of Pure Reason*: the Self, the World, and God. If God is the principle of demonstration, it is because Kant defines God as the master of the disjunctive syllogism: God is the *ens realissimum*, the sum total of all possibility, and the 'reality' of each thing is derived from this originary material through the enactment of disjunctive (either-or) syllogisms. See LS, 176, 296. Deleuze is here following Nietzsche (and others) in suggesting that traditional metaphysics is derived from (and led into 'transcendent illusions' by) language and its grammar, that is, from the most general structure of propositions.

The limitation of much philosophy of language is not only that it has tended to focus primarily on the relation of denotation or reference, that is, on the way in which propositions can designate a state of affairs, which determines the truth value of a proposition. The deeper problem is that it has tended to focus on propositions in fully formed and already developed languages—that is, on the tertiary arrangement of language—without posing the question of their *genetic* conditions. In biology, for instance, one does not discover the nature of the organism by simply examining a fully formed individual, since the individual itself is the result or effect of a complex set of processes, starting with the genetic code and passing through a series of developmental processes. The same is true of language: one is led astray if one analyzes language in its full blown, adult state, so to speak, without adopting a *genetic* point of view—although ultimately this genetic standpoint is a static standpoint, and not a developmental one. (As we shall see, Deleuze distinguishes between the *dynamic* genesis, which we are here discussing, and the formal, transcendental, or static genesis of the event.) What then is this genetic element of language?

3. The Secondary Organization of Language (Sense and Nonsense)   This question brings us to the third stage of the dynamic genesis, the third element of language, which lies 'between' the primary order of language (pure noise) and its tertiary arrangement (in propositions). This is what Deleuze calls the secondary organization of language, which is the domain of *sense*. Why is sense the genetic element of language? Deleuze is here indebted to the genius of thinkers like Frege and Russell, who discovered that the condition of truth (or denotation) lies in the domain of *sense*: in order for a proposition to be true it must have a sense. Yet Frege and Russell betrayed this thesis at the moment they discovered it, Deleuze argues, because they fell into the circularity of the method of *conditioning*. One of Deleuze's essential theses in both *Difference and Repetition* and *Logic of Sense* was that, in transcendental philosophy, the Kantian method of *conditioning* (which elucidates the conditions of possible experience) must be replaced by a method of *genesis* (which elucidates the conditions of *real* experience). In Frege and Russell, sense is defined as the condition of the true, but it is granted an extension *larger* than truth in order to account for the possibility of error. A false or erroneous proposition nonetheless remains a proposition endowed with sense, whereas a proposition that does not have a sense can neither be true nor false—it is simply non-sensical. For instance, the famous opening line of Lewis Carroll's *Jabberwocky* ('Twas brillig, and the slithy toves did gyre and gimble in the wabe') is neither true nor false, but lacks sense. But in this manner, although the sense-nonsense relation is deemed to be prior to the truth-falsity relation, sense only grounds the truth of a proposition by remaining *indifferent* to what it grounds—and the values of truth and falsity are allowed to continue in the same state as before, as if they were independent of the condition assigned to them (truth is still a matter of adequation or reference).

This then is what Deleuze calls 'the most general problem of a logic of sense' (LS, 68): 'What would be the purpose of rising from the domain of truth to the domain of sense, if it were only to find between sense and nonsense a relation analogous to that of the true and the false?' We cannot simply presume the existence of 'truth' as a fact, and then seek its conditions. Deleuze thus alters the formulation of the problem of truth in terms of the problem of *genesis*: 'Truth and falsity do not concern a simple designation, rendered possible by a sense which remains indifferent to it. The relation between a proposition and what it designates must be established *within sense itself*: the nature of ideal sense is to point beyond itself towards the object designated.'[6] Rather than utilizing a method of conditioning, which would presume truth as a 'fact' and then seek its conditions, Deleuze holds that philosophy must adopt a method of genesis: truth must be seen to be a matter of production within sense (method of genesis) rather than adequation to a state of affairs (method of conditioning).

How then does this secondary organization of language (sense and non-sense) function with regard to the dynamic genesis of language? According to Deleuze, sense can be said to function simultaneously on two quite different registers. On the one hand, sense is what has been called the 'expression' of a proposition, something that is irreducible to the other three dimensions of the proposition. In Frege's famous example, 'Venus is the morning star' and 'Venus is the evening star' are both true and both refer to the same state of affairs, yet they have different senses. Similarly, I can attribute the proper name 'Battle of Waterloo' to a particular state of affairs, but the battle itself exists nowhere but in my proposition. (e.g., 'The Battle of Waterloo took place in 1815'). What we find in the state of affairs are *bodies* mixing with one another—spears stabbing flesh, bullets flying through the air, cannons firing, bodies being ripped apart—and the battle itself is simply the *effect* of the intermixing of these bodies. The battle itself exists nowhere except in my proposition, which attributes the name 'Battle of Waterloo' to this particular state of affairs, this particular mixture of bodies. Deleuze is not referring here to a nominalism of universals, but rather to the singularity of proper names. Put differently, the Battle of Waterloo itself does not 'exist' per se, but is something that merely 'insists' or 'subsists' in my proposition. One of the fundamental theses of *Logic of Sense* is that sense is to propositions what attributes like 'Waterloo' are to states of affairs: they subsist or insist at their surface, they lie at the surface or border-line between propositions and states of affairs. Yet this first aspect of sense is only one aspect of Deleuze's book, and not even the most important one, although it is perhaps the one most frequently commented on. For on the other hand, the second aspect concerns sense as the element of the *genesis* of propositions, and no longer simply the *effect* of propositions. (Indeed, the complex relation between these two aspects of sense is the primary problem Deleuze tries to address in the book.) How then does sense function as an element of genesis?

An infant is born into what Deleuze calls the primary order of language: noise, the primary affects (and sounds) of the body, with all its intensive variations. Simultaneously, in the midst of this primary order, the infant hears the Voice on High, that is, the voices of those speaking an already constituted language (Freud himself stressed the acoustic origins of the superego). The problem of the dynamic genesis concerns the means by which the infant moves from the primary order of the body to the tertiary arrangement of language. Deleuze's claim is that this movement can be effectuated only by passing through the secondary organization of sense. It is obvious that, for the infant, the Voice on High already has all the dimensions of the 'tertiary organization' of language, which pre-exists the life of the infant: it *manifests* the emotional variations of the speaker (the voice that loves and reassures, attacks and scolds, withdraws and keeps silent, complains about being wounded), it *denotes* states of affairs in the world, including good objects (breast) and introjected objects (food); and it *signifies* something, namely, all the classes and concepts that structure this domain of the Voice that pre-exists the infant. Yet the infant itself does not know what the Voice is denoting, manifesting, or signifying. For the child, the Voice 'has the dimensions of language without having its condition; it awaits the *event* that will make it a language. It is no longer a noise, but is not yet language' (LS, 194). In other words, the Voice does not yet have a *sense*. Whereas the Noise of the depths is an *infra-sense*, an under-sense, an *Untersinn*, the Voice from the heights is a *pre-sense*; it still awaits the 'event' that functions the genetic element of language itself.

But as Deleuze notes, this is not simply an experience of infants. The passage from noise to voice is re-lived when the sounds reaching sleeping people are organized into the voice ready to wake them. More obviously, we experience it when we encounter someone speaking a foreign language. The Greeks called non-Greeks 'barbarians' (*barbaros*) because when they heard foreigners speak, all they heard were nonsensical syllables ('bar bar'). They heard the Voice, and they could see that it 'made sense,' that it *had* a sense, but they lacked access to the sense of the foreign language. Similarly, Americans tend to caricature the sound of French as extremely vowely, just as the French tend to characterize American speech in term of a hot potato in one's mouth, since most American vowel sounds are diphthongs.

Yet how does one gain access to this domain of sense? For the infant to accede to the tertiary arrangement of language (the Voice), it must pass through the secondary organization of language, which is the construction of the surface dimension of *sense*, entailing a certain period of apprenticeship on the child's part. From the continuous flow of the Voice which comes from above, the child will begin to cut out, to extract, elements of different orders, to free them up in order to give them a function that nonetheless remains 'pre-linguistic' (LS, 230). This is an early formulation of the theory of flows that Deleuze will develop in *Anti-Oedipus*: the voice is a flow from which elements, which are purely non-signifying, are extracted and recombined. The first words of the infant are not formed linguistic units, but merely formative elements: phonemes, morphemes, semantemes.

In Deleuze's analysis, the construction of the surface organization of sense can be distinguished into at least three moments, which are defined by three types of series or syntheses (the connective, conjunctive, and disjunctive synthesis). In the first moment (connection), the child extracts pure phonemes from the current of the Voice, and connects them together in what linguists call 'a concatenation of successive entities' (ma ma, da da, bay bee, etc.), which can then enter into more complex relations, or even an alignment of clusters (LS, 231). In the second moment (conjunction), there is the construction of *esoteric words* out of these phonemes, a formation that is brought about not by a simple addition of preceding phonemes, but rather through the *integration* of the phonemes into convergent and continuous series ('Your royal highness' is contracted into 'y'reince'). In the third moment (disjunction), the child starts making these esoteric words enter into relation with other divergent and independent series. Yet even here, the elements (singularities) are not yet organized into formed linguistic units that would be able to denote things, manifest persons, and signify concepts. Taken together, then, these three syntheses constitute the production of the *surface of sense* out of the Voice. If the first moment of the dynamic genesis is the movement from Noise to the Voice, the second moment is the movement from the Voice to Speech. This is the fundamental operation of the dynamic genesis, at least with regard to language: the extrication of pure phonemes—which are themselves expressed in differential relations, such as bat/cat—from the flow of the Voice. 'If the child comes to a pre-existing language which it cannot understand,' Deleuze writes, 'perhaps conversely, it grasps that which we no longer know how to grasp in our own language, namely, the phonemic relations, the differential relations of phonemes' (LS, 230). Deleuze elsewhere makes a similar point with regard to the biological domain: 'There are "things" that only an embryo can do, movements that it alone can undertake or even withstand'—movements of folding and migration, for instance, that would tear an adult organism apart (DR, 215). The implication is the same in both domains: we are led astray in our analyses if we focus on fully-formed individuals (in biology) or fully-formed languages (in linguistics).

What then, within the dynamic genesis, is required in order for one to move from the primary order of noise to the tertiary arrangement of language? Deleuze's response is that the genetic condition of language is what he calls the 'pure event,' which is nothing other than the secondary organization of sense itself, or what Deleuze calls 'the transcendental field.' The concept of a *transcendental field* was first proposed by Husserl in his own writings on the status of sense. 'Phenomenology, alone of all philosophies, talks about a transcendental field,' Merleau-Ponty would later write in *Phenomenology of Perception*. 'The process of *making explicit* . . . is put into operation on the "lived-through" world itself, thus revealing, *prior* to the phenomenal field, the transcendental field.'[7] The *Logic of Sense* has close affinities with the *Phenomenology of Perception*, except that Deleuze is attempting to isolate the field of sense rather than the field of perception. Deleuze, however, would critique the Husserlian conception of the transcendental field of sense—which is inscribed with 'centers of individuation and individual systems, monads and points of view, and *Selves* in the manner of Leibniz' (LS, 99)—and instead follow Sartre's call for an *impersonal* transcendental field.[8] *Difference and Repetition* (1968) and *Logic of Sense* (1969) are the primary works in which Deleuze attempts to explore and define the nature of this transcendental field. 'The idea of singularities . . . which are impersonal and pre-individual,' he writes in *Logic of Sense*, 'must now serve as our hypothesis for the determination of this domain and its genetic power' (LS, 99). Indeed, one could list an entire open-ended list of empirico-transcendental concepts that Deleuze develops to define the transcendental field: determinable elements, differential relations, singularities, convergent and divergent series with their differing syntheses (connective, conjunctive, disjunctive), the dark precursor, virtuality/actuality, differentiation/differenciation, multiplicity, indiscernibility, and so on. In this regard, the *Logic of Sense* is an exploration of only one aspect of the transcendental field, albeit an important one: 'The surface is the transcendental field itself, the locus of sense and expression' (LS, 125).

The dynamic genesis thus finds its *real* condition in what Deleuze calls the *static genesis*, which resolves what Deleuze considers to be one of the fundamental problems of the logic of sense: 'How can we maintain both that sense *produces* even the states of affairs in which it is embodied, and that it is itself *produced* by these states of affairs or the actions and passions of bodies?' (LS, 124). On the one hand, the question of the dynamic genesis concerns the means by which sense is produced from the depths of bodies and their states of affairs— that is, sense is the means through which sounds are separated from bodies and organized into propositions (the expressive function); on the other hand, it is only through sense itself that states of affairs are constituted and attributed to bodies (e.g., the battle of Waterloo). Although Žižek sees these two conceptions of sense as 'fundamentally incompatible' (OwB, 20), the entire goal of the *Logic of Sense* is to elucidate the exact nature of their relation and their ultimate compatibility.

Sense is what separates sounds from bodies and organizes them into propositions, freeing them for the expressive function. 'In the surface organization which we called secondary, physical bodies and sonorous words are separated and articulated at once by an incorporeal frontier. This frontier is sense, representing, on one side, the pure 'expressed' of words, and on the other, the logical attribute of bodies' (LS, 91). The organization of sense constitutes what Deleuze calls 'the transcendental field.' In describing his project, Deleuze writes, 'We seek to determine an impersonal and pre-individual transcendental field, which does not resemble the corresponding empirical fields [already-constituted languages, or the tertiary order of language], but which nevertheless is not confused with an undifferentiated depth [the primary order of noise].'[9] Sense lies at the logical genesis of the three dimensions of the proposition (denotation, manifestation, signification), but also at the ontological dimensions of the three relata (the denoted, the manifested, the signified). Sense forms a boundary or frontier between words and things that allows the two to relate to each other without reducing this relation to one of isomorphism or representation. Sense is, as it were, the a priori structure that conditions the dynamic genesis.

What then accounts for the shift in Deleuze's thinking between *Logic of Sense* and *Anti-Oedipus?* Why was Deleuze compelled to move from the surface-depth problem, in *Logic of Sense*, to the problem of the body without organs, in *Anti-Oedipus?* The issue, it seems to me, revolves around the question of the mode of access we have (or do not) to the primary order of language (noise). For the implicit presupposition of *Logic of Sense* seems to be that we do *not* have access to the primary order, since this is precisely the domain of language that belongs to the mad.

Nothing makes this clearer than the profound thirteenth series of *Logic of Sense* ('Of the Schizophrenic and the Little Girl'), which compares the uses of language found in Lewis Carroll and Antonin Artaud respectively, each of whom exemplifies a very different type of nonsense. The first type of nonsense, found in Lewis Carroll, operates entirely within the secondary organization of sense. Carroll's technique is to take the already-given formative elements of language (sense), and to establish new syntheses between. The word 'snark,' for instance (in 'The Hunting of the Snark'), is formed through a conjunctive synthesis of 'snake' and 'shark.' Carroll's famous poem 'Jabberwocky' begins with a series of such portmanteau words: ''Twas brillig, and the slithey toves did gyre and gimble in the wabe, all mimsy were the borogroves, and the mome raths outgrabe.' To which Alice responds, 'Somehow it seemed to fill my head with ideas—only I don't exactly know what they are!'[10] The poem seems to make 'sense' to Alice because Carroll combines the elements of language in a way that still retains their sense, even though they are made to enter into a new synthesis. The term 'slithey' is a synthesis of 'slimy' and 'lithe,' and thus seems to have a sense, even though it is a non-sensical combination of elements.

But Deleuze also identifies a second, and more profound, type of non-sense, which is found in the poetry and writings of Antonin Artaud. Artaud considered Lewis Carroll's poems to be so much 'pigshit,' since Carroll was content to remain at the surface, making poems out of a little combinatorial game (snark = snake + shark). But that kind of non-sense is nothing—absolutely nothing—compared to the non-sense of the body, with its pure intensities and noises, which Artaud expressed in his *cris-souffles* ('scream-breaths') 'in which all literal syllabic, and phonetic values have been replaced by *values that are exclusively tonic*' (LS, 88)—and which are tied, moreover, to a profound pathology, an extraordinary lived experience. In a sense, Artaud follows the reverse path of the infant (though 'regression' is hardly an appropriate concept for this process): the infant starts in the primary order of the body, and attains the tertiary arrangement of language by passing through—or rather constructing—the secondary organization of sense. But Artaud's schizophrenic pathology took him in exactly the opposite direction. The tertiary arrangement of language (the proposition) is 'grounded' in the 'secondary organization' of sense (which is what Carroll plays with); and yet, following what Deleuze sometimes calls the 'bend' in sufficient reason, the dimension of sense itself threatens to collapse into the un-grounded primary order of noise (Artaud).[11] This is why Deleuze insists that 'we would not give a single page of Artaud for all of Carroll' (LS, 93).

We are all aware of the fundamental fragility of this domain of sense, and the fact that it can break down at any moment. If I were reading this chapter to you, speaking in propositions, you would comprehend me because those propositions are sustained by the element of sense. Sense is the surface, the boundary, the frontier that exists between, on the one hand, the noises of my body (creaking joints and cracking knuckles, rumbling stomachs, clearing throats, etc.) and, on the other hand, the expressive sense that those noises take on in language, such that the noises coming out of my mouth right now participate fully in the linguistic world we all share, this tertiary arrangement of language. As Merleau-Ponty showed, the same is true for the entirety of my body, which is 'expressive' through and through, having a 'sense' in every one of its gestures.[12]

Indeed, does not Artaud's greatness—and his great pathos—lie in the fact that, to some degree, he was able to speak, and to write, out of the depths of the primary order of the body? Nietzsche, for his part, seemed unable to do so, and lapsed into silence. Yet, is Nietzsche's or Artaud's experience any different from that of our own? In a sense, yes, absolutely yes, since both Artaud and Nietzsche suffered a profound pathology most of us will never have to confront. But in another sense, no, things are not so different, since stumbling over a single word (parapraxes) would be enough to reveal the fragility of the sense that sustains what I am saying—the chaos that constantly threatens to bubble up and subsume everything, making us fall into 'the undifferentiated abyss of a groundlessness which only permits the pulsation of a monstrous body' (LS, 120).

A revealing passage in *Logic of Sense* shows Deleuze's hesitations about remaining at the surface, while remaining fully aware of the dangers of plunging into the depths—the depths into which Nietzsche himself 'perished in his own manner' (LS, 108). Deleuze muses aloud about the situation of a philosopher like himself, writing on Artaud's schizophrenia, Nietzsche's collapse, Hölderlin's madness, Woolf's suicide, Fitzgerald's breakdown, Lowry's alcoholism—all the while remaining on the surface, dipping his toes in the

water, but not diving into the depths himself. 'All these questions point to
the ridiculousness of the thinker . . . Are we to speak always about Bousquet's
wound, about Fitzgerald and Lowry's alcoholism, Nietzsche and Artaud's madness while remaining on the shore? Are we to become the professionals who
give talks on these topics? Are we to take up collections and create special
journal issues? Or should we go a short way further to see for ourselves, to be
a little alcoholic, a little mad, a little suicidal, a little of guerilla—just enough
to extend the crack, but not enough to deepen it irremediably? Wherever we
turn, everything seems dismal. Indeed, how are we to stay at the surface without staying on the shore?' (LS, 157–8).

In *Anti-Oedipus*, one might say, Deleuze took the plunge and dove into the
depths. This is what separates *Anti-Oedipus* from the *Logic of Sense*. *Anti-Oedipus*
explicitly takes the most extreme form of psychosis—schizophrenia—as its
model for the unconscious, and it unhesitatingly attempts to write about the
'depths' in a straightforward manner. In this, Deleuze seemed to have taken
a cue from Jacques Lacan, who had insisted that the unconscious—or the
Real—is revealed in its purest and least mediated form in psychosis, rather
than in neurosis or perversion (neurosis, perversion, and psychosis being the
three main categories in Lacan's diagnostic schema). In this sense, Deleuze
seems to have seen both *Logic of Sense* and *Masochism: Coldness and Cruelty* as
somewhat timid books, approaching the question of the unconscious through
still-safe models drawn from perversion—the pervert having achieved a 'mas-
tery of surfaces.'[13] Lacan himself, however, never used psychosis directly as a
model for the unconscious. Psychotics resist entry into the Symbolic (foreclosure) because they mistake words for things; and they resist therapeutization
because they have a libido that is too liquid or viscous. In this sense, the dimension of the Real can at best only appear as a 'gap' or a 'rupture' in the Symbolic.
But rather than seeing foreclosure as a resistance of the ego, Deleuze sees it as
the intensive outcry of what he calls 'desiring-production' (AO, 67). Indeed,
Deleuze's term for the Real is 'schizophrenia as a pure process' (which must
be distinguished from the schizophrenic as a clinical entity), and it is with this
concept that Deleuze can be seen to have taken Lacan's thought to its limit and
conclusion. 'It is this entire reverse side of the [symbolic] structure that Lacan
discovers . . . schizophrenizing the analytic field, instead of oedipalizing the
psychotic field' (AO, 309).

Hence, following directions hinted at by Lacan himself, *Anti-Oedipus*
attempts to use the model of schizophrenia to describe the Real in all its positivity: differential partial objects or intensities that enter into indirect syntheses; pure positive multiplicities where everything is possible (transverse
connections, polyvocal conjunctions, included disjunctions); signs of desire
that compose a signifying chain, but which are themselves non-signifying,
and so on (AO, 309). The domain of the Real is a 'sub-representative field,'
but Deleuze does not hesitate to claim that 'we have the means to penetrate

the sub-representational.'[14] Some of Deleuze's most insightful texts on schizo-phrenics—such as 'Louis Wolfson; or, The Procedure'—are those that analyze the specifically schizophrenic uses of language, which push language to its limit and undo its significations and designations.[15] Deleuze suggests that the usual negative diagnostic criteria that have been proposed for schizophrenia—dissociation, detachment from reality, autism—are above all useful terms for *not listening* to schizophrenics. But in the end, this problem is not specific to schizophrenics: 'we are *all* libidos that are too viscous and too fluid . . .' (AO, 67; cf. 312).

Whereas *Logic of Sense* was content to remain at the surface of sense (Lewis Carroll), *Anti-Oedipus* can be said to have plunged into the depth of bodies (Artaud). Why then does Deleuze no longer speak of the 'depths' in *Anti-Oedipus*? At the very least, the concept of depth has relevance only from the viewpoint of a theory of surfaces; outside of that context, the notion of depth loses its relevance. Once Deleuze ensconces himself in the depths, so to speak, he requires a new conceptual apparatus. This is why, in *Anti-Oedipus*, the surface-depth problem of *Logic of Sense* is replaced with the problem of the body without organs, and the flows that traverse it. The concept of the 'body without organs,' which Deleuze derives from Artaud, had already appeared in *Logic of Sense*, but only as a means of describing the largely undifferentiated status of the depths of bodies—'an organism without parts which operates entirely by insufflation, respiration, evaporation, and fluid transmission' (LS, 88). In the depth of bodies, the possible uses of language are altered accordingly: 'In this primary order of schizophrenia, the only duality is that between the actions and passions of bodies. . . . Here everything happens, acts, and is acted upon beneath sense and far from the surface—sub-sense, a-sense, *Untersinn*. . . . The word becomes the action of a body without parts, instead of being the passion of a fragmented organism. . . . There is no longer anything to prevent propositions from falling back onto bodies and from mingling their sonorous elements with the body's olfactory, gustatory, or digestive affects' (LS, 89–91). In the *Logic of Sense*, in other words, the transcendental field is the surface of sense itself, and the depths of bodies is a largely undifferentiated abyss into which one falls once the surface gives way. Artaud managed to give us a glimpse into the depths, but he is the great exception: 'Artaud is alone in having been an absolute depth in literature, and in having discovered a vital body and the prodigious language of this body. As he says, he discovered them through suffering. He explored the infra-sense, *which is still unknown today*' (LS, 93, emphasis added).

Anti-Oedipus attempts to explore the nature of this still-unknown dimension of infra-sense—the transcendental field is pushed into the depths. If Deleuze abandons the surface-depth terminology, it is no doubt because the notion of depth carries a somewhat negative connotation—as an undifferentiated groundlessness in relation to the constituted surface dimension of sense. *Anti-Oedipus* instead focuses on the specific element of depth that Artaud had discovered and named: the body without organs. In *Anti-Oedipus*, however, the body without organs is no longer linked with the depths, but rather is constituted by and constitutes its own transcendental field, which Deleuze characterizes in terms of the logic of the passive syntheses. Summarizing briefly, one could say that Deleuze assigns three fundamental components to the concept of the body without organs:

1. Organs-parts   Schizophrenics experience their organs in a non-organic manner, that is, as elements or singularities that are connected to other elements in the complex functioning of a 'machinic assemblage' (connective synthesis). In *The Empty Fortress*, for example, Bruno Bettelheim presents a portrait of little Joey, a kind of 'child-machine' who could live, eat, defecate, breathe, and sleep only by plugging himself into motors, carburetors, steering wheels, lamps, and real or imaginary circuits. 'He had to establish these imaginary electric circuits [*raccordements*] before he could eat, for only the current could make his digestive tract work. He executed this ritual with such dexterity that we had to double check to make sure he had neither cord nor socket.'[16]

2. The Body Without Organs   But the breakdowns in the functioning of these organ-machines reveals a second theme—that of the body without organs as such, a non-productive surface upon which the an-organic functioning of the organs is stopped dead in a kind of catatonic stupor (disjunctive synthesis). In this sense, the body without organs is a model of death (the death instinct), albeit a death that is coextensive with life. Authors of horror stories, like Edgar Allen Poe, know this well, when they appeal to the terror, not of the organic corpse, but of the catatonic schizophrenic: the organism remains intact, with its vacant gaze and rigid postures, but the vital intensity of the body has been suspended, frozen, blocked.

3. Intensities   These two poles—the vital an-organic functioning of the organs and their frozen catatonic stasis, with all the variations of *attraction* and *repulsion* that exist between them—can be said to translate the entire anguish of the schizophrenic. These two poles are never separate from each other, but generate between them various forms in which sometimes repulsion and sometimes attraction dominates: the paranoid form of schizophrenia (repulsion) and its miraculating or fantastic form (attraction). This is the third theme of schizophrenia: the theme of *intensive variation* (conjunctive synthesis). Schizophrenics tend to experience these oscillating intensities (manic rises in intensity, depressive falls in intensity . . .) in an almost pure state. Beneath the hallucinations of the senses ('I see,' 'I hear') and the deliriums of thought ('I think'), there is something more profound, a feeling of intensity, that is, a *becoming* or a transition ('I feel'). A gradient is crossed, a threshold is surpassed or retreated from, a migration is brought about: 'I feel that I am becoming woman,' 'I feel that I am becoming god,' 'I feel that I am becoming pure matter. . . .'

The innovation of *Anti-Oedipus*, beyond *Logic of Sense*, is to have penetrated into this sub-representative, schizophrenic domain of the body without organs, and made use of it as the model for the unconscious itself. The analysis of this unconscious will entail a corresponding practice that Deleuze and Guattari will call 'schizoanalysis.' In developing his model of the body without organs, Deleuze admitted his debt to the work of Pierre Klossowski, notably the latter's *Nietzsche and the Vicious Circle*. Klossowski showed how we get a glimpse into Nietzsche's delir-ium in the letters and postcards he wrote before his collapse. In them, language took on a purely *intensive* use, insofar as it directly expressed the 'primary order' of Nietzsche's body and its impulsive states. In Nietzsche's last writings, each of these states received its own proper name—some of which designated Nietzsche's 'attractive' allies, or manic rises in intensity (Prado, Lesseps, Chambige, 'hon-est criminals,' Dionysus), while others designated his 'repulsive' enemies, or depressive falls in intensity (Caiaphus, William, Bismark, the 'antisemites,' the Crucified)—a chaos of pure oscillations ultimately invested by 'all the names of history.'[17] Yet was it not this very experience that Nietzsche confronted through-out all his writings, long before his breakdown?[18] In any case, in *Anti-Oedipus*, Artaud no longer appears as the exception—the one who was able to speak from the 'depths,' and Deleuze is able to appeal to a long list of writers and thinkers who, as Klossowski shows, pushed the use of language to its intensive limits.

With this reading of Deleuze's own movement from *Logic of Sense* to *Anti-Oedipus* in hand, it should perhaps be clear why a Lacanian like Žižek would almost inevitably have to characterize *Anti-Oedipus* as Deleuze's worst book, and as a betrayal of Lacan. The issue revolves around the status of what Lacan called the 'Real.' For an 'orthodox' Lacanian, the Real is the name for a 'gap' in the Symbolic, a moment of radical negativity that can never be approached in itself, but can only be discerned in its effects. Although Lacan himself insisted that psychosis provides the most direct access to the unconscious, the access psych-otics have to the symbolic is necessarily 'foreclosed.' It is this orthodox inter-pretation of the Real that Deleuze and Guattari contest in *Anti-Oedipus*. The Real is indeed the internal limit to any process of symbolization, but Deleuze insists that Lacan was never content to describe the Real, negatively, as a resist-ant kernel within the symbolic process upon whose internalized exclusion the symbolic is constituted (negation or exclusion as constitutive). Rather, Lacan was pushing psychoanalysis to 'the point of its self critique,' where the Real would be able to appear in all its positivity: 'the point where the structure, beyond the images that fill it [fantasies] and the Symbolic that conditions it within representation, reveals its reverse side as a positive *principle of nonconsist-ency* that dissolves it' (AO, 310, 311). What Lacan discovered (and what psychosis makes manifest most directly) is the *reverse side* of the symbolic structure, and Deleuze can say that he was simply following directions indicated by Lacan him-self when, in *Anti-Oedipus*, he and Guattari attempted to describe the Real in all its positivity: differential partial objects or intensities that enter into indirect syntheses; pure positive multiplicities where everything is possible (transverse connections, polyvocal conjunctions, included disjunctions); signs of desire that compose a signifying chain, but which are themselves non-signifying, and so on. The fundamental question no longer concerns the means by which a transcendent 'gap' is constituted within the Symbolic, but the immanent means by which the Real is betrayed and converted into a symbolizing structure. Put simply, one could say that psychoanalysis begins with the symbolic and seeks out the gaps which mark the irruption of an 'impossible' Real, whereas schizo-analysis starts with the Real as the immanent process of desire, and seeks to mark both the mechanisms by which the process is interrupted (reterritorializations) and the conditions under which it can be continued and transformed (becomings, intensities . . .). It is perhaps in this sense that, as Deleuze himself said in the *Abécédaire* interviews of 1998–99, *Anti-Oedipus* is 'a book still to be discovered,' above all by readers of Lacan.[19]

Notes

[1] Žižek, S. (2004), *Organs Without Bodies: On Deleuze and Consequences* (New York and London: Routledge), 21; hereafter referred to as OwB. See Deleuze, G. (1988), *Logic of Sense*, trans. Mark Lester and Charles Stivale; ed. Boundas, C. V. (New York: Columbia University Press), hereafter referred to as LS, and *Anti-Oedipus: Capitalism and Schizophrenia* (1983), trans. Robert Hurley, Mark Seem, and Helen Lane (Minneapolis: University of Minnesota Press), hereafter referred to as AO.

[2] Deleuze, *Logic of Sense*, p. 124. See also p. 96: 'How are we to reconcile these two contradictory aspects [of sense]? On one hand, we have *impassibility* in relation to states of affairs and neutrality in relation to propositions; on the other hand, we have the power of *genesis* in relation to propositions and in relation to states of affairs themselves.'

[3] In short, Žižek is suggesting that *Logic of Sense* anticipates Badiou's distinction between Being and Event: Being is the domain of corporeal causality, whereas the event corresponds to the domain of incorporeal effects, which introduces 'a gap in corporeal causality,' 'an irreducible crack in the edifice of Being' (*Organs Without Bodies*, 27, 41).

[4] Deleuze, G. (2004), *Desert Islands and Other Texts, 1953–1974*, ed. David Lapoujade, trans. Michael Taormina (New York: Semiotext(e)), 261, in the discussion following 'Nomad Thought.'

[5] Daniel N. Stern (1990), *Diary of a Baby* (New York: Basic Books), 14: 'a sudden increase in interest; a rising, then a falling wave of hunger pain; an ebbing of pleasure.'

[6] Deleuze, G. (1994), *Difference and Repetition*, trans. Paul Patton (New York: Columbia University Press), 154. Hereafter, DR.

[7] Merleau-Ponty, M. (1962), *Phenomenology of Perception*, trans. Colin Smith (London and New York: Routledge; rev. ed. 2003), 71, 69. In *Logic of Sense*, Deleuze

criticizes Husserl for defining the transcendental field in terms of 'centers of individuation and individual systems, monads and points of view, and *Selves* in the manner of Leibniz' (LS, 99).

8 See LS 98–9 and 343–4, as well as Jean-Paul Sartre (1991), *The Transcendence of the Ego: An Existential Theory of Consciousness*, trans. Forrest Williams and Robert Kirkpatrick (New York: Farrar, Straus, and Giroux).

9 Deleuze, LS, 102. See also Merleau-Ponty, *Phenomenology of Perception*, 71, 69: 'Phenomenology, alone of all philosophies, talks about a transcendental field. . . . The process of making explicit . . . is put into operation upon the "lived-through" world itself, thus revealing, prior to the phenomenal field, the transcendental field' (71, 69).

10 Lewis Carroll (1979), *Through the Looking-Glass*, in *The Complete Works of Lewis Carroll* (New York: Modern Library), 153–5.

11 On the relation between these three orders of language, see *Logic of Sense*, p. 120.

12 See Merleau-Ponty, *Phenomenology of Perception*.

13 Deleuze, *Logic of Sense*, 92. See Deleuze, G. (1991), *Masochism: Coldness and Cruelty*, trans. Jean McNeil (New York: Zone Books).

14 Deleuze, 'The Method of Dramatization,' in *Desert Islands*, p. 115.

15 See Deleuze, G. (1997), 'Louis Wolfson; or, The Procedure,' in *Essays Critical and Clinical*, trans. Daniel W. Smith and Michael A. Greco (Minneapolis: University of Minnesota Press), 7–22. See also *Anti-Oedipus*, 310: 'Elisabeth Roudinesco has clearly seen that, in Lacan, the hypothesis of an unconscious-as-language does not closet the unconscious in a linguistic structure, but leads linguistics to the point of its auto-critique, by showing how the structural organization of signifiers still depends on a despotic Great Signifier acting as an archaism.'

16 Bettelheim, B. (1972), *The Empty Fortress: Infantile Autism and the Birth of the Self* (New York: Free Press). See also AO 37–8.

17 Klossowski, P. (1997), *Nietzsche and the Vicious Circle*, trans. Daniel W. Smith (Chicago: University of Chicago Press), especially chapter nine, 'The Euphoria of Turin.'

18 See, for instance, Nietzsche, *Beyond Good and Evil*, §296, 426–7: 'Alas, what are you after all, my written and painted thoughts! Alas, only Alas, always only what is on the verge of withering and losing its fragrance! Alas, always only storms that are passing, exhausted, and feelings that are autumnal and yellow! Alas, always only birds that grew weary of flying and flew astray and how can be caught by the hand—by *our* hand. We immortalize what cannot live and fly much longer—only weary and mellow things!'

19 See Gilles Deleuze, 'Abécédaire,' 'D as in Desire,' available online in a summary by Charles J. Stivale at http://www.langlab.wayne.edu/CStivale/D-G/ABCs.html.

Part III

Deleuze and the Arts

Chapter 8

Deleuze, Philosophy, and the Materiality of Painting

Darren Ambrose

It's a very very close and difficult thing to know why some paint comes across directly onto the nervous system and other paint tells you a story in a long diatribe through the brain . . . A painting has a life completely of its own. It lives on its own, like the image one's trying to trap; it lives on its own, and therefore transfers the essence of the image more poignantly . . . In the way I work I don't in fact know very often what the paint will do, and it does many things which are very much better than I could make it do . . . Paint is so malleable that you never do really know. It's such an extra-ordinary supple medium that you never do quite know what paint will do. I mean, you even don't know that when you put it on wilfully, as it were, with a brush—you never quite know how it will go on.[1]

Francis Bacon

We do not listen closely enough to what painters have to say.[2]

Gilles Deleuze

These incisive remarks, made by the painter Francis Bacon when in conversation with the art critic David Sylvester, serve as an excellent illustration of his lifelong obsession with the question of what paint can say, with what problems, meanings, intensities and sensations actually happening through the material of paint itself. Indeed it is precisely Bacon's artistic efforts to think in and through paint, his effort to elaborate a specifically painterly logic of sensation through a peculiar and arresting form of abstract figural work, which so drew the philosopher Gilles Deleuze toward his paintings. In Deleuze's 1981 study of Bacon, *The Logic of Sensation*, the artist becomes con-figured as the modern paradigm of a painter concerned with the expressive materiality of paint and the conveyance of intense modes of sensation which are distanced from the auspices of representation and narration. Bacon's work circumvents narrative relations between Figures and concentrates on 'matters of fact' or 'the brutality of fact,' and for Deleuze this enables Bacon to begin to present the possibilities of what can be done with the materiality of paint on its own. His understanding of Bacon's paintings rests on understanding them as conveying a very special type of *violence,* a violence not of representation but of *sensation.* For Deleuze this is a violence associated with 'colour and line, a static or potential violence, a violence of reaction and expression' (LS, x). Bacon's paintings are to be understood as an interlocking series of experimental rhythmic assemblages in vivid colors of flesh and bone. Here the broken tones of flesh and bone operate as limits to a complex rhythmic interplay, where each push the other to its limit—bone expands in and through flesh in spasmodic movements and flesh compresses and descends into bone in order to give birth to a heightened sense of the 'brutality of fact.' As Deleuze writes in his 1968 work *Difference and Repetition,* it is only through a certain abandonment of figuration and representation, signaled by much contemporary art, 'that we find the lived reality of a sub-representational domain.'[3] Yet at the same time, as Deleuze recognizes, this distancing from figuration and representation in Bacon's work seemingly occurs within simultaneous elevation of the Figure: the disruption of narrative form emerges from the instantiation of entirely new modes of relation between the Figures on the canvas, modes which Deleuze denotes as primarily 'rhythmic.' The composed Figure, Field, objects and other Figures on the canvas, Deleuze argues, 'interrelate in a way that is free of any symbolic undercurrent' (LS, xiv). Indeed, for Deleuze, they are to be understood as rhythmic experiments in painting sensation, a form of ceaseless experimentation held at a certain distance from the operative constraints of representation and narration in order to better explore the possibilities of what can be achieved with the materiality of paint alone.

For Deleuze, the matter of paint itself has increasingly become the crucial expressive component in the art of painting. A painting is after all made of paint, and for Deleuze painters recognize that paint has its own specific logic, or indeed multiple logics, its own meanings, its own expressions, its own analogical language. Deleuze recognizes that the raw material of paint is often felt by the painter to be something deeply alive, to be full of thought and expressive meaning, even before it is formed into the resemblance of a head, a landscape, an animal, or other object.[4] It is a matter of returning to a primal act of painting. Deleuze argues that we must learn to listen to artists and the language that they use. In fact our task becomes one of essentially suspending judgment regarding works of art in order to learn to measure the full implication of the materials and the techniques through which the artist has had to negotiate, mediate, and 'create.'

In this chapter, I will attempt to provide a detailed account of Deleuze's theory of the materiality of art in an effort to better understand his very precise understanding of the art of painting, and in particular his work on Francis Bacon. This will involve beginning with a necessary overview of Deleuze's ontology (i.e., his philosophical theory of Being as Becoming) and the intimate role that a sophisticated consideration of the work of art plays within it. This will serve to situate my account of Deleuze's very specific understanding of the materiality of painting and its analogical language of sensation.

Deleuze (often in conjunction with Félix Guattari) developed a radical materialist philosophy by focusing upon what might be called the material *forces* of life, that is, the radically impersonal and non-human forces of life. In the most general sense Deleuze attempts to think *beyond* the human condition, and as a result attempts to commune with the profoundly irrational, ineffable, chaotic and unspeakable forces of *becoming* in life and to elaborate a philosophical understanding of the conditions of individuation. As a philosopher Deleuze attempts to go beyond the surface fixities of the actual (the existing conditions of current culture and society) and creatively assemble a conceptual discourse capable of conveying those pre-individual impersonal forces, transversal affects, energies, fluxes, flows, and sensations that specific actual socio-historical situations block, reify, and domesticate into rational or conceptual schema/systems and clichéd patterns of representation and intelligibility. In contrast, Deleuze's philosophy represents nothing less than an extraordinarily rigorous attempt to comprehend, either through (created) concepts or radically revitalized existing concepts, the impersonal (virtual) forces and flows of becoming: to discover the *real* conditions of ontological genesis and actuality. In *Difference and Repetition* Deleuze writes that it is a matter of, in the style of Nietzsche, thinking 'an interior of the earth opposed to the laws of its surface' (DR, 7). Ontology thus becomes a philosophy of the subterranean processes of individuation, or a philosophy concerned with the very *genesis* of individuated entities; it becomes *ontogenesis*, an ontology of becoming. This is explicitly configured as a *creative* philosophical ontology of what Deleuze terms the 'virtual.' For Deleuze the virtual is the embryonic and intensive multiplicity of forces immanent to the real, and in contrast to the actual: 'The virtual must be defined as strictly a part of the real object—as though the object had one part of itself in the virtual into which it plunged as though into an objective dimension' (ibid. 260).

Deleuze's approach remains profoundly philosophical (indeed it ultimately becomes a theory of what philosophy actually *is*—namely a vegetal network of thought that is rhizomatic instead of arborescent[5]) because it posits a rigorous approach to the creation and development of precise concepts in an effort to think these embryonic and impersonal virtual forces of becoming. It thus delineates the activity of philosophy, through the *creation* of concepts, as the liberation of thought from pre-existing 'images of thought' (the actual) and the construction of new 'images of thought' (the virtual).

Philosophy is thus no longer concerned with providing fixed definitions of essences associated with the actual, but with thinking virtual 'events' and 'processes' as the transcendental condition of possibility of the actual. The virtual field is a pre-individual and totally impersonal zone beyond (or prior to) any idea of consciousness. It is the real (yet virtual) condition of emergence of actualized phenomena; the real condition of ontological actuality. This movement of ontogenesis, from virtual to actual, 'always takes place by difference, divergence or differenciation' (DR, 264). Deleuze consistently pursues the emergent and divergent paths of differenciation and becoming from the virtual to the actual; these are lines of creation, 'each of which corresponds to a virtual section and represents a manner of solving a problem, but also the incarnation of the order of relations and distribution of singularities peculiar to the given system' (ibid.). Genuine creation is always born of the virtual, which it taps as a reservoir. Deleuze writes:

> Actualisation breaks with resemblance as a process no less than it does with identity as a principle. Actual items never resemble the singularities they incarnate. In this sense, actualisation or differenciation is always a genuine creation . . . For a potential or virtual object to be actualised is to create divergent lines which correspond to—without resembling—a virtual multiplicity. (ibid.)

For Deleuze each philosophical creation, as an activity of 'thinking the virtual' immanently, must be enacted as a counter-effectuation of the phenomenal real: so from the actual, or the existing phenomenal state of affairs, the philosophical concept returns upstream to the event, or the virtual. This is where the philosophical concept is truly 'at home.' Thus, philosophical concepts themselves must be wrested from, rather than being represented on the basis of, the phenomenon. This return upstream, the movement back to the pre-individual, problematic conditions of experience[6] amounts to a work of the most careful forensic detection[7] and creation, a work of invention on the part of the philosopher since there can be no pre-existing means (or art) for doing so. The result of this countereffectuating gesture means that for Deleuze there is nothing of the pre-existing personal in art or in philosophy: thus what announces itself in the sensible, what calls for thinking in the violence of the shock, and opens onto the act of creation, or invention, is radically impersonal—cosmic and virtual. However, it is never merely a question of attempting to 'break out' of the world that exists,[8] but of creating the right conditions for the exposition of other possible worlds, the heterocosmic—to 'break in' in order to introduce new variables into the world that exists, causing the quality of its reality/actuality to undergo modification, change, and becoming. As he and Guattari write in *A Thousand Plateaus*: 'It is through a meticulous relation with the strata that one succeeds in freeing lines of flight, causing conjugated flows to pass and escape and bringing forth continuous intensities . . . Connect, conjugate, continue' (TP, 161). It is in this sense that we can, I believe, certainly trace Deleuze's debt to the ideas of the painter Paul Klee. Klee writes in his 1924 lecture *On Modern Art*:

> The artist surveys with penetrating eye the finished forms which nature places before him. The deeper he looks, the more readily he can extend his views from the present to the past, the more deeply he is impressed by the one essential image of creation itself, as genesis, rather than by the image of nature, the finished product. He says to himself, thinking of life around him: this world at one time looked different and, in the future, will look different again. Then, flying off to the infinite, he thinks: it is very probable that, on other stars, creation has produced a completely different result. Chosen are those artists who penetrate to the region of that secret plane where primeval power nurtures all evolution. There, where the power-house of all time and space—call it brain or heart of creation—activates every function; who is the artist who would not dwell there? In the womb of nature, at the source of creation, where the secret key to all lies guarded. What springs from this source, whatever it may be called, dream, idea or phantasy—must be taken seriously only if it unites with the proper creative means to form a work of art. Not only do they add more spirit to the seen, but they also make secret visions visible.[9]

Klee understood that the artistic plane of composition must be understood as being involved in directly engaging a transcendental principle of Life (akin to Deleuze's virtual 'plane of immanence' or 'interior forces of the Earth') in an enterprise of co-creation. For Klee the process of actualization in Life is everywhere to be understood as a becoming 'actual' of something primeval, something 'virtual,' that is, as a process of organic individuation. Thus, the fundamental process of creation in nature is as a continuous actualization of a 'virtual' force. However, this 'virtual' is always in some sense held back in reserve in *absolute immanence* (for Klee it is the 'secret place where primeval power nurtures all evolution'). As such the 'virtual' entails an ongoing and ceaseless creative force of natural composition *through* which the virtual 'becomes' actual. So there is a virtual dimension of force that is always immanent within, yet does not resemble the virtual's subsequent actualization or individuation. While the virtual's actualization ceaselessly occurs in actual bodies as a dynamic process of organic individuation, there is, *immanent* to that process, a *passive* non-resembling force of the virtual. The virtual in itself always remains something distinct as the self-forming form, which is grasped independently of any actualization—and it is this virtual as a compositional principle of self-forming form that is engaged in an *ongoing* process of individuation through 'difference, divergence or differenciation' (DR, 264). The 'virtual' thus becomes actualized, but also always remains something immanent *within* the actual, a virtual multiplicity always in reserve, still to come.

In their final collaborative work, *What is Philosophy?*, Deleuze and Guattari make it clear that as far as they are concerned *both* the natural plane of composition and the artistic plane of composition are to be recognized as creative planes of nature—planes of the actualization of virtual self-forming forms. The artistic plane is a metamorphic 'plane of composition of Being' and its object is to engage life in an enterprise of *co-creation*. Art's 'possible' is the embodied embryonic virtual, 'the event as alterity engaged in an expressive matter.' Art's universe is that of an expressive matter attempting to render the sensations of the embryonic virtual's passage into the actual something palpable or sensible. Art seeks to transfigure the virtual's force and energy upon its own plane of aesthetic composition. In this sense the artist must allow, through an act of co-creation, for a passage of the virtual into her work, for it to become as 'sensation.' In order to achieve this passage the dominant structures of recognition and rationality must in some sense be suspended, or countereffected by the artist. As Bacon says—'Painting will only catch the mystery of reality if the painter doesn't know how to do it . . . I know what I want to do but don't know how to bring it about' (BF, 102). Once such a countereffectuation has been achieved the forces of virtual multiplicity must become something to be struggled with aesthetically and its productive differential vitality put to work. It must be allowed to breed its different forms, its multiplicities, and its foldings, in the visual space of the work, without its chaotic and anarchic energy destroying the overall cohesion of that work. For Deleuze artists understand the creative potential of the sub-representational virtual multiplicity—'Great artists of the fold . . . already have a presentiment of a certain kind of animal rhizome with aberrant paths of communication.'[10] It is precisely the notion of co-creation that is so important with regard to understanding the metamorphic 'theatre' of art. For Deleuze and Guattari the aberrant processes undertaken by modernist artists, such as Klee, Cezanne, or Bacon, to embody the virtual immanent to the natural plane (within actual Life) is in some way absolutely fundamental to all forms of art. The task of all art is to make new forces visible, to formulate the problems they pose, and to incite a kind of creative and experimental activity of thinking around them. As John Rajchman writes:

> Artworks complicate things . . . create more complex nervous systems no longer subservient to the debilitating effects of clichés, to show and release the possibilities of a life . . . They rewire the nervous system, revitalise the brain, releasing us, in mind as in body, from the heaviness of grounded identities and habitual forms.[11]

It is via a similar type of radical cognitive experimentation involving a suspension of the apparatus of conventional categorical representation, a systematic disruption of all the faculties that the philosopher must strive toward a genuine thought of the virtual.

When 'creating' a concept to 'think' the virtual in philosophy that 'concept' is never something simply formed or fabricated within what might be considered as a pre-existing 'art of philosophy' (which entails what Deleuze calls in *Difference and Repetition*, a dominant pre-existing 'image of thought'); rather philosophy is to be recognized as nothing less than the discipline of the dynamic, vital, and rhizomatic concept '*creation*.' Deleuze and Guattari repeatedly insist that one can really think only where what is to be thought is not already given, when what is to be thought is not governed by the 'forces of recognition.' So the 'art of philosophy' *is* the creation of concepts emerging from a 'fundamental encounter' rather than a pre-existing field with a pre-supposed 'image of thought' that is seen as 'enabling' the 'creation of concepts.' Clearly what Deleuze and Guattari understand here by 'creating' involves the activity of the philosopher (whom they describe in *What is Philosophy?* as the 'friend of the concept'[12]); however, this creative activity is separate from (and thus in a process of mediation with) an 'outside' realm (the 'plane of immanence') which 'creatively' and 'autonomously' self-posits, that is, the vital and infinite self-movement of pure thought (which is also for them the field of sensible being—understood as anorganic vitality). In *Difference and Repetition* Deleuze had written of this 'outside realm' as that which 'forces us to think,' as that which is at the basis of a 'fundamental encounter':

> Its primary characteristic is that it can only be sensed. In this sense it is opposed to recognition . . . It is not a sensible being but the being of the sensible. It is not the given but that by which the given is given. It is therefore in a certain sense the imperceptible . . . Sensibility, in the presence of that which can only be sensed (and is at the same time imperceptible) finds itself before its own limit, the sign, and raises itself to the level of a transcendental exercise: to the nth power. (DR, 176)

For Deleuze and Guattari the realm of pure thought must be recognized as a 'pure movement'—here 'movement' is considered to be an infinite movement or rather the movement of the infinite (WP, 35–40). Since all philosophical concepts have to be first 'created' this pure movement of thought (and being) must itself be radically 'conceptless.' As Jean-Clet Martin writes: 'The concept takes place in silence, in that twilight moment when we are no longer sure what it was we were supposed to understand, when communication is blocked and reflection comes up against its own stupidity—a moment when we don't really know what to think, a moment of difficulty for thought.'[13]

The 'plane of immanence' Deleuze and Guattari initiate here is an 'image of thought' as a purely 'conceptless' plane of infinity (as opposed to the history of Western metaphysics that had always operated with a finite 'image of thought' always already infested with concepts, sometimes explicitly, sometimes implicitly):

> The plane of immanence is not a concept that is or can be thought but rather the image of thought, the image thought gives itself of what it means to think, to make use of thought, to find one's bearings in thought . . . Thought demands only movement that can be carried to infinity. What thought claims by right, what it selects, is infinite movement or the movement of the infinite. It is this that constitutes the image of thought. (WP, 37)

Indeed they maintain a strict separation between the conceptual realm and what they call the pre-philosophical plane of pure thought (akin to Heidegger's pre-ontological understanding of Being [WP, 40]), but crucially this is a differentiation maintained *within* philosophy. For them the realm pure thought (as the 'plane of immanence') is an utterly impersonal self-positing field of forces which constitutes the possibility of all philosophical thought (i.e., the subsequent creation of concepts and their movement). 'If philosophy begins with the creation of concepts, then the plane of immanence must be regarded as pre-philosophical . . . or even as non-philosophical, the power of a One-All like a moving desert that concepts come to populate' (WP, 40–1). In *Difference and Repetition* Deleuze goes so far as to say that 'thought is primarily trespass and violence, the enemy, and nothing presupposes philosophy: everything begins with misosophy' (DR, 176). This pure movement of thought (and being) is thus the crucial 'non-philosophical' (misosophy) element implicated within every conceptually creative act of philosophy. This pure movement (or 'plane of immanence') is essentially a virtual field in which concepts are produced, circulate, and collide with one another. Not thinkable by itself, it can only be defined and mapped with reference to the concepts which populate it. The 'plane of immanence' is a kind of intuitive ground whose 'infinite movements' are fixed by 'co-ordinates' constructed by the finite movements of the concepts. The construction of concepts always refers back to this pre-philosophical field of the plane of immanence. Deleuze and Guattari write:

> The 'plane of immanence' is given as the internal condition of thought, it is thought's 'non-philosophical' image, which does not exist outside of philosophy although philosophy must always presuppose it. It is presupposed not in a way that one concept may refer to others but in a way that concepts themselves refer to a non-conceptual understanding. (WP, 40)

The plane of immanence has to be philosophically constructed, yet it is also that which constructs itself through philosophy (i.e., it is self-positing); it is at once then 'always already there' or presupposed; and something that has to be 'laid out' or 'constructed'; which is to say, posed. In other words, the 'plane of immanence' is presupposed only insofar as it 'will have been' posed; but posed only insofar as it 'will have been' presupposed:

> Philosophy defined as the creation of concepts implies a distinct but insepar-able presupposition. Philosophy is at once concept creation and instituting of the plane. The concept is the beginning of philosophy, but the plane is its instituting. The plane is clearly not a program, design, end, or means: it is a plane of immanence that constitutes the absolute ground of philosophy, its earth or deterritorialisation, the foundation on which it creates its concepts. Both the creation of concepts and the instituting of the plane are required, like two wings or fins. (WP, 41)

For Deleuze and Guattari a philosophy's power is not only measured, as Deleuze claims in his early Spinoza book, 'by the concepts it creates, or whose meaning it alters,' but also by the degree to which it is able to maintain an internal-ized non-philosophical plane of thought (i.e., thought as a pure conceptless and immanent self-movement). The 'creative' activity of the philosopher (the 'friend of the concept') involves an ongoing process of mediation with (and the inclusion of) the vitality of the non-philosophical plane of thought (or being), 'the plane of pure immanence.' Indeed, conceptual 'creation' as an act of the philosopher *and* the autonomously self-positing/immanent movement of thought (or being) are mutually implied; or, in other words, are two aspects of one and the same process. This process is obviously not just confined to the co-creative activities of the philosophical realm—anything which is 'created,' whether it be a living organism, a work of art, or indeed a 'concept,' has what Deleuze and Guattari call this 'autopoetic characteristic' (i.e., an autonomous and immanent movement of becoming) whereby they self-posit or realize themselves. So that which emerges, that which is realized, from a free and cre-ative act, is also, they suggest, that which also necessarily *posits itself.*

As Deleuze writes in *Difference and Repetition*: 'Do not count upon thought to ensure the relative necessity of what it thinks. Rather, count upon the contingency of an encounter with that which forces thought to raise up and educate the absolute necessity of an act of thought or a passion to think' (DR, 176).

And in *What is Philosophy?* Deleuze and Guattari write:

> THE plane of immanence is that which must be thought and that which cannot be thought. It is the nonthought within thought. It is the base of all planes, immanent to every thinkable plane that does not succeed in thinking it. It is the most intimate within thought and yet the absolute outside—an outside more distant than any external world because it is an inside deeper than any internal world: it is immanence . . . Perhaps this is the supreme act of philosophy: not so much to think THE plane of immanence as to show

that it is there, unthought in every plane, and to think it in this way as the outside and the inside of thought, as the not-external outside and the not-internal inside—that which cannot be thought and yet must be thought. (WP, 59–60)

Deleuze and Guattari clearly reconfigure philosophy as having to preserve the plane of immanence through misosophy, to maintain it through an irreducible relationship to the non-philosophical fields of both the arts and sciences. More importantly, they argue that the vital creativity associated with philosophy and its conceptual movement in some sense rests upon it being necessarily intertwined and co-implicated with the autopoiesis (the element that creatively 'self-posits') of those non-philosophical realms.[14] As Rajchman recognizes: 'His aesthetic is thus involved in a kind of "intraphilosophical struggle"; and in all his criticism, we find a peculiar procedure that consists in calling upon the arts to show philosophy the way out of the "dogmatic image of thought" under which it has laboured' (DC, 116).

For Deleuze contemporary philosophy constructs its concepts upon the planes expressed by science, art, literature and, most recently, modern cinema. Common sense and the powers of recognition are no longer posed as the beginning of a philosophical construction, in the sense that they no longer provide the ground of philosophy itself. Rather, for Deleuze, contemporary philosophy has taken on other measures—even those measures that 'belong to the order of dreams, of pathological processes, esoteric experiences, drunkenness and excess' (WP, 41). To an even greater degree contemporary philosophy erects itself on the ground of 'something that does not think,' an unthinkable and imperceptible exteriority.[15] This something that does not think in us returns as a question concerning the possibility of thought itself, the possibility that 'I am not yet thinking.' And to a greater and greater degree, contemporary philosophy poses its own ground in what is 'other than' or 'exterior to' consciousness, or what stubbornly remains 'outside' the powers of conventional representation, which, Deleuze argues, 'calls forth forces in thought which are not the forces of recognition, today or tomorrow, but the powers of a completely other model, from an unrecognised and unrecognisable *terra incognita*' (DR, 172).

Such a task involves what Deleuze and Guattari term in *What is Philosophy?*, a 'pedagogy of the concept' (WP, 12); or, in other words, how to go about 'creating' new types of divergent concept, that is, concepts of difference that 'move,' rather than merely forming or fabricating copies or clichés of existing ones. For Deleuze and Guattari if we are ever to begin to approach an answer to this problem it must be through analyzing the non-philosophical, preserved in its difference from the philosophical (from the conceptual). Crucial to this task of the 'pedagogy of the concept' is a rigorous analysis of the 'conditions of creativity' associated with philosophical activity, which must necessarily make reference to the vital and sovereign activities of the non-philosophical (i.e., the sciences and the arts) (each of which presents its own distinct strategies for 'thinking' and 'creating'). As Rajchman writes:

> For Deleuze art may be said to 'make sense' before it acquires significa-tions, references or 'intentions' identified through the institutions of a public 'Sinn' or a 'common sense' . . . In all art there is a violence of what comes before the formation of codes and subjects, which is a condition in an expressive material of saying and seeing things in new ways. (DC, 124)

So one finds throughout all their work a rigorous exploration of the vital corre-spondences and mutual implications between philosophy and non-philosophy (science and art), all of which is pursued under the auspices of a reconfigured task of the 'pedagogy of the concept.' They thus pursue the specific 'logics of sensation' associated with the different fields of art (such as painting [which we will come to soon], music, literature, cinema, etc.) as part of a pedagogic effort to open up the multiple paths of creative differentiation (or what Deleuze and Guattari call 'lines of flight'), of divergent concept creation and movement. Hence the multiple nomadic paths associated with these different logics of sensation seek to *modulate* the definition of philosophy and its task of 'creating' concepts and movement in thought.

The essential affinity here resides precisely in the notion of 'creativity,' that is, the *creation* of concepts in philosophy and the *creation* of what they term 'percepts' and 'affects' in works of art (WP, 163–99). Deleuze and Guattari's engagement with the arts in *What is Philosophy?* rests upon the view that 'cre-ativity' is primarily a prerogative of the arts, in that within the arts there is a ceaseless process of countereffectuation with regard to the creative reproduc-tion of the phenomenal real, toward a ceaseless experimental thinking, under-taken through material, of the forces of the 'virtual' (the conceptless plane of immanence).[16] So their work seeks to emphasize not the conditions under which a specific work of art is created (i.e., historical, sociological, cultural, etc.—a somewhat tedious academic exercise), but rather how the work of art can reveal something to philosophy about the conditions of creative activity, of creative practice itself. A constant focus of their attention with regard to the different misosophical fields of art are questions of expression, creativity, sensibility, and intuition. They thus privilege in their analyses the specifically 'autopoetic' forces and rhythms present in the work of art, that is, what they consider to be the intrinsic self-ordering and creative self-positing associated with the different materials utilized by artists in the fields of art—paint, stone, sound, cinematic movement-image, cinematic time-image, and language.

Deleuze and Guattari argue that all art, from its inception, has sought to invent or create means for rendering visible certain intensities of Life—affects, energies, rhythms, and forces. For them art, through its creative and invent-ive activity is capable of reaching, traversing, and penetrating the virtual

movement of difference and of becoming, the chaotic plane of virtual multiplicity (for Klee it is the 'womb of nature . . . the source of creation, where the
secret key to all lies guarded.' (*On Modern Art*) In fact they argue that all art
becomes creatively vital precisely through plunging into the pure immanence
of Life, by immersing itself within the field of virtual forces and intensities
(within Klee's 'womb of nature'). As I've already mentioned, this field of virtual multiplicity is a field *without* concepts or forms, indeed it is a field capable of dissolving all settled organic forms into pure zones of intensities where
one can no longer tell what is human, animal, vegetable, or mineral. It is the
countereffectuated real. Deleuze and Guattari argue that the artist must literally 'create' certain plastic methods and techniques for handling the different
materials involved in the multiple practices of art in order to engage in an act
of 'co-creation' with the vital and 'autopoetic' forces of immanence. This act
of co-creation is common to all the arts, according to Deleuze and Guattari,
and is to be broadly understood as involving firstly the 'capture' of the virtual and invisible forces associated with the plane of immanence and then
the rendering of these invisible forces as something actual and sensible, something visible, audible, or legible (or as Deleuze and Guattari sometimes term
it, something 'consistent'). In explaining this crucial function of the work of
art they constantly cite Klee who had claimed that the task of modern art was
no longer to merely render the already visible (the pre-existing 'actual'), but to
'render visible' that which was invisible (the 'virtual'). This becomes extrapo-
lated by Deleuze and Guattari into being the fundamental task of *all* art; for all
art it is not the mere reproduction of pre-existing visible forms that is primary
but rather the 'capture' and 'rendering visible' of the non-visible forces acting
behind or beneath these forms, namely the 'virtual multiplicity':

> It is now a question of elaborating a *material* charged with harnessing forces
> of a different order: the visual material must capture nonvisible forces.
> Render visible, Klee said; not render or reproduce the visible . . . The forces
> to be captured are no longer those of the earth, which still constitute a great
> expressive Form, but the forces of an immaterial, nonformal, and energetic
> Cosmos. (TP, 342)

Thus the arts must capture intensive forces (i.e., from the virtual field of multiplicity) as a 'bloc of sensations' which are transfigured and transcribed into
the different materials associated with each of the specific fields. Specific
fields of art, through their own specific material, have to create what they call
a consistent 'being of sensation.' Each work of art has to become individuated as (using a term borrowed from Duns Scotus) a *heacceity*—or a material
'bloc of sensations' as an impersonal 'thisness'.[17] The work of art is thus radically non-human or pre-human yet totally inseparable from human experience. Successful works of art must be capable of standing alone, that is, they

must be independent of any specific perception, affection, and sentiments linked to the human. Yet they must also be capable of presenting us with an affective 'fundamental encounter,' with the transcendentally empirical or the imperceptibly sensible. Thus the work of art produces, through 'percepts' and 'affects' (the 'beings of sensation' that are extracted from the perceptions and affections of everyday corporeal experience) a 'bloc of sensations' that we perceive and that affects us beyond the concepts associated with the human. It is these 'inhuman' capacities that Deleuze claims the artwork instantiates. As Rajchman writes: 'Art is less the instantiation of a lifeworld than a strange construct we inhabit only through transmutation or self-experimentation, or from which we emerge refreshed as if endowed with a new optic or nervous system. A painting is such a construct rather than an incarnation' (DC, 135).

In this way the work of art is capable of addressing our nervous system directly; it thereby creates a 'being of sensation' that exists in and of itself, outside the habitually human, and as such reveals to us a revitalized state of becoming-nonhuman. This notion of a 'bloc' or 'compound' or 'assemblage' of sensation suggests a sense of independence, a 'standing apart from,' a 'standing alone,' of sensation. To put it another way, for Deleuze and Guattari the artist must express pure perceptions and sensations (percepts and affects) that are *independent* of the pre-existing conceptual identity of any given thing. These pure perceptions and sensations (percepts and affects) have the effect of destabilizing us, of drawing us out of ourselves, of taking us beyond ourselves by expressing (or bringing to expression) a world, or more precisely, a plane, of potential movements and changes that associate our actual existence with something different or external to it (i.e., the virtual field), or as Rajchman writes, 'to show and release the possibilities of a life': 'The artist is always adding new varieties to the world. Beings of sensation are varieties, just as the concept's beings are variations . . . In relation to the percepts or visions they give us, artists are presenters of affects, the inventors and creators of affects. They not only create them in their work, they give them to us and make us become with them, they draw us into the compound' (WP, 175).

Percepts are not 'ordinary' perceptions: (according to Deleuze and Guattari they are 'independent of a state of those who undergo them')—thus the percept 'is the landscape before man, in the absence of man' (WP, 169). Equally, affects do not arise from pre-existing subjects but instead pass through them, revitalizing and reconstructing them. The affect is the 'becoming-other,' not as a passage from one pre-existing lived state to another but man's vital nonhuman becoming. Affects are not 'ordinary' affections. 'Affects are the non-human becomings of man . . . we are not in the world, we become with the world; we become by contemplating it. We become universes. Becoming-animal, plant, molecular, becoming zero' (WP, 169).

The formation or creation of artworks takes place upon what Deleuze and Guattari call a 'plane of composition,' which they subdivide into the 'technical plane of composition' (which concerns the material of artworks) and the 'aesthetic plane of composition' (which concerns sensations). Within the first plane, they argue, 'the sensation realises itself in the material' (WP, 193), that is, the sensation adapts itself to a well-formed, organized, and regulated matter. So in painting, for example, this is the mode of representational, naturalistic, and perspectival art, in which sensations are projected upon a material plane or surface that is *always already* inhabited by spatial schemata and coordinates that structure the morphology of the figure. It is a kind of graphic hylomorphism—(hylomorphism being the doctrine that the order displayed by material systems is due to the form projected in advance by an external producer, a form which organizes what would otherwise be chaotic or passive matter). On the second plane 'it is the material that passes into the sensation' (WP, 193), and here we are able to think the autopoetic 'self-ordering' potentials of matter itself. So, rather than sensation being projected upon the readily striated (i.e., spatially determined and overcoded) material surface, the material itself rises up into a metamorphic plane of forces and discloses what they call 'smooth space.' The 'Smooth' space of the virtual is defined as a relatively undifferentiated and continuous topological space (hence 'Smooth') which is incessantly undergoing discontinuous differentiation and transitions and is progressively acquiring determination until it condenses into a measurable and divisible metric space (hence 'Striated').[18] For them, in contrast with a hylomorphic model, matter is never simply a homogenous substance that passively receives forms but is itself composed of 'intensive' and 'energetic' virtual traits.

'Percepts' and 'affects' become the compositional elements with which an artist creates, elements that the artist shapes and forms on a purely aesthetic plane of composition and renders as perceptible through *materials* that have now themselves been configured or rendered *expressive*. So, in the 'veritable theatre of metamorphosis and permutations' of modern art, it becomes much more a matter of concentrating upon the way in which the specific material being used, such as paint, can become inherently expressive of sensation rather than merely a vehicle for a pre-existing idea of a specific sensation; thus, it is here that the genuinely 'self-ordering' potentials of matter (i.e., paint) are able to be 'thought' aesthetically.

Within modernist painting, where abstraction comes to prominence, the materiality of the paint itself comes to articulate and express these 'forces'—matter itself becomes the crucial expressive component in the artwork. Matter-movement carries with it virtual 'singularities' as implicit or virtual forms and it is the potential for material self-ordering with which the artist must negotiate. 'Form' is something suggested by the material itself. Forms are 'created' out of these suggested virtual potentials of the matter rather than being something which is preconceived by the artist and then imposed on a passive matter. Hence the significance for Deleuze of Bacon's type of diagrammatic figuration—the creation of resemblance but through profoundly non-resembling means. The artist on the 'aesthetic plane of composition,' such as a painter like Bacon, in some sense *surrenders* to the matter of paint and follows its virtual singularities. By attending to these traits the artist allows it to speak to their 'instinct' and then devises a range of practical strategies to bring out these virtualities, to actualize them as sensible 'possibilities,' as heterocosmic 'facts.'

So to briefly restate before turning our attention to Bacon and the materiality of painting, Deleuze and Guattari argue that there are, intrinsic to the different and varied materials of art, certain vital 'autopoetic' forces and rhythms; and the matter of the artwork itself is never simply a homogeneous substance that passively receives preconceived forms but is an emergent autopoetic line of divergent becoming. It is precisely these implicit or virtual intensive traits that make the self-formation of all matter possible (its ontogenetic process of becoming as the movement from the virtual to the actual), and which, according to Deleuze and Guattari, provide the means by which forms of matter can be so continually self-modulating and self-differentiating. In painting it is thus the materiality of the paint itself (i.e., its multiple virtual material traits) which comes to articulate and express such 'forces'—the matter of paint itself becomes the crucial expressive component in the artwork.

There is an analogous effort to elucidate the specific and peculiar logic of paint developed by painters undertaken by James Elkins in an extraordinary study of painting called *What Painting Is.*[19] In this work Elkins pursues this logic through the mobilization of a fascinating type of fluid resonance between alchemy and painting. For Elkins painting has a deep affinity with alchemy insofar as both concern an ongoing logical development emerging from a negotiation with different fluid materials 'which are worked on without knowledge of their properties, by blind experiment.' For Elkins the ongoing dialogue with the material of paint by the painter, and the development of a thinking in paint or a specifically painterly logic of sensation, 'is an unspoken and uncognized dialogue where paint speaks silently.' In a wonderfully Deleuzian passage worth citing here Elkins writes:

A painting is made of paint—of fluids and stone—and paint has its own logic, and its own meanings . . . To an artist, a picture is both a sum of ideas and a blurry memory of 'pushing paint', breathing fumes, dripping oils and wiping brushes, smearing and diluting and mixing. Bleary preverbal thoughts are intermixed with the nameable concepts, figures and forms that are being represented. The material memories of a picture—every painting captures a certain resistance of paint, a prodding gesture of the brush, a speed and insistence in the face of mindless matter: and it does so at the same moment, and in the same thought, as it captures the expression of a face. (JE, 2–3)

For Deleuze too the raw material of paint is often felt by the painter to be something deeply alive, to be full of thought and expressive meaning, even before it is formed into the resemblance of a head, a landscape, or other object. It is in this sense that both Elkins and Deleuze, as aesthetic theorists, echo the injunction of the painter Malevitch, who claimed that a painter is said to be a painter and nothing but a painter, and argues that the task of the painter is to ceaselessly struggle with the 'powers' of painting in order to make paintings rather than merely paint objects and reproduce the existing forms of nature. It is a matter of returning to a primal act of painting.

Deleuze's work on Bacon, for example, is marked by an extraordinary effort to listen to how Bacon continues a certain return to this primal act of painting, how he 'thinks in paint,' often drawing at length from the interviews Bacon conducted with David Sylvester. In the *Logic of Sensation* Deleuze spends considerable time considering the specific utilization of the 'catastrophe' (a 'catastrophe' somehow implicit within the art of painting, and what Deleuze terms, after Bacon, the 'graph' or 'diagram') in Bacon's work. Hence he spends a great deal of time analyzing in detail Bacon's specific handling of the conflicts between chaos and order, chance and control, and the realm of the unthought within the art of painting; in other words Bacon's specific handling of the autopoetic traits of the material of paint, his efforts to productively utilize the 'virtual' traits immanent within the very material itself as a means for creative fabulation and figuration. Deleuze argues that Bacon utilizes the 'diagram' precisely as a way to constitute an *analogical* language in paint and of paint, a painterly logic of sensation emerging from a negotiation with the autopoetic material traits of paint itself. This utilization of the 'Diagram' in painting by Bacon consists of these three distinct stages:

1. In contrast with the two extremes of contemporary abstraction, Bacon begins with a figurative form (i.e., the extent to which one has to, because of the inevitable figural givens inhabiting the canvas, prevalent through photography etc.)

2. Bacon then produces a catastrophic intervention of the 'diagram' to scramble it (through the introduction (over the top of these 'pre-pictorial' figurations, images, etc.) of purely accidental material components of paint—that is, thrown, scrubbed, rubbed, scraped injections of paint. For Bacon a fundamental act of painting is defined as precisely making random material marks (lines-traits); cleaning, sweeping, brushing, or wiping the canvas to clear out locales or zones (color-daubs); throwing paint from various angles and at various speeds). So it is precisely through the introduction of these purely 'material traits' that the pre-pictorial givens (clichés) are able to be removed. The 'diagram' is thus a fundamental pre-figural preparation of a canvas—the series of shades, colors, scratches, and layers of painterly material set down prior to the actual delineation of the Figure.

For Bacon this process consists of a series of haphazard lines, colored spots, and pitched paint. Such a physical rather than a visual act of painting lays down a ground that is in contradiction with the pre-planned figure, a kind of physical or material catastrophe that underlies the production of figuration in paintings—it serves to destroy the nascent figuration and give the Figure a chance to emerge.

3. Bacon then utilizes this catastrophe of the 'diagram' to allow the materiality of the paint (the accidental injection of brute material) to facilitate the emergence of a form of a completely new type of figural resemblance, which Deleuze terms the Figure. (As I mentioned earlier, Bacon's peculiar painterly logic of sensation is thus understood as the production of a type of figural resemblance through a radically un-resembling means.) For Deleuze the 'diagram' allows the emergence of another world into the visual world of figuration, another form of creative individuation. However, being itself a catastrophe, the 'diagram' must not be permitted to merely create a catastrophe. Being a zone of scrambling, the 'diagram' must not be permitted to utterly scramble the painting. The 'diagram' must be grasped as an inherently fecund zone, (a zone of the virtual) with what emerges from it coming both gradually and all at once. The 'diagram' is indeed a chaos, a catastrophe, but it is also a germ of rhythmic order.[20] It is a violent chaos in relation to the figurative givens, but it is a germ of rhythm in relation to the new order of the painting. As Bacon says, it 'unlocks areas of sensation.' This lack of control and restraint is, for Deleuze, the failure of abstract expressionism.

So for Deleuze the process of painting exemplified by Bacon's route involves a continual injection of the manual 'diagram' into the visual whole, as a 'slow leak' of catastrophe. The 'diagram' thus initiates the genuinely creative act of painting. Deleuze claims that of all the arts painting is undoubtedly the only one that necessarily, 'hysterically,' integrates its own material catastrophe, and consequently is constituted as a flight forward through material. In creating, painters must pass through the material catastrophe themselves, embrace the virtual multiplicity and chaos of the material of paint, and try to negotiate, create, and invent with its autopoetic power and force:

Painting needs more than the skill of the draftsman who notes resemblances between human and animal forms and gets us to witness their transformation: on the contrary, it needs the power of a ground that can dissolve forms and impose the existence of a zone in which we no longer know which is animal and which human, because something like the triumph or monument of their nondistinction rises up . . . The artist must create the syntactical or plastic methods and materials necessary for such a great undertaking, which re-creates everywhere the primitive swamps of life. (WP, 173–4)

And:

> The hysteria of painting—painting directly attempts to release the pres-
> ences beneath representation, beyond representation. With painting hys-
> teria becomes art. Painting makes presence immediately visible. It liberates
> lines and colours from their representative function, but at the same time
> it also liberates the eye from its adherence to the organism, from its charac-
> ter as a fixed and qualified organ: the eye becomes virtually the polyvalent
> indeterminate organ that sees the body without organs, as a pure presence.
> Painting is able to discover the material reality of bodies with its line-colour
> systems and its polyvalent organ, the haptic eye. (LS, 52)

Where painters obviously differ is in their respective manners of embracing
this non-figurative chaos, in their evaluation of the pictorial order to come,
and the relation of order with this chaos. Thus, different painters utilize the
'diagram' in order to constitute what Deleuze calls an 'analogical language
of paint,' a kind of radically presubjective material expression with its own
specific 'sense' and 'logic.'[21] For example, cries, groans, grunts, growls, sighs,
whispers, and moans can function as elements of an uncoded analogical language and have profound significance, yet whose sounds obviously lack the
conventional and discrete organization of a coded natural language. In much
the same way, Deleuze argues, painting is able to utilize the expressive traits of
the material of paint to elaborate color and line schemas to the state of a language, an 'analogical language,' for example, Bacon's violence of 'line and colour.' In painting it is the 'diagram' that creates the possibility of this analogical
language, uncoded and affective—hence a language capable of conveying and
bearing sensation—yet structured according to its own autonomous order, as
opposed to pregiven exterior orders. In Chapter 13 of *The Logic of Sensation*
Deleuze tentatively identifies three essential dimensions or elements of painting's own autonomous analogical language—planes, colors, and bodies. In
such a conception of painting the primacy of variable autonomous connections or junctures of planes replace the externally fixed relations of classical
perspective; variable autonomous color relations of tonality replace externally
fixed relations of value based on light and shades (chiaroscuro); and the mass
and disequilibrium of the body replaces stable figurative representations and
traditional figure-ground relations. A painter's negotiation with the catastrophe of the Diagram thus has the capacity to destroy the figurative coordinates
of conventional representations, and release the multiple possibilities of invention according to an uncoded and autonomous analogical language.

The Diagram acts as a modulator for the painter. The Diagram and its
involuntary manual order will have been used to break all the figurative

coordinates; but it is through this very action that it defines possibilities of fact, by liberating lines for the armature and colours for modulation. Lines and colours are then able to constitute the Figure or the Fact, that is, to produce the new resemblance inside the visual whole, where the Diagram must operate and be realised. (LS, 120–1)

The 'diagram' functions as a modulator of forces, a temporally varying mold that directs and orients the construction of each new painting. There is then a triple liberation or countereffectuation here—of the body, of the planes, and of color. Such liberation can occur only by passing through the material catastrophe of painting, that is, through the 'diagram' and its involuntary irruption, that is, through the necessary negotiation with the autopoetic virtual traits of the material of paint itself. As a result of this irruption a new figuration is able to emerge, one where bodies are thrown off balance, where they are in a state of perpetual fall; where planes collide with each other and colors become confused and no longer delimit a fixed represented object. However, in order for this rupture with figurative resemblance to avoid merely perpetuating the catastrophe, thus in order for it to succeed in producing a more profound resemblance of the Figure in painting, the planes, starting with the Diagram, must maintain their junction; the body's mass must integrate the imbalance in a deformation; and above all, modulation must find its true meaning and technical formula as the law of Analogy. In painting, the 'diagram' must act as a variable, continuous, and productive mold, which allows for a highly controlled, disciplined, and rigorous negotiation with the materiality of paint and allows for the creation and invention of a new type of figuration through paint.

In conclusion, what Deleuze's careful analyses of the materiality of paint (the autopoesis associated with the material of paint and the elaboration of an analogical language of paint as a pre-representational 'logic of sensation') emphasize, within the context of his broader ontology of art, is the degree to which philosophers must be acutely attentive to the type of problems associated with the specificity of the materiality of painting, to be attentive to the painter's understanding of its pre-verbal meaning, its associations, its powers, its virtualities, and its unthought possibilities. Philosophers need to listen to how artists articulate their different ways of negotiating with the radically self-positing element of the material they utilize, how they hold themselves in a dynamically creative relationship with the unthought of paint, controlling and utilizing it at the same time as being continually astonished, affected, and modified by it. Philosophers need to listen to how different painters understand what 'happens' when they 'create' in and through paint—when they attempt to 'think in and through paint,' they must be attentive to its infinite movement, in order that lessons for philosophy, and its own efforts toward a ceaseless creative activity of 'thinking the virtual' can be genuinely learnt.[22]

Notes

[1] Sylvester, D. ed. (1987), *The Brutality of Fact: Interviews with Francis Bacon*, Third Enlarged Edition (London: Thames and Hudson) [hereafter BF].

[2] Deleuze, G. (2003), *Francis Bacon: The Logic of Sensation*, trans. D. W. Smith (London: Continuum), 99 [hereafter LS].

[3] Deleuze, G. (2004), *Difference and Repetition*, trans. P. Patton (London: Continuum), 83 [hereafter DR]. In LS Deleuze claims that the work of Cézanne is marked by one of the most significant attempts to put us in communication with a pre-objective phenomenal reality in which the world emerges with *us*, a radically pre-human world. Cézanne initially encounters this world as chaos from which his canvas will, after significant struggle, arise.

[4] Indeed, Bacon says—'There are standards set up as to what appearance is or should be, but there's no doubt that the ways appearance can be made are very mysterious ways, because one knows that by some accidental brushmarks suddenly appearance comes in with a vividness that no accepted way of doing it would have brought about. I'm always trying through chance or accident to find a way by which appearance can be there but remade out of other shapes . . . If the thing seems to come off at all, it comes off because of a kind of darkness which the otherness of the shape which isn't known, as it were, conveys to it' (BF, 105–7).

[5] See Deleuze, G. and Guattari, F. (1988), *A Thousand Plateaus*, trans. B. Massumi (London: The Athlone Press), 3–25 [hereafter TP].

[6] Deleuze, following Bergson, writes of the virtual realm as the realm of an original and primary problematic—'The virtual possesses the reality of a task to be performed or a problem to be solved: it is the problem which orientates, conditions and engenders solutions, but these do not resemble the conditions of the problem' (DR, 264).

[7] Deleuze famously talks of philosophy as a strange hybrid between the genre of detective fiction and science fiction. Why detective fiction? Manuel de Landa posits the following—'The virtual leaves behind traces of itself in the intensive processes it animates, and the philosopher's task may be seen as that of a detective who follows these tracks or connects these clues and in the process, creates a reservoir of conceptual resources to be used' Delanda, M. (2002), *Intensive Science & Virtual Philosophy* (London: Continuum), 44.

[8] Deleuze rejects such extreme nihilism, since it can only lead to death, madness, nothingness, or catastrophe. In particular see Deleuze and Guattari's comments in TP, 160–1.

[9] Klee, P. (1924), *On Modern Art* (London: Faber and Faber).

[10] In TP (255) Deleuze and Guattari write at length of this single and abstract animal rhizome as the plane of immanence—'There is a pure plane of immanence, univocality, composition, upon which everything is given, upon which unformed elements and materials dance that are distinguished from one another only by

their speed and that enter into this or that individuated assemblage depending on their connections, their relations of movement. A fixed plane of life upon which everything stirs, slows down or accelerates. A single Abstract animal for all the assemblages that effectuate it.'

[11] Rajchman, J. (2000), *The Deleuze Connections* (Cambridge, MA: MIT), 139 [hereafter DC].

[12] Deleuze, G. and Guattari, F. (1994), *What is Philosophy?*, trans. G. Burchell and H. Tomlinson (London: Verso), 5 [hereafter WP]—'The philosopher is the concept's friend; he is potentiality of the concept.'

[13] Martin, J.-C. (1999), 'Deleuze's Philosophy of the Concrete' in I. Buchanan (ed.), *A Deleuzian Century* (London: Duke University Press), 241.

[14] In the short preface to the 1994 English translation of DR a text contemporaneous with WP Deleuze writes—'Philosophy . . . creates and expounds its own concepts only in relation to what it can grasp of scientific functions and artistic constructions . . . The scientific or artistic content of a philosophy may be very elementary, since it is not obliged to advance art or science, but it can advance itself only by forming properly philosophical concepts from a given function or construction, however elementary. Philosophy cannot be undertaken independently of science or art.' DR, xiv.

[15] Hence, as we will see later in this paper, the precise relevance of Deleuze's discussion of what he calls the essential 'catastrophe' and 'hysteria' implicit within the art of painting in LS. Here Francis Bacon is embraced by Deleuze as a painter who celebrates and productively negotiates with and maintains the irrational, the unthinkable, and the imperceptible, via the implicit 'catastrophe' and 'hysteria' within painting. Indeed Bacon says—'one of the things I've always tried to analyse is why it is that, if the formation of the image that you want is done irrationally, it seems to come onto the nervous system much more strongly than if you knew how you could do it. Why is it possible to make the reality of an appearance more violently in this way than by doing it rationally.' BF, 104.

[16] As we will outline, with regard to Deleuze's discussion of painting in LS, this is discussed as painting's ongoing and ceaseless struggle with the 'catastrophe' and 'hysteria' implicit within it, the threat of ruination, of chaos and confusion that haunts it. It is this necessary traversal from the chaos (or what Deleuze will term in his work the 'Diagram') to the painting which becomes so significant for Deleuze. As Bacon says—'I want a very ordered image but I want it to come about by chance.'

[17] 'There is a mode of individuation very different from that of a person, subject, thing, or substance. We reserve the name haecceity for it . . . in the sense that they consist entirely of relations of movement and rest between molecules or particles, capacities to affect and be affected' (TP, 261).

[18] For a more detailed treatment of the 'Smooth' and the 'Striated' see TP, 474–500.

[19] Elkins, J. (1999), *What Painting Is* (London: Routledge), referred later on as JE.

[20] When referring to this diagrammatic function of the production of differenciation in art in DR Deleuze writes of this initiation of a new order—'The actualisation of the virtual appears to take the form of the creation of divergent lines, each of which corresponds to a virtual section and represents a manner of

solving a problem, but also the incarnation of the order of relations and distribution of singularities peculiar to the given section in differenciated species and parts' 264.

[21] 'Painting is the analogical art par excellence. It is even the form through which analogy becomes a language, or finds its own language: by passing through a diagram' (LS, 117).

[22] This chapter is a version of a paper first delivered at The Royal College of Art, London in June 2005. Thanks go to Kamini Vellodi and Emily Harding.

Chapter 9

Deleuze and Merleau-Ponty
Aesthetics of Difference

Henry Somers-Hall

The purposes of this chapter are twofold. First, to show the importance within Deleuze's aesthetics of the notion of the Gestalt, conceived of as a figure against a background, and second to show the degree to which the recognition of the importance of this notion leads to sympathy for the themes of Merleau-Ponty within his work. After showing the motivations for Merleau-Ponty's adoption of the concept of the Gestalt, and its application within *Eye and Mind*, I want to show that despite the similarities in their analyses, Merleau-Ponty's analysis is ultimately incapable of providing a complete description of the work of art.

Merleau-Ponty's early philosophy is an attempt to provide an ontological foundation to the Gestalt. 'A figure on a background is the simplest sense-given available to us,' and as such 'is the very definition of the phenomenon of perception' (PP, 4). Traditional Gestalt psychology's grounding in the isomorphism between the results of modern physics and the structure of the organism must be seen as inadequate, as it requires us to unreflectively presuppose scientific ontology wholesale. Merleau-Ponty, of course, solves this problem of foundations by invoking the transcendental reduction. The bracketing of the natural attitude, and the reduction of the world to a field of immanence, enables us to construct a descriptive ontology, which does not rely on the theoretical suppositions of general science. Husserl, however, follows the transcendental reduction with another reduction, the eidetic reduction, a move which allows the study of the world as essence. Through the reduction, phenomenology grants access to the flow of singularities before consciousness. These 'matters of fact,' according to Husserl, are not adequate to the founding of a pure science, and instead, we need to seek the atemporal essence of the phenomenon, that which underlies it and encompasses 'the entire *wesengehalt* of the phenomenon, from its largest generality down to its seemingly most innocuous differences' (TPD, 57). This is achieved through a monstrous, potentially infinite, series of deformations of the object by the faculty of phantasy. This process doesn't destroy the identity found at the level of essence by showing the object to be a 'heterogeneous multiplicity,' but instead points to a deeper identity, a plane upon which the deformations take place marking the limits of the intelligibility of the deformations. Phantasy therefore defines the essence by providing the boundaries beyond which the object can no longer be grasped as such by consciousness. It reduces the heterogeneous multiplicity to a homogenous multiplicity (TPD, 59). This reliance on the underlying plane in order to produce identity cannot be used to define a self-identical essence, however, as the Gestalt *is* precisely the interplay between the figure and the ground. As such, any variation in the figure itself will cause reciprocal topological variations in the underlying field itself. Husserl's error is in not realizing that the ground itself is a part of the figure. The process of individuation which creates objects necessarily draws them together into communities. The ground and figure are different in kind, but also, as is shown by the possibility of infinite regress, infinite reversibility preventing their reduction to a homogenous plane. This naturally reduces the power of the phenomenological method, and as Merleau-Ponty states, 'since our reflections are carried out in the temporal flux on to which we are trying to seize, there is no thought which embraces all our thought' (PP, xiv).

Instead of dealing with the extent to which Deleuze's criticisms of phenomenology can be applied to Merleau-Ponty's work, I want to show the similarity between Deleuze's and Merleau-Ponty's work in regard to the Gestalt and the work of art. While phenomenology must normally be seen as a science of the actual, Deleuze recognizes the possibility of Merleau-Ponty moving beyond this limitation in his later work *Eye and Mind*. As he puts it, 'Erwin Strauss, Merleau-Ponty, or Maldiney need Cezanne or Chinese painting' (WP, 149). Of course, such an analysis still must begin at the level of the actual, as 'Apollo, the clear-confused thinker, is needed in order to think the Ideas of Dionysus' (DR, 214). The difficulty is to go beyond this language, to push our analysis to the level of the 'closest noumenon' which is the level of the virtual. Such a movement is of course a break with classical phenomenology.

While in his early work, Merleau-Ponty uses the notion of the Gestalt to characterize the actual, in *Eye and Mind* he attempts to move further to the point of actualization of the Gestalt itself. As he argues, the mutual dependence of things moves us toward the substitution of the space of dimensions for that of depth. Depth becomes the first dimension, if it can even still be considered in terms of dimensions, as it is through depth that things maintain their independence through their relations with the field of objects that are around them. Merleau-Ponty's conception of Depth here comes close to the Bergsonian conception of time. Depth is not a space in the conventional sense of a series of dimensions through which the movements of objects can be measured, but a place where relationships between objects as differential processes are formed. As such, it is closer to the idea of a place where bodies come to be through their interrelations than a spatially extended area where objects can be moved around, measured, and compared with those about them. Things maintain themselves by the pushing forward and holding back of relations with other things, thus prohibiting the isolation and analysis of any one from its milieu. This notion of depth, which is key to the understanding of Cezanne for Merleau-Ponty, maintains the idea of the Gestalt as a process. With Cezanne we find a study of perception which does not already presuppose the nature of that which allows perception to take place. Cezanne's suicide, 'aiming for reality while denying himself the means to attain it,' mirrors the move from Gestalt psychology to the *Phenomenology of Perception*: it is a recognition that the insights of impressionism require a revolution in order for their implications to be brought into the open (CD, 63). This revolution amounts to giving back to the world its weight, as well as keeping the depth which the impressionists had found with its loss. Cezanne's realization is that 'space must be shattered—the fruit bowl must be broken' (EM, 140). It is this breaking up of objective space that leads us to the origin of the Gestalt itself. This is the 'deflagration of Being,' the burning up of the visible, which aims at tearing a fissure in being precisely at the point between things themselves. Clearly such an approach requires a move away from traditional painting techniques. Following Deleuze, we can say that Cezanne is searching for a certain virtuality within his work, an attempt to present 'not some confused determination, but a completely determined structure formed by its genetic differential elements, its "virtual" or "embryonic' elements"' (DR, 209). Cezanne's answer to this problem of finding a path to the root of being is a return to pure forms, forms which, 'taken together, as traces or cross-sections of the thing, let it appear between them like a face in the reeds' (EM, 140). These cross sections must be understood in terms of the n-dimensional fields of the virtual, within which the real idea of the determined entity exists, different in kind from its actualized descendent. It is traces of these forces which are found within the middle period of Cezanne. In moving to the level of depth, we necessarily require a change in the language we use. Cezanne finds it necessary to put 'Being's solidity on one side and its variety on the other' (EM, 140). As such, we find ourselves forced to use the two languages of Deleuze, the clear-confused (which is the language of the actual) and the obscure-distinct (which pertains to the virtual). Through this division, Cezanne is hoping to create a double description of the object, which encompasses both its virtual and actual tendencies.

Of course, the study of color itself cannot get us to the heart of things. It is indeed a breaking of the 'skin of things,' but the heart is 'beyond the colour envelope just as it is beyond the space envelope' (EM, 141). The exploration of the thing through color is a form of trying to bring to expression that part of the virtual which 'must be defined as strictly a part of the real object' (DR, 209). Merleau-Ponty is clearly attempting to move beyond the world of perception to the real conditions for the experience of perception. What he is searching for is the origin of the Gestalt in that 'relation between a perceiving body and a sensible . . . and not perspectival world' (VI, 206). The intention is to penetrate beyond perception through perception, an intention which has

clearly been taken up in the world of art, as shown by the ability of the artist
to transpose his work from one field to an other—an ability which shows that
what the artist is attempting to grasp is not an aspect of perception, but that
which gives rise to the relation between the subject and the Gestalt. The move
from Cezanne to Klee, and the emphasis on the line, clarifies this change of
position. It is the line that 'renders visible,' not as the contour of the Gestalt
(the line which is brought into existence at the same moment as the fusion
of the figure with its horizon), but instead as the line which is the generating
power of the Gestalt itself. Such a line is the 'blueprint of the genesis of things.'
The attempt being made here is to paint the *idea* of the thing under consideration. The line curls itself through the different planes of the idea, mirroring
the phase portrait of a system to such a degree that it is necessary to 'leave it
up to the title to designate by its prosaic name the entity thus constituted.' In
that Klee's painting 'subtends the spatiality of a thing quite as much as a man
or an apple tree,' we are in a situation where the dimensionality of the painting no longer matters to the underlying content. While the multiplication of
dimensions is necessarily replaced with the multiplication of lines, necessary
to give the painting sensible form, the lines themselves attempt the task of
putting forth the differential relations which hold beneath the painting itself.
The factor that governs the nature of the lines within the work is that it is 'the
line's relation to itself . . . [that] will form a meaning of the line.' What Klee is
trying to produce is a line that 'is intrinsically defined, without reference to
a uniform space in which it would be submerged.' The line thus becomes the
'complex theme' of an internal multiplicity which defines the actualized thing.
It is an attempt to render visible that which is behind the visible. This explains
Klee's statement that to give a generating axis of a man the painter 'would
have to have a network of lines so entangled that it could no longer be a question of a truly elementary representation.' The work of Klee therefore seems
to meet the criteria set up by Deleuze for the notion of an idea, which is at the
heart of the language of the virtual. The first of these criteria is that of a lack
of conceptual significance, the idea that an idea does not contain within itself
its own meaning (thus allowing the idea to be actualized in different contexts).
This criterion is met by the fact that the name becomes a necessary identifier
of the work. Without the title, the work can no longer be seen to signify anything in particular. It should be noted that the title of the work does not give
meaning to the painting, however, but instead actualizes an indeterminate
virtual meaning already present (EM, 143). Second, the interrelation between
elements must be intrinsically spatial, as opposed to extrinsically spatial. As we
have seen from Merleau-Ponty's notion of depth, the thing can no longer be
seen to merely reside in space, but instead draws space around it. The painting
of the lines forms its own space, a space within depth that is necessarily composed by the juxtaposition of the lines themselves. The third criterion, the criterion that the Idea must be actualized in diverse spatio-temporal situations,

which guarantees the nature of the idea as a structure, is met by the painting before it is given a name. The name of the painting delineates a path of actualization, ties it to one actualized state of affairs. This feature of the work is not integral to the painting itself, however; the latter requires a name precisely on the basis that before it is thus determined, its meaning is unknown precisely because of its ability to be actualized in a variety of contexts.

We have seen how Merleau-Ponty's analysis of the work of art comes close to the recognition of the virtual. There is clearly something that is between, or behind, the actual differential structure of perception. There is the movement, in the analysis of the work of Cezanne, toward a division at the heart of language. A segregation of the clear-confused from the distinct-obscure. This division, however, is quickly rejected by Merleau-Ponty. 'We must seek space and its content together' (EM, 143). It is here that we finally come to an understanding of the Deleuzian comment that 'phenomenology is never more in need of . . . a "rigorous science" than when it invites us to renounce it' (WP, 149). Merleau-Ponty has made tremendous progress in the illumination of the actual, primarily through the breaking down of the conventional concept of space-time, and the recognition that the Gestalt is not its own foundation. The difficulty is that the notion of depth attempts to fulfill two functions. It attempts to explain the actualization of the Gestalt, and also to explain the Gestalt as actualized. As such, the two parts of the Gestalt, the virtual and the actual, become conflated. These two parts provide two radically different origins of Gestalt structure: First through its actual origin, that is, the fact that a Gestalt naturally appears from an already existent Gestalt (a corollary of the fact that the Gestalt is the simplest unit of perception); and second through the origin of the Gestalt as the actualizing of an intertwining/integration of a pre-individual field of singularities. Merleau-Ponty's attempt to explain the virtual origin of the Gestalt figure is doomed to failure because the language of phenomenology forces him to describe this origin in terms of the actual. As such the virtual is sought between figures, where, as I have shown, one can only find other Gestalt structures. He reaches a stage where the Gestalt loses its stability, where it starts to break down, but such an analysis is still an analysis of the flesh. To move to the final level of analysis, we need to give up searching between the Gestalt, at the point of the contour, for its origin. Instead, what is necessary is that we move to a language at which the Gestalt itself is already broken, or rather, is yet to be formed. This is the level of the dissolved Gestalt, the Gestalt at, or before the brink of corporeality. This is not to disregard Merleau-Ponty's work. It is not a flawed analysis of the virtual, and was never meant to be, but rather an analysis of the non-perspectival nature of the actual, of the flesh, that is the source of particular instantiations of the Gestalt within the world. What Merleau-Ponty has found is the *function* through which the Gestalt of the flesh unravels its temporal structure. A complete analysis of perception, however, must take account of the work of Deleuze in *The Logic of Sensation*.

'Painting's eternal object' writes Deleuze, 'is this: to paint forces' (WP, 182). This movement away from the actual gives us the opportunity to clarify the Gestalt's origin within the virtual. The move to the notion of force within art does not do away with the need to deal with the Gestalt. As we can see from the beginning of Deleuze's work on Francis Bacon, the Gestalt takes prominence within his work, in the form of a circle, which 'often delimits the place where the person—that is to say, the figure—is seated, lying down, doubled over, or in some other position' (FB, 1). The Gestalt, in the work of Deleuze, however, is in a constant mode of flight, a constant mode of trying to get beyond itself. The depth of the background behind the figure is made to be as shallow as possible. The spasm—the trademark of Bacon—is seen by Deleuze as an attempt on the part of the flesh to 'flow out of itself,' to escape from its background. The effect of the attempt to escape the Gestalt is seen further in the flattening of the figure against the background, threatening to dissipate itself 'like a lump of fat in a bowl of soup,' or the final possibility, the disappearance of the figure in its entirety, leaving behind nothing but a trace of its former self (FB, xii). It is clear here that there is an effort to free art from the restrictions of the actual, to move beyond the Gestalt, but a move which purports to open up, through the remnants left on the canvas, the origin of the Gestalt. Thus, 'neither the tactile-optical world nor the purely optical world are stopping points for Bacon' (FB, 136). The work of Bacon, furthermore concerning itself with the body, with contorted figures, gives Deleuze the possibility of forming a new critique of the work of Merleau-Ponty. The work of Bacon makes explicit the theme of the flesh falling away from the bone, the theme which is at the heart of Deleuze's debate with Merleau-Ponty.

The painting of Bacon institutes two separate movements. First, the movement described just now, which is the attempt at the dissolution of the Gestalt structure through a variety of methods which disrupt the field/figure relation. This movement, mirroring Merleau-Ponty's analysis, takes place at the point of the contour, that is, between the figure and its background. The contour also precipitates a second movement, that between the material structure and the figure. This is the figure's attempt to escape through the contour itself, which is the recognition of a 'vanishing point' within the Gestalt, where the figure, under 'all the pressures of the body' attempts to escape from itself (FB, 16). Thus within the body we find the root of a second exchange. This time the exchange becomes the source of an immobile movement, an 'intense motionless effort' of the figure that is not in the realms of 'the place, but rather of the event' (FB, 15). The dissolution of the Gestalt at the level of the actual necessarily opens up the possibility of reaching that which underlies the Gestalt. Thus, the collapse of the figure/background relation forces the figure to make a similar move, an effort to return to the preindividual field which is its origin. This movement of 'de-actualization' 'releases the presences beneath representation' (FB, 52). These presences beneath representation cannot themselves be seen as spatial entities, even as entities within a field of depth. To do so would be to misconstrue the relation between the clear-confused and the distinct-obscure. 'It . . . is not the force which is sensed, since the force "gives" something completely different from the forces that condition it' (FB, 56). This means that the study of art becomes the attempt to see what precisely is not manifest within the painting. The collapse of the Gestalt, which simply leaves 'traces' on the canvas is this opening to the non-manifest. The dissipation of the figure goes 'from the figure to the structure' (FB, 33), a structure which is pre-individual, as individuation necessitates the formation of a Gestalt structure. Instead, these relations between the traces of forces on the canvas are differential relations. At the body's attempt to escape itself, and through the tension which swirls across the surface of the flesh, we arrive at the purely internal relations within color. These relations, however, give us everything. As this analysis is not far from Merleau-Ponty's analysis of Klee, we need to understand what Deleuze wants to achieve by it. The key is Deleuze's comment that 'flesh, however firm, descends from bones; it falls or tends to fall away from them' (FB, ix).

For Merleau-Ponty, the flesh is the element of the world. For Deleuze, we could perhaps define the world through the notion of force. It is for this reason that the house, the work of architecture comes to prominence, and why Cezanne, with his 'world as nature' is Merleau-Ponty's signifier, while Bacon, with his 'world as artefact' signifies the philosophy of Deleuze. Deleuze is not rejecting the notion of the flesh, but instead is calling for the recognition that the element of the flesh is only the world seen under one of its aspects. There is a coexistence of flesh and bone, the one residing within the other. The bone is therefore that which shows itself in the work of art which is not flesh, but it necessarily coexists with the flesh, and provides the flesh with its structure. This notion is the virtual, that which provides the structure to the actual/flesh/Gestalt. The link between bone and the virtual becomes explicit in a sentence from *What is Philosophy?* 'The second element is not so much bone or skeletal structure as house or framework' (WP, 179). Here then is a clarification of the fact that flesh retains its position for Deleuze, as well as a reference to the true nature of bone. The notion of bone as found in Bacon is here tied to the notion of architecture, a play of, and with forces. The human flesh of Bacon recedes and dissolves itself, revealing the virtual structure which supported it. Beneath the flesh is not bone but force.

We must now ask how this relates to what we have said of Merleau-Ponty. The difficulty is that there are two languages at play within philosophy, the one which deals with the level of the actual, with phenomena as they are given to us (the level of the clear-confused) and the other which deals with the virtual. This second level is the level of the distinct-obscure, a level where the Gestalt is yet to be formed, and where description takes the form of the analysis of a field of forces. This is the level of the shattered space of Cezanne, of the fragmented Gestalt where the foreground and background dissolve into one another. The languages cannot be confused with each other, for to do so would be to risk conflating these two aspects of the Gestalt. This would lead to a consideration of the virtual in terms of the actual, and to a perpetuation of the Gestalt beyond its proper place. It is for this reason that Merleau-Ponty ultimately rejects Cezanne's solution, arguing that we need to 'seek space and content together' (EM, 140). Once this statement is accepted, the possibility of an analysis of perception traversing the virtual is cut away from us. It is true that at the level of the actual, the Gestalt cannot be separated from the space it itself forms, from the planes which radiate out from it; but such an analysis can only move us half way toward the nature of the differential structures. The other half of the enquiry does not take place, as Merleau-Ponty recommends, between the figures, but instead at the point where the figure dissolves itself, where the contour starts to fall apart, and where we see traces of that which is behind the Gestalt.

References

Beistegui, M. (2000), 'Toward a phenomenology of difference?,' *Research in Phenomenology* 30. Cited as TPD.

Deleuze, G. (1994), *Difference and Repetition*, trans. P. Patton (London: Athlone Press). Cited as DR.

—(2003), *Francis Bacon: The Logic of Sensation*, trans. Daniel Smith (London: Continuum Press). Cited as FB.

Deleuze, G. and Guattari, F. (2004), *What is Philosophy?*, trans. G. Burchell and H. Tomlinson (London: Verso). Cited as WP.

Johnson, G. (Ed.) (1993), *The Merleau-Ponty Aesthetics Reader* (Evanston: Northwestern University Press).

Merleau-Ponty, M. (1962), *The Phenomenology of Perception*, trans. Colin Smith (London: Routledge & Kegan Paul). Cited as PP.

—(1993), *Eye and Mind*, in G. Johnson (ed.), *The Merleau-Ponty Aesthetics Reader* (Evanston: Northwestern University Press). Cited as EM.

—(1993), 'Cezanne's Doubt,' in G. Johnson (ed.), *The Merleau-Ponty Aesthetics Reader* (Evanston: Northwestern University Press). Cited as CD.

—(1968), *The Visible and the Invisible*, trans. A. Lingis (Evanston: Northwestern University Press). Cited as VI.

Chapter 10

From the Death of the Author to the Disappearance of the Reader

Bruce Baugh

The story goes that when Elizabeth I watched a staging of Shakespeare's *Richard II*, she exclaimed (with some dismay), 'Richard is me!' That 'shock of recognition' and of identification is probably familiar to any reader: we can all exclaim, in this respect, '*Elizabeth* is me!' In a literary work, actions and characters often reveal to us uncomfortable truths about ourselves: in Hamlet's indecision we see our own dithering, in Oedipus' reckless pursuit of the truth we recognize our own obstinate self-ignorance in the name of principles; there are endless examples (pick your own), including examples represented within literature, as when Hamlet hopes that the tragedy enacted by the players will 'catch the conscience of the king,' and reveal to Claudius his own guilt in the murder of Hamlet's father. But literature also provides other examples, offering a different lesson: Don Quixote mistaking himself for a 'knight errant,' Emma Bovary mistaking herself for the heroine of a romantic novel. Often, the shock of recognition is a shock of misrecognition, where the characters and actions in a literary work are identified not with who we are, but with an imaginary self, whether that self is what we would like to be but aren't (as in Don Quixote's case), or the self we dread becoming or fear represents some basic, and base, truth about ourselves. Of course, Don Quixote was mad, as was Emma Bovary, after her fashion. But what if every identification with a literary character was a misidentification, every recognition a misrecognition? Elizabeth, for all her imaginings about her weakness as a 'prince,' was, after all, *not* Richard II. There is an element of madness in any act of identification with a literary character, whether fictional or real. The 'shock of recognition' is the effect of an illusion, and above all of the primary and inevitable illusion of the unified 'self' that results from our childhood habit of identifying ourselves with the unified image of the face and body that looks out at us from the mirror. This is the first misrecognition, and the problem with it is not so much that it is mistaken and mad, but that in placing us within the constraints of a well-defined 'identity,' it is not nearly mad enough.

Since Barthes proclaimed 'the death of the author,' and since Foucault relegated the 'author' to a legal-critical function, we have got quite used to separating the author from the work, the writer from the author, and the writer from the flesh-and-blood individual who did other things besides write. We no longer look to the work to reveal the truth of the author, or to the author to reveal the truth of the work—at least, not when we are reading in a critically informed and self-consciously 'academic' way. But we still seem to look to literature to find the truth of *the reader*: we expect literature to show us 'who we really are,' for good or ill, 'warts and all.' Instead of making an inference from work to author, we make an inference from work to reader: what if both inferences were equally questionable? What if, indeed, there were another way to read, which did not lead us back into ourselves (or into some 'human condition' we share with everyone else), but away from ourselves, into the unknown?

Gilles Deleuze offers a theory of writing and of reading that makes both activities 'lines of flight,' a movement away from the familiar and the known, an act of 'deterritorialization.' The aim of literature is not to help us get our bearings or to find ourselves, but to lose our bearings and our 'selves,' to *get lost*. Deleuze says that 'to create is to lighten, to unburden life, to invent new possibilities of life,'[1] and that 'the only end of writing is life,' 'an impersonal yet singular life' that is beyond the personality or character of the person who lives it,[2] 'a non-personal power,'[3] 'beyond the perceptual states and affective transitions of the lived,'[4] a 'more than personal life' beyond 'the poverty of the imaginary and the symbolic' (D, 51). Writing and reading are not voyages of self-discovery, based on the desire to have oneself and one's claims recognized by others, but a pure 'voyage out' in which one loses one's identity, and slips through 'the objective determinations which fix us, put us into a grille, identify us and make us recognized' (D, 45). Writing as a line of flight is a way out, not 'out of the world' and into the imaginary, but out of identity, 'the known,' established orders of meaning and of 'right,' always moving from the defined to the undefined, from a dominant term to a 'minor' one (CC, 1). Rather than cementing or confirming an identity, writing and reading unsettle it: 'It is always a question of freeing life wherever it is imprisoned or of tempting it into an uncertain combat' (WIP, 171), of discovering 'the splendor of *l'On*,'[5] 'the power of an impersonal' third-person beneath the apparent persons 'that strips us of the power to say "I" ' (CC, 3). 'One has to disappear, to become unknown' (D, 45).

This may sound reassuringly familiar to connoisseurs of the modern; it seems to resemble the pursuit of the exotic and the foreign in Conrad, Melville, or T. E. Lawrence. Yet, despite Deleuze's admiration for Melville and Lawrence, writing's line of flight is not a trip that takes a self or identity intact from one place to another (D, 37). However 'exotic,' 'strange,' or 'surprising' the destination, a destination is an end-point, something that can be located and 'plotted,' and which retrospectively defines and determines the line leading toward it. It is no use fleeing one identity for another, like the Americans and

Europeans who sought their 'primitive' selves in the colonial outposts of the South Pacific, Africa, or Asia: this is to journey from the known to the known, even if the 'known' and defined term toward which one flees is something with which one is unacquainted, and therefore 'strange.' It is not a matter of assuming masks or identities, like an 'imposter' who seeks to become 'someone else' in order to claim new powers, a new territory, a new order, in the manner of Conrad's Lord Jim or Kurz (see D, 11 5). Exoticism's discovery of new selves, or of a foreign self that reveals the secret heart of darkness in the familiar self, is not getting lost or getting rid of one's self.

Odysseys, however 'estranging,' nevertheless retain the pattern of Homer's original, and a 'line of flight' is the opposite of an Odyssey. Odysseus remains himself throughout his voyages (unlike, say, his crew, who are really transformed into beasts), and returns home to reclaim his rightful place: his kingdom, his household, his servants, his wife: the subject reclaiming the *properties* that define him. His homecoming is complete when he is *recognized*: when all the masks fall away, and his identity is revealed, when he is no longer the wayfaring stranger because the marks and signs have been deciphered, his secret uncovered. In that respect, the *Odyssey* is the model of tragic drama, the pivotal moment always being that of 'recognition and reversal,' whether recognition leads to destruction (*Oedipus the King, Lord Jim*) or a 'return' to where one belongs (*Odyssey*).[6] Whether for good or ill, every tragedy effects a return to one's 'true' self, and it is this structure of estrangement and return that makes the tragic plot a unified whole, with a beginning, a middle, and a conclusion.

Modern literature's line of flight, by contrast, effects what F. Scott Fitzgerald calls 'a clean break': 'A clean break is something you cannot come back from; that is irretrievable because it makes the past cease to exist.'[7] A true voyage out is where 'you can't go home again' because neither you nor home any longer exist. What Deleuze calls 'deterritorialization' is this departure without arrival or return, a voyage that is always *in media res*, without beginning or ending, but purely and simply 'in the middle' of a path, *en route* (D, 30): 'There is no terminus from which you set out, none which you arrive at or ought to arrive at' (D, 2). Not only in the modern novel, but from its inception, 'the novel has always been defined by the adventures of lost characters who no longer know their name, what they are looking for, or what they are doing,' from Chrétien de Troyes knights errant to Beckett's Molloy.[8] These characters cannot be recognized because they are not attached to the particularities or properties that would mark them and which they could claim as their own (CC, 87) but are 'without references, without possessions, without properties, without qualities, without particularities . . . without past or future' (CC, 74; see D, 31, 38, 43), existing only in the midst of the open road or the open sea, leading a life without seeking salvation, voyaging without any particular aim, with freedom as their sole fulfillment (CC, 87). 'All referents are lost': Melville's Ahab cannot return home and cannot find refuge in a new port or haven because he is fleeing from everywhere (CC, 77), carried off on a line of flight where he and the whale enter into a zone of proximity, indistinction, indiscernibility or ambiguity (CC, 78), each losing himself in the other as much as the other loses itself in him, such that neither can be reduced or assimilated to the other (D, 2; WIP, 173). This is not finding one's true self—through either personal or collective memory, or recognition (see CC, 66)—or a new self, but losing the self in a process of becoming that confuses and destabilizes all the terms, a demonic passage *between* terms (D, 42) 'in which each pushes the other, draws it into its line of flight in a combined deterritorialization' (D, 44), 'where I can no longer be distinguished from what I am becoming' (CC, 65). As Deleuze so pithily puts it: ' "See me as I am": all that stuff is over' (D, 47–8).

Of course, this raises a number of questions. Why would a dissolution of the self be salutary? Would it not also be dangerous? How exactly does literature effect such a dissolution? What's wrong with the reader identifying with literary characters, anyway?

Deleuze, following certain trends in French psychoanalysis, regards the ego or Me (*le Moi*) as a result of a process of identification, whereby in identifying with another, one consolidates the Self and establishes certain boundaries of inclusion and exclusion. In a sense, Deleuze agrees with Locke's equation of the self with property—every man has a property in his own person—*private* property, fenced around and marked with 'No trespassing' signs. The boundaries of the self are established by a subject imitating the image or model it identifies with; the subject tries 'to assume a form, to appropriate the image, to adapt itself to this image and the image to itself' (CC, 76), an effort at which the subject 'either succeeds or fails' (CC, 78), and which 'always risks falling into neurosis or turning into narcissism' (CC, 76). The self defined by how successfully it imitates a model or image is from the outset a false self, just as 'an invariable model, a fixed form' is itself false (CC, 104), since what is absent from both is 'the power of metamorphosis' or creative activity: not a fixed form, but a process of trans-formation, of pure becoming, 'a surging forth of life' (CC, 105). The ego, then, as a mere reflection of a dead model, is 'already dead' (CC, 51); it is therefore necessary to 'stop thinking of yourself as an ego in order to live as a flow, a set of flows in relation with other flows, outside of oneself and within oneself' (CC, 51), a life of forces and flows that is always traversing points rather than being confined within a fixed boundary. In great writing, says Deleuze, a 'character' is a unique, chance combination of forces, 'collections of intensive sensations,' 'Individuation without a subject' (D, 39–40), revealing that 'At the most profound level of subjectivity, there is not an ego, but rather a singular composition, an idiosyncrasy . . . marking the unique chance that . . . *this* combination had been thrown and not another' (CC, 120).

It might seem that identification with a character would release the flow of life between one person and the other, but such identifications really amount to an attempt to appropriate and absorb the other, 'recovering persons and possessions' by relating impersonal life forces to 'me' and 'mine' (CC, 65). In this, the reader who identifies with a character is much as Milan Kundera describes two people having a conversation:

> First one of them does all the talking, the other one breaks in with 'That's just like me, I . . .' and goes on talking about himself until his partner has a chance to say 'That's just like me, I . . .'. [This] may look like a form of agreement, a way of carrying the other party's idea further, but that is an illusion. What they really are is . . . a battle for the ears of others.[9]

When a reader identifies with a character in a novel—'that's just like me, I . . .'—the reader is not trying to force the character to listen, of course, but is trying to force the literary character within the familiar grid of the reader's own self, seeing in the character only what the reader sees in herself, and seeing in herself only an image imitated from a model. This is narcissism, in every sense of the term, and even a kind of hysteria (D, 43), and definitely a kind of *ressentiment* in which the self affirms itself by negating what is not it, and seeks to subdue or capture the other. The movement here is from fixed term to fixed term, with the 'self' as the 'centre,' even though the self is formed through imitation of a model. Identification is assimilation of everything to the model, to 'criteria that preexist for all time (to the infinity of time), so that it can neither apprehend what is new in an existing being, nor even sense the creation of a mode of existence' (CC, 135).

If there is a good way for the reader to 'identify' with literature at all, it is by linking up with those forces in it that carry out 'a cold and concerted destruction of the ego,' and lead characters 'far from [their] own country' (CC, 117). By finding affective and perceptual links with characters who are lost, who lose themselves, we can take up a broken line that cannot be retraced, extending a line of flight already begun elsewhere by someone or something else (D, 39) and which lead not just outside of the ego, but beyond the human subject altogether, as when we enter into 'the subjectivity of the milieu itself,' with all its 'qualities, substances, powers, and events: [such as] the street, . . . with its materials (paving stones), its noises (cries of merchants), its animals (harnessed horses) or its dramas (a horse slips, a horse falls down, a horse is beaten)' (CC, 61). Mrs. Dalloway no longer judges or categorizes either others or herself ('She would not say of any one in the world now that they were this or were that . . . She would not say of herself, I am this, I am that')[10] because she has become indistinguishable from 'life; London; this moment in June' (4) 'outside looking on' (9) from the point of view of the life of London's streets: 'somehow in the streets of London, on the ebb and flow of things, here, there, she survived' (9), 'invisible; unseen; unknown' (11). Her 'self' has entered into a 'zone of indiscernibility' with London's streets on 'this moment in June,' her life indistinguishable from that of the milieu, she perceives and feels from the point of view of the milieu, and has thereby journeyed far from her own country, even while remaining 'at home' (see WIP, 169).

One does not have to journey far in space to journey far from self, and it is best to move 'in place,' in a 'stationary flight of intensity' rather than the false freedom of movement in space[11]—to be always away and on the way, in 'the middle and not the beginning or the end' (D, 31). Although it is true that certain milieus lend themselves to journeys without fixed points of reference—the open sea, the desert (CC, 117)—when Ahab perceives and feels from the point of view of the sea he inhabits with the whale, when T. E. Lawrence perceives and feels from the point of view of the desert he inhabits with the Arabs, they too lose themselves by merging with the subjectivity of the milieu, but no more and no less than does Mrs. Dalloway the purely interior journey that dislocates the fixed landmarks of London and of her life. It is always a question of getting lost without being found again, of 'becoming imperceptible' (WIP, 169; CC, 26, D, 45), and so to be able to find (*trouver*) something new, that is, to really *find* something, 'under the ruins of [one's] devastated ego' (CC, 117), instead of just re-finding (*retrouver*) one's self.

There is no guarantee that a voyage without a destination will have a happy ending, for either the novelistic character or the reader. That is not the point. Anyway, it would be a bit daft to think that Ahab goes to sea the way Gilligan does, that Lawrence goes to the desert the way a hippie goes to Morocco, or that Mrs. Dalloway goes to London the way my daughter goes to the mall. These characters do not *choose* their voyages the way a consumer does at the travel agency; they are swept away by a line of flight that runs through them and takes them out of themselves, not by choice, but by necessity. Whether or not their ends are fatal, as sometimes happens, there is a fatality governing their becomings: they *must* undertake these voyages out. Such voyages expose them to encounters with other forces—other people, milieus, land- and seascapes—that can enhance or decrease their powers of living; or more precisely, encounters can increase an impersonal power of life that runs through them and beyond them, producing new effects and inventing new variations (D, 39–40, 49–50, 51–2, 57, 59–60).

Our role as readers is not to imitate these characters or their becomings, but to experiment with the intensities of affect and perception they release, searching for those that carry us off on our own lines of flight; in short, the reader's aim should be to experiment with the different possible encounters with the different aspects of the novel, seeking out those encounters that increase our power of life, and which take us out of ourselves: a 'process through which force enriches itself by seizing hold of other forces and joining itself to them in a new ensemble: a becoming' (CC, 132).

'Experiment, never interpret' (D, 48). Reading ought to be 'a series of experiments for each reader in the midst of events that have nothing to do with books,'[12] and where books are themselves used as 'an experimental machine, a machine for effects, as in physics.'[13] Both the reader and the book are composites in a system of relations expressing 'a power of existing or acting,'[14] and when two bodies' parts intermingle in such a way that their characteristic relations can be harmoniously combined, this results in an increase in their powers of existing, experienced affectively in a feeling of joy (CC, 148).[15] Reading is 'a kind of test . . . a physical or chemical test, like that whereby workmen test the quality of some material' (EPS, 317), a test of the powers of the reader and the book at the moment of their encounter.

It is impossible to know in advance whether the encounter will turn out well for either party: in any experimental encounter, the result is unforeseen (D, 47), and can just as well result in destruction as in an increase in power. Experimentation knows 'nothing of meaning and aims,' it is a 'pure process that fulfills itself, and that never ceases to reach fulfillment at it proceeds,'[16] 'an impersonal process' bringing together different 'voyagers and becomers [*devenants*]' (CC, 66). There is always the risk of being destroyed by a life too strong for one, a risk undertaken first by the writer, whose 'irresistible and delicate health' results from experiencing a life liberated from its imprisonment in man, organisms, and genera (CC, 3), a vitality that provides a perspective on both health and illness, a 'great health' (D, 5)[17] that also bears witness to the writer's experience of 'something in life that is too much for anyone, too much for themselves, and has put on them the quiet mark of death' (WIP, 172–3). But for the writer, this risk, this voyage, is as necessary as it is for their characters; they must risk their lives for 'the more than personal life' that they bear witness to (CC, 45): 'to write is trace lines of flight which are not imaginary, and which indeed one is forced to follow' (D, 43). It is this involuntary openness to 'nonorganic vitality . . . the relation of the body to the imperceptible forces and powers that seize hold of it' (CC, 131) that makes great writers *grands vivants*, in and through the frail physical and psychological health that comes from being too weak for the life that runs through them (D, 50).

Writing is not a choice, but 'the impossibility of another choice' (D, 51). 'Without a set of impossibilities, you wouldn't have a line of flight, the exit that is creation,' and a writer creates her own impossibilities in order to create a way out, but out of necessity, because these impossibilities grab her by the throat.[18] Kafka, faced with the triple impossibility of not writing, of not writing in German (since like other Czech Jews, Kafka is not fluent in Czech, disdains Yiddish, and can only dream of the ancient and future language of Hebrew), and of writing in German (that 'paper language' of the Imperial bureaucracy), is forced to invent a 'minor' use of German within and against the 'major' and official German of the Empire;[19] Virginia Woolf, faced with the impossibility of living and the impossibility of not living, dissolves herself into her characters and her characters into their living milieu. In both cases, it is a matter of finding a way out. All the figures in Kafka—blocked passages, doors to nowhere, humans metamorphosing into animals, interminable 'processes' (trials, *Prozess*)—express the condition of a man caught like a rat in a maze, and whose only hope of escape is to *become* a rat: to think rat-wise, to adopt all the rat maneuvers. To not get trapped, to escape: these are the vital imperatives of the writer, necessities, not choices.[20] The greatest trap is that of the self, and the greatest problem is 'How can we rid ourselves of ourselves [*nous défaire de nous-mêmes*], and demolish ourselves?'[21]

For the reader, the same imperative obtains: 'One must resist both of the traps, the one which offers us the mirror of contamination and identifications, and the one which points out to us the observation of the understanding' (D, 53), the traps of 'Richard is me!' and of passing judgment on a work or its characters. Both operations keep us firmly within our own fixed reference points, our would-be timeless and fixed criteria of evaluation. But it is not a question of judging or misjudging but of sensing whether other beings increase or diminish the impersonal power of life within us (CC, 135), 'we can only assemble among assemblages' (D, 53), experimentally combine ourselves with others, and enter into a 'becoming' along with them. Whatever the risks of getting lost, the risks of being broken by a 'great health' or impersonal vitality are *necessary* risks. Whatever the risks, 'all mistranslations are good—always provided that . . . they relate to the use of the book, that they multiply its use' (D, 5).

Novalis somewhere remarks that 'philosophy is really homesickness; it is the urge to be at home everywhere,'[22] and Georg Lukács, in his pre-Marxist days, decried that 'transcendental homelessness' of the modern era.[23] Deleuze finds in literature not 'the literary form of the transcendent homelessness of the idea'[24] but the antidote for this *Heimweh*. Let's get lost: we have nothing to lose but ourselves.

Notes

[1] Deleuze, G. (1965), *Nietzsche* (Paris: Presses Universitaires de France), 20.

[2] Deleuze, G. (1995), 'L'immanence: une vie . . .', *Philosophie* 47 (September 1), cited in Smith, D. W. (1997), ' "A Life of Pure Immanence": Deleuze's "Critique et clinique" Project,' the 'Introduction' to Deleuze, *Essays Critical and Clinical*, trans. Daniel W. Smith and M. A. Greco (Minneapolis: University of Minnesota Press), xii–xiv; hereafter referred to as CC.

[3] Deleuze, G. and Parnet, C. (1987), *Dialogues*, trans. H. Tomlinson and B. Habberjam (New York: Columbia University Press), 50; hereafter referred to as D.

[4] Deleuze, G. and Guattari, F. (1994), *What is Philosophy?*, trans. H. Tomlinson and G. Burchell (New York: Columbia University Press), 171; hereafter referred to as WIP.

[5] Deleuze, G. (1990) *The Logic of Sense*, trans. M. Lester M. with C. Stivale ed. C. V. Boundas (New York: Columbia University Press), 297; *Logique du sens* (Paris: Minuit, 1969), 345. Both hereafter referred to as LS, with reference to the English translation first.

⁶ Aristotle, *Poetics* 50b24–55a21; trans. R. Janko (Indianapolis: Hackett, 1987), 10–22.

⁷ Fitzgerald, F. S. (1965), *The Crack Up, with other Pieces and Stories* (Harmondsworth: Penguin), 52–3; cited as D 38.

⁸ Deleuze, G. and Guattari, F. (1987), *A Thousand Plateaus*, trans. B. Massumi (Minneapolis: University of Minnesota Press), 173–4; hereafter referred to as ATP.

⁹ Kundera, K. (1981), *The Book of Laughter and Forgetting*, trans. M. H. Heim (Harmondsworth: Penguin), 79–80.

¹⁰ Woolf, V. (2000), *Mrs. Dalloway* (London: Penguin), 8–9; further references given in parentheses in the text.

¹¹ Deleuze, D. and Guattari, F. (1986), *Kafka: Toward a Minor Literature*, trans. D. Polan (Minneapolis: University of Minnesota Press), 13.

¹² Deleuze, G. (1995), *Negotiations*, trans. M. Joughin (New York: Columbia University Press), 8–9.

¹³ Bensmaïa, R. (1986), 'Foreword' to Deleuze G. and Guattari, F. *Kafka: Toward a Minor Literature*, xi.

¹⁴ Deleuze, G. (1990), *Expressionism in Philosophy: Spinoza*, trans. M. Joughin (New York: Zone Books), 89–90; hereafter referred to as EPS.

¹⁵ See Deleuze, G. (1988), *Spinoza: Practical Philosophy*, trans. R. Hurley (San Francisco: City Light Books), 40, 63–5.

¹⁶ Deleuze, G. and Guattari, F. (1983), *Anti-Oedipus: Capitalism and Schizophrenia*, vol. 1, trans. R. Hurley, M. Seem and H. R. Lane (Minneapolis: University of Minnesota Press), 370–71.

¹⁷ Deleuze, *Nietzsche*, 9–10.

¹⁸ Deleuze, *Negotiations*, 133.

¹⁹ Deleuze and Guattari, *Kafka: Toward a Minor Literature*, 15–16, 20, 23.

²⁰ Deleuze and Guattari, *Kafka*, 13.

²¹ Deleuze, G. (1986), *Cinema I: The Movement-Image*, trans. H. Tomlinson and B. Habberjam (Minneapolis: University of Minnesota Press), 66.

²² Cited by Lukács, G. (1971), *History and Class Consciousness*, trans. R. Livingstone (Boston: MIT Press), 29.

²³ Lukács, G. *Theory of the Novel*, trans. A. Bostock (London: Merlin Press), 41.

²⁴ Lukács, *Theory of the Novel*, 121.

Part IV

Deleuze: The Ethical and the Political

Chapter 11

Affirmation versus Vulnerability
On Contemporary Ethical Debates

Rosi Braidotti

At the end of postmodernism politics is in decline, whereas ethics triumphs in the public debate. This is not in itself a progressive move as once again the charge of moral and cognitive relativism is moved against any project that shows a concerted effort at displacing or decentering the traditional, humanistic view of the moral subject. This attitude asserts the belief in the necessity of strong foundations, such as those that a liberal view of the subject can guarantee. Doxic consensus is set: without steady identities resting on firm grounds, basic elements of human decency, moral and political agency, and ethical probity are threatened. In opposition to this belief, which has little more than longstanding habits and the inertia of tradition on its side, I want to argue in this chapter that a post-humanistic and nomadic vision of the subject can provide an alternative foundation for ethical and political subjectivity.

This argument is framed by a larger dispute, which I will not explore here—that of the thorny relationship between poststructuralist ethics in Continental philosophy, on the one hand, and the dominant, mostly Anglo-American traditions of moral philosophy on the other. Todd May (1995) argued persuasively that moral philosophy as a discipline does not score highly in poststructuralist philosophy or in French philosophy as a whole. This is no reason, however, to move against it the lazy charges of moral relativism and nihilism. One only has to look across the field of French philosophy—Deleuze's ethics of immanence (1972; 1980), Irigaray's ethics of sexual difference (1984), Foucault's attempt to self-style the ethical relationship, Derrida's and Lévinas' emphasis on the receding horizons of alterity—to be fully immersed in ethical concerns. It is the case that ethics in poststructuralist philosophy is not confined to the realm of rights, distributive justice, or the law; it rather bears close links with the notion of political agency, freedom, and the management of power and power-relations. Issues of responsibility are dealt with in terms of alterity or the relationship to others. This implies accountability, situatedness, and cartographic accuracy. A poststructuralist position, therefore, far from thinking that a liberal individual definition of the subject is the necessary precondition for ethics, argues that liberalism at present hinders the development of new modes of ethical behavior.

The proper object of ethical enquiry is not the subject's moral intentionality, or rational consciousness, as much as the effects of truth and power that his/her actions are likely to have upon others in the world. This is a kind of ethical pragmatism, which is conceptually linked to the notion of embodied materialism and to a non-unitary vision of the subject. Ethics is therefore the discourse about forces, desires, and values that act as empowering modes of being, whereas morality is the established sets of rules. Philosophical nomadism shares Nietzsche's distaste for morality as sets of negative, resentful emotions and life-denying reactive passions. Deleuze joins this up with Spinoza's ethics of affirmation to produce a very accountable and concrete ethical line about joyful affirmation.

There is no logical reason why Kantians should have a monopoly on moral thinking. In moral philosophy, however, one touches Kantian moral universalism at one's peril. From the Habermasian school and its American branch— Benhabib (2002), Young and Fraser (1996)—to the hard-core Kantianism of Martha Nussbaum (1999), a rejection of poststructuralist theories in general and ethics in particular has taken place. Lovibond (1994) expresses her concern with the loss of moral authority that is entailed by a non-unitary vision of the subject and reasserts the necessity of a Kantian agenda as the only source of salvation after the debacle of postmodernism.

I want to take the opposite road and attempt to read poststructuralist philosophy in its own terms rather than reduce it to the standards of a system of thought—in this case the Kantian tradition—that shares so few of its premises. There are serious advantages to the anti-representational slant of contemporary poststructuralist philosophy, in that it entails the critique of liberal individualism and its replacement by an intensive view of subjectivity. The ethics of nomadic subjectivity rejects moral universalism and works toward a different idea of ethical accountability in the sense of a fundamental reconfiguration of our being in a world that is technologically and globally mediated. One of the most pointed paradoxes of our era is precisely the clash between the urgency of finding new and alternative modes of political and ethical agency, on the one hand, and the inertia or self-interest of neoconservatism on the other. It is urgent to explore and experiment with more adequate forms of non-unitary, nomadic, and yet accountable modes of envisaging both subjectivity and democratic, ethical interaction. Two crucial issues arise: the first is that, contrary to the panic-stricken universalists, an ethics worthy of the complexities of our times requires a fundamental redefinition of our understanding of the subject in his/her contemporary location and not a mere return to a more or less invented philosophical tradition. Second, an alternative ethical stance based on radical immanence and becomings is capable of a universalistic reach, if not a universalistic aspiration. It just so happens to be a grounded, partial form of accountability, based on a strong sense of collectivity and community building. In what follows I want to argue for the relevance of a Deleuzian approach to this urgent ethical project.

The following main discursive alignments can be seen at present in post-structuralist ethical thought. Besides the classical Kantians (see Habermas' recent work on human nature, 2003), we have a Kantian-Foucauldian coalition that stresses the role of moral accountability as a form of bio-political citizenship. Best represented by Nicholas Rose (2001) and Paul Rabinow (2003), this group works with the notion of 'Life' as *bios*, that is to say as an instance of governmentality that is as empowering as it is confining. This school of thought locates the ethical moment in the rational and self-regulating accountability of a bio-ethical subject and results in the radicalization of the project of modernity.

A second grouping takes its lead from Heidegger and is best exemplified by Agamben (1998). It defines *bios* as the result of the intervention of sovereign power, as that which is capable of reducing the subject to 'bare life,' that is to say *zoe*. The latter is, however, contiguous with Thanatos or death. The being-aliveness of the subject (*zoe*) is identified with its perishability, its propensity, and vulnerability to death and extinction. Bio-power here means Thanatos-politics and results in the indictment of the project of modernity.

Another important cluster in this brief cartography of new ethical discourses includes the Lévinas-Derrida tradition of ethics, which is centered on the relationship between the subject and Otherness in the mode of indebtedness, vulnerability, and mourning (Critchley 1992). I have enormous respect for this school of thought, but the project I want to pursue takes as the point of reference *bios-zoe* power defined as the non-human, vitalistic, or post-anthropocentric dimension of subjectivity. This is an affirmative project that stresses positivity and not mourning.

The last discursive coalition, to which this project belongs, is inspired by the neo-vitalism of Deleuze, with reference to Nietzsche and Spinoza (Ansell-Pearson 1997, 1999). Bio-power is only the starting point of a reflection about the politics of life itself as a relentlessly generative force. Contrary to the Heideggerians, the emphasis here is on generation, vital forces, and natality. Contrary to the Kantians, the ethical instance is not located within the confines of a self-regulating subject of moral agency, but rather in a set of inter-relations with both human and inhuman forces. These forces can be rendered in terms of relationality (Spinoza), duration (Bergson), immanence (Deleuze), and, in my own terms, ethical sustainability. The notion of the non-human, inhuman, or post-human emerges therefore as the defining trait of this new kind of ethical subjectivity. This project moves altogether beyond the postmodern critique of modernity and is especially opposed to the hegemony gained by linguistic mediation within postmodernist theory.

Transformative Ethics

At the core of this ethical project is a positive vision of the subject as a radically immanent, intensive body, that is, an assemblage of forces or flows, intensities, and passions that solidify in space and consolidate in time, within the singular configuration commonly known as an 'individual' self. This intensive and dynamic entity is rather a portion of forces that is stable enough to sustain and undergo constant though non-destructive fluxes of transformation. It is the body's degrees and levels of affectivity that determine the modes of differentiation. Joyful or positive passions and the transcendence of reactive affects are the desirable mode. The emphasis on 'existence' implies a commitment to duration and conversely a rejection of self-destruction. Positivity is built into this program through the idea of thresholds of sustainability. Thus, an ethically empowering option increases one's *potentia* and creates joyful energy in the process. The conditions that can encourage such a quest are not only historical; they concern processes of transformation or self-fashioning in the direction of affirming positivity. Because all subjects share in this common nature, there is a common ground on which to negotiate the interests and the eventual conflicts.

It is important to see that this fundamentally positive vision of the ethical subject does not deny conflicts, tension, or even violent disagreements between different subjects. The legacy of Hegel's critique of Spinoza is still looming large here, notably the criticism that a Spinozist approach lacks a theory of negativity, which may adequately account for the complex logistics of interaction with others. It is simply not the case that the positivity of desire cancels or denies the tensions of conflicting interests. It merely displaces the grounds on which the negotiations take place. The Kantian imperative of not doing to others what you would not want done to you is not rejected as much as enlarged. In terms of the ethics of *conatus*, in fact, the harm that you do to others is immediately reflected in the harm you do to yourself, in terms of loss of *potentia*, positivity, self-awareness, and inner freedom. Moreover, the 'others' in question are non-anthropomorphic and include planetary forces. This move away from the Kantian vision of an ethics that obliges people, and especially women, natives, and others to act morally in the name of a transcendent standard or universal rule is not a simple one. I defend it as a forceful answer to the complexities of our historical situation; it is a move toward radical immanence against all Platonizing and classical humanistic denials of embodiment, *mater*, and the flesh.

What is at risk, however, in nomadic ethics is the notion of containment of the other. This is expressed by a number of moral thinkers in the Continental tradition, such as Jessica Benjamin (1988) in her radicalization of Irigaray's horizontal transcendence, Lyotard in the 'differend' (1983) and his notion of the 'unattuned,' and Butler (2004) in her emphasis on 'precarious life.' They stress that moral reasoning locates the constitution of subjectivity in the inter-relation to others, which is a form of exposure, availability, and vulnerability. This recognition entails the necessity of containing the other, the suffering and the enjoyment of others in the expression of the intensity of our affect-ive streams. An embodied and connecting containment as a moral category could emerge from this, over and against the hierarchical forms of contain-ment implied by Kantian forms of universal morality.

The objection that a Spinozist ethics fails to account for the interaction with the Other is predictable, and it is connected, on the one hand, to the issue of the negotiations of boundaries, limits, and costs and, on the other, to affectiv-ity and compassion. The nomadic view of ethics takes place within a monistic ontology that sees subjects as modes of individuation within a common flow of *zoe*. Consequently there is no self-other distinction in the traditional mode, but variations of intensities, assemblages set by affinities and complex syn-chronizations. Bio-centered egalitarianism breaks the expectation of mutual reciprocity that is central to liberal individualism. Accepting the impossibil-ity of mutual recognition and replacing it with one of mutual specification and mutual codependence is what is at stake in nomadic ethics of sustainabil-ity. This is against both the moral philosophy of rights and the humanistic tradition of making the anthropocentric Other into the privileged site and inescapable horizon of otherness.

If the point of ethics is to explore how much a body can do, in the pur-suit of active modes of empowerment through experimentation, how do we know when we have gone too far? How does the negotiation of boundaries actually take place? This is where the non-individualistic vision of the sub-ject as embodied and hence affective and interrelational, but also fundamen-tally social, is of major consequence. Your body will thus tell you if and when you have reached a threshold or a limit. The warning can take the form of opposing resistance, falling ill, feeling nauseous, or it can take other somatic manifestations, like fear, anxiety, or a sense of insecurity. Whereas the semiotic-linguistic frame of psychoanalysis reduces these to symptoms awaiting inter-pretation, I see them as corporeal warning signals or boundary markers that express a clear message: 'too much!' One of the reasons why Deleuze and Guattari are so interested in studying self-destructive or pathological modes of behavior, such as schizophrenia, masochism, anorexia, various forms of addiction, and the black hole of murderous violence, is precisely in order to explore their function as thresholds or boundary markers. This assumes a qualitative distinction between, on the one hand, the desire that propels the subject's expression of his/her conatus—a neo-Spinozist perspective is implicitly positive in that it expresses the essential best of the subject—and, on the other hand, the constraints imposed by society. The specific, context-ually determined conditions are the forms in which the desire is actualized or actually expressed.

Bodily entities are not passive, but rather dynamic and sensitive forces forever in motion, which 'form unities only through fragile synchronization of forces' (Lloyd 1994, 23). This fragility concerns mostly the pitch of the synchronization efforts, the lines of demarcation between the different bodily boundaries, the borders that are the thresholds of encounter and connection with other forces, the standard term for which is 'limits.' Because of his monistic understanding of the subject, Spinoza sees bodily limits as the limits of our awareness as well, which means that his theory of affectivity is connected to the physics of motion. Another word for Spinoza's *conatus* is therefore self-preservation, not in the liberal individualistic sense of the term, but rather as the actualization of one's essence, that is to say, of one's ontological drive to become. This is neither an automatic nor an intrinsically harmonious process, insofar as it involves interconnection with other forces and consequently also conflicts and clashes. Negotiations have to occur as stepping-stones to sustainable flows of becoming. The bodily self's interaction with his/her environment can either increase or decrease that body's *conatus* or *potentia*. The mind as a sensor that prompts understanding can assist by helping to discern and choose those forces that increase its power of acting and its activity in both physical and mental terms. A higher form of self-knowledge by understanding the nature of one's affectivity is the key to a Spinozist ethics of empowerment. It includes a more adequate understanding of the interconnections between the self and a multitude of other forces, and it thus undermines the liberal individual understanding of the subject. It also implies, however, the body's ability to comprehend and to sustain physically a greater number of complex interconnections, and to deal with complexity without being overburdened. Thus, only an appreciation of complexity and of increasing degrees of complexity can guarantee the freedom of the mind in the awareness of its true, affective, and dynamic nature.

This is expressed by Spinoza in terms of achieving freedom through an adequate understanding of our passions and consequently of our bondage. Coming into possession of freedom requires the understanding of affects or passions by a mind that is always already embodied. The desire to reach an adequate understanding of one's *potentia* is the human being's fundamental desire or *conatus*. An error of judgment is a form of misunderstanding (the true nature of the subject) that results in decreasing the power, positivity, and activity of the subject. By extension, reason is affective, embodied, dynamic; understanding the passions is our way of experiencing them and making them work in our favor. In this respect, Spinoza argues that desires arise from our passions. Because of this, they can never be excessive, given that affectivity is the power that activates our body and makes it want to act. The human being's built-in tendency is toward joy and self-expression, not toward implosion. This fundamental positivity is the key to Deleuze's attachment to Spinoza.

Lloyd argues that Spinoza's treatment of the mind as part of nature is a source of inspiration for contemporary ethics. Spinozist monism acts 'as a basis for developing a broader concept of ethology, a study of relations of individual and collective and being affected' (Lloyd 1996, 18). Clearly, it is a very non-moralistic understanding of ethics that focuses on the subject's powers to act and to express their dynamic and positive essence. An ethology stresses the field of composition of forces and affects, speed, and transformation. In this perspective, ethics is the pursuit of self-preservation, which assumes the dissolution of the self: what is good is what increases our power of acting, and this is what we must strive for. This results not in egoism but in mutually embedded nests of shared interests. Lloyd calls this 'a collaborative morality' (Lloyd 1996, 74). Because the starting point for Spinoza is not the isolated individual, but complex and mutually depended co-realities, the self-other interaction also follows a different model. To be an individual means to be open to being affected by and through others, thus undergoing transformations in such a way as to be able to sustain them and make them work toward growth. The distinction activity/passivity is far more important than that between self and other, good and bad. What binds the two is the idea of interconnection and affectivity as the defining features of the subject. An ethical life pursues that which enhances and strengthens the subject without reference to transcendental values, but rather in the awareness of one's interconnection with others.

About Pain and Vulnerability

This vision of ethics involves a radical repositioning or internal trans-formation on the part of subjects who want to become-minoritarian in a productive and affirmative manner. It is clear that this shift requires changes that are neither simple nor self-evident. They mobilize the affectivity of the subjects involved and can be seen as a process of transformation of negative into positive passions. Fear, anxiety, and nostalgia are clear examples of the negative emotions involved in the project of detaching ourselves from familiar and cherished forms of identity. To achieve a post-identity or non-unitary vision of the self requires the dis-identification from established references. Such an enterprise involves a sense of loss of cherished habits of thought and representation, and thus is not free of pain. No process of consciousness-raising ever is.

The beneficial side effects of this process are unquestionable and in some way they compensate for the pain of loss. Thus, the feminist questioning and in some cases rejection of gender roles triggers a process of dis-identification with established forms of masculinity and femininity, which has fuelled the political quest for alternative ways of inhabiting gender and embodying sexuality (Braidotti 2002). In race discourse, the awareness of the persistence of racial discrimination and of white privilege has led, on the one hand, to the critical reappraisal of blackness (Gilroy 2000; Hill Collins 1991) and, on the other, to radical relocation of whiteness (Griffin and Braidotti 2002).

In a Spinozist vein, these are transformative processes that not only rework the consciousness of social injustice and discrimination but also produce a more adequate cartography of our real-life condition, free of delusions of grandeur. It is an enriching and positive experience which, however, includes pain as an integral element. Migrants, exiles, refugees have first-hand experience of the extent to which the process of dis-identification from familiar identities is linked to the pain of loss and uprooting. Diasporic subjects of all kinds express the same sense of wound. Multi-locality is the affirmative translation of this negative sense of loss. Following Glissant (1990), the becoming-nomadic marks the process of positive transformation of the pain of loss into the active production of multiple forms of belonging and complex allegiances. What is lost in the sense of fixed origins is gained in an increased desire to belong, in a multiple rhizomic manner which transcends the classical bilateralism of binary identity formations.

The qualitative leap through pain, across the mournful landscapes of nostalgic yearning, is the gesture of active creation of affirmative ways of belonging. It is a fundamental reconfiguration of our way of being in the world, which acknowledges the pain of loss but moves further. This is the defining moment for the process of becoming-ethical: the move across and beyond pain, loss, and negative passions. Taking suffering into account is the starting point; the real aim of the process, however, is the quest for ways of overcoming the stultifying effects of passivity, brought about by pain. The internal disarray, fracture, and pain are the conditions of possibility for ethical transformation. Clearly, this is an antithesis of the Kantian moral imperative to avoid pain or to view pain as the obstacle to moral behavior. Nomadic ethics is not about the avoidance of pain; rather it is about transcending the resignation and passivity that ensue from being hurt, lost, and dispossessed. One has to become ethical, as opposed to applying moral rules and protocols as a form of self-protection. Transformations express the affirmative power of Life as the vitalism of *bios-zoe*, which is the opposite of morality as a form of life insurance.

The awakening of ethical and political consciousness through the pain of loss has been acknowledged by Edgar Morin (1996) in his account of how he relinquished Marxist universalism to embrace a more 'situated perspective' (Haraway 1997) as a European. He describes his 'becoming-European' as a double affect. The first concerns the disappointment with unfulfilled promises of Marxism. The second is compassion for the uneasy, struggling, and marginal position of post-war Europe, squashed between the United States and the USSR. The pain of this awareness that Europe was ill loved and a castaway results in a new kind of bonding, and a renewed sense of care and accountability. This produces a post-nationalistic redefinition of being a European in a minoritarian mode, which defines the European space-time location as a zone of mediation and transformation (Balibar 2002).

The sobering experience—the humble and productive recognition of loss, limitations, and shortcomings—has to do with self-representations. Established mental habits, images, and terminology railroad us back toward established ways of thinking about ourselves. Traditional modes of representation are legal forms of addiction. To change them is not unlike undertaking a disintoxication cure. A great deal of courage and creativity is needed to develop forms of representation that do justice to the complexities of the kind of subjects we have already become. We already live and inhabit social reality in ways that surpass tradition: we move about, in the flow of current social transformations, in hybrid, multicultural, polyglot, post-identity spaces of becoming (Braidotti 2002). We fail, however, to bring them into adequate representation. There is a shortage on the part of our social imaginary, a deficit of representational power, which underscores the political timidity of our times.

The real issue is conceptual: how do we develop a new post-unitary vision of the subject, of ourselves, and how do we adopt a social imaginary that does justice to the complexity? How does one work through the pain of dis-identification and loss? Given that identifications constitute an inner scaffolding that supports one's sense of identity, how do changes of this magnitude take place? Shifting an imaginary is not like casting away a used garment, but more like shedding an old skin. It happens often enough at the molecular level, but in the social it is a painful experience. Part of the answer lies in the formulation of the question: 'we' are in this together. This is a collective activity, a group project that connects active, conscious, and desiring citizens. It points toward a virtual destination: post-unitary nomadic identities, floating foundations, and so on but it is not utopian. As a project it is historically grounded, socially embedded, and already partly actualized in the joint endeavor, that is, the community, of those who are actively working toward it. If this be utopian it is only in the sense of the positive affects that are mobilized in the process: the necessary dose of imagination, dreamlike vision, and bonding without which no social project can take off.

Steps toward an Ethics of Affirmation

The ethics of affirmation, with its emphasis on moving across the pain and transforming it into activity, may seem counter-intuitive. In our culture people go to great lengths to ease all pain, but especially the pain of uncertainty about identity, origin, and belonging. Great distress follows from not knowing or not being able to articulate the source of one's suffering, or from knowing it all too well, all the time. People who have been confronted by the irreparable, the unbearable, the insurmountable, the traumatic and inhuman event will do anything to find solace, resolution, and also compensation. The yearning for these measures—solace, closure, justice—is all too understandable and worthy of respect. Nowadays, this longing is both supported and commercially exploited by genetics and its application to tracking of racial and territorial origins.

The ethical dilemma was already posed by Jean-François Lyotard in *Le Differend* and, much earlier, by Primo Levi about the survivors of Nazi concentration camps: the kind of vulnerability human beings experience in the face of events on the scale of high horror is something for which no adequate compensation is even thinkable, let alone applicable. There is an incommensurability of the suffering involved for which no measure of compensation is possible—a hurt or wound beyond repair. This means that the notion of justice in the sense of a logic of rights and reparation is not applicable in a quantifiable manner. For Lyotard, in keeping with the poststructuralist emphasis on the ethical dimension of the problem, ethics consists in accepting the impossibility of adequate compensation, and living with the open wound. On the contrary, contemporary culture has taken the opposite direction: it has favored, encouraged, and rewarded a public morality based on the twin principles of claims and compensation, as if financial settlements could provide the answer to the injury suffered, the pain endured, and the long-lasting effects of the injustice. Cases that exemplify this trend are the compensation for the Shoah in the sense of restitution of stolen property, artworks, and bank deposits. Similar claims have been made by the descendants of slaves forcefully removed from Africa to North America (Gilroy 2000), and more recently compensation for damages caused by Soviet communism, notably the confiscation of properties across eastern Europe, from Jewish and other former citizens.

The ethics of affirmation is about suspending the quest for both claims and compensation, resisting the logic of retribution of rights and taking instead a different road. In order to understand this move it is important to de-psychologize the discussion of affirmation. Affectivity is intrinsically understood as positive: it is the force that aims at fulfilling the subject's capacity for interaction and freedom. It is Spinoza's *conatus,* or the notion of *potentia* as the affirmative aspect of power. It is joyful and pleasure-prone, and it is immanent in that it coincides with the terms and modes of its expression. This means concretely that ethical behavior confirms, facilitates, and enhances the subject's *potentia,* as the capacity to express his/her freedom. The positivity of this desire to express one's innermost and constitutive freedom (*conatus, potentia,* or becoming) is conducive to ethical behavior, however, only if the subject is capable of making it endure, thus allowing it to sustain its own impetus. Unethical behavior achieves the opposite: it denies, hinders, and diminishes that impetus or is unable to sustain it. Affirmation is therefore not naive optimism or Candide-like unrealism. It is about endurance and transformation. Endurance is self-affirmation. It is also an ethical principle of affirmation of the positivity of the intensive subject—its joyful affirmation as *potentia.* The subject is a spatio-temporal compound which frames the boundaries of processes of becoming. This works by transforming negative into positive passions through the power of an understanding that is no longer indexed upon a phallogocentric set of standards, but is rather unhinged and therefore affective.

This sort of turning of the tide of negativity is the transformative process of achieving freedom of understanding through the awareness of our limits, of our bondage. This results in the freedom to affirm one's essence as joy, through encounters and minglings with other bodies, entities, beings, and forces. Ethics means faithfulness to this *potentia*, or the desire to become. Deleuze defines the latter with reference to Bergson's concept of 'duration,' thus proposing the notion of the subject as an entity that lasts, that endures sustainable changes and transformation and enacts them around him/herself in a community or collectivity. Affirmative ethics rests on the idea of sustainability as a principle of containment and tolerable development of a subject's resources, understood environmentally, affectively, and cognitively. A subject thus constituted inhabits a time that is the active tense of continuous 'becoming.' Endurance has therefore a temporal dimension: it has to do with lasting in time—hence duration and self-perpetuation. But it also has a spatial side to do with the space of the body as an enfleshed field of actualization of passions or forces. It evolves affectivity and joy, as in the capacity for being affected by these forces, to the point of pain or extreme pleasure, which come to the same; it means putting up with hardship and physical pain.

The point, however, is that extreme pleasure or extreme pain—which may score the same on a Spinozist scale of ethology of affects—are of course not the same. On the reactive side of the equation, endurance points to the struggle to sustain the pain without being annihilated by it. It also introduces a temporal dimension about duration in time. This is linked to memory: intense pain, a wrong, a betrayal, a wound are hard to forget. The traumatic impact of painful events fixes them in a rigid, eternal present tense out of which it is difficult to emerge. This is the eternal return of that which precisely cannot be endured and returns in the mode of the unwanted, the untimely, the unassimilated or inappropriate/d. They are also, however, paradoxically difficult to remember, insofar as remembering entails retrieval and repetition of the pain itself.

Psychoanalysis, of course, has been here before (Laplanche 1976). The notion of the return of the repressed is the key to the logic of unconscious remembrance, but it is a secret and somewhat invisible key which condenses space into the spasm of the symptom and time into a short-circuit that mines the very thinkability of the present. Kristeva's notion of the abject (1980) expresses clearly the temporality involved in psychoanalysis—by stressing the structural function played by the negative, the incomprehensible, the unthinkable, the other of understandable knowledge. Deleuze calls this alterity 'Chaos' and defines it ontologically as the virtual formation of all possible form. Lacan, on the other hand—and Derrida with him, I would argue—defines Chaos epistemologically as that which precedes form, structure, and language. This makes for two radically divergent conceptions of time and negativity. That which is incomprehensible for Lacan, following Hegel, is the virtual for Deleuze, following Spinoza, Bergson, and Leibnitz.

This produces a number of significant shifts: from negative to affirmative; from entropic to generative; from incomprehensible, meaningless, and crazy to virtual waiting to be actualized; from constituting constitutive outsides to a geometry of affects that require mutual synchronization; from a melancholy and split to an open-ended web-like subject; from the epistemological to the ontological turn in poststructuralist philosophy.

This introduces a temporal dimension into the discussion that leads to the very conditions of possibility of the future, to futurity as such. For an ethics of sustainability, the expression of positive affects is that which makes the subject last or endure. It is like a source of long-term energy at the affective core of subjectivity (Grosz 2004). Nietzsche has also been here before, of course. The eternal return in Nietzsche is the repetition, yet neither in the compulsive mode of neurosis nor in the negative erasure that marks the traumatic event. It is the eternal return of and as positivity (Ansell-Pearson 1999). This kind of ethics addresses the affective structure of pain and suffering but does not locate the ethical instance within it, be it in the mode of compassionate witnessing (Bauman 1993; 1998) or empathic co-presence. In a nomadic, Deleuzian-Nietzschean perspective, ethics is essentially about transformation of negative into positive passions, that is, about moving beyond the pain. This does not mean denying the pain but rather activating it, working it through. Again, the positivity here is not supposed to indicate a facile optimism or a careless dismissal of human suffering.

What is positive in the ethics of affirmation is the belief that negative affects can be transformed. This implies a dynamic view of all affects, even those that freeze us in pain, horror, or mourning. Affirmative nomadic ethics puts the motion back into emotion and the active back into activism, introducing movement, process, and becoming. This shift makes all the difference to the patterns of repetition of negative emotions.

What is negative about negative affects is not a value judgment (any more than it is for the positivity of difference), but rather the effect of arrest, blockage, and rigidification that comes as a result of an act of violence, betrayal, a trauma—or which can be self-perpetuated through practices that our culture simultaneously chastises as self-destructive and cultivates as a mode of discipline and punishment: all forms of mild and extreme addictions, differing degrees of abusive practices that mortify and glorify the bodily matter, from binging to bodily modifications. Abusive, addictive, or destructive practices do not merely destroy the self but harm the self's capacity to relate to others, both human and non-human others. Thus they harm the capacity to grow in and through others and become others. Negative passions diminish our capacity to express the high levels of interdependence, the vital reliance on others, which is the key to a non-unitary and dynamic vision of the subject. What is negated by negative passions is the power of life itself, as the dynamic force, vital flows of connections and becomings. This is why they should not be encouraged, nor should we be rewarded for lingering around them too long. Negative passions are black holes.

An ethics of affirmation involves the transformation of negative into positive passions: resentment into affirmation, as Nietzsche put it. The practice of transforming negative into positive passions is the process of reintroducing time, movement, and transformation into a stifling enclosure saturated with unprocessed pain. It is a gesture of affirmation of hope in the sense of affirming the possibility of moving beyond the stultifying effects of the pain, the injury, the injustice. This is a gesture of displacement of the hurt, which fully contradicts the twin logic of claims and compensation. This is achieved through a sort of de-personalization of the event, which is the ultimate ethical challenge. The displacement of the ego-indexed negative passions or affects reveals the fundamental senselessness of the hurt, the injustice, or injury one has suffered. 'Why me?' is the refrain most commonly heard in situations of extreme distress. This expresses rage as well as anguish at one's ill fate. The answer is plain: for no reason at all. Examples of this are the banality of evil in large-scale genocides like the Holocaust (Arendt 1963), and the randomness of surviving them (think of Primo Levi who could/not endure his own survival). There is something intrinsically senseless about the pain or injustice: lives are lost or saved for all and no reason at all. Why did some go to work in the WTC on 9/11 while others missed the train? Why did Frida Kahlo take that tram which crashed so that she was impaled by a metal rod, and not the next one? For no reason at all. Reason has nothing to do with it. That is precisely the point.

Contrary to the traditional morality that follows a rationalist and legalistic model of possible interpretation of the wrongs one suffered to a logic of responsibility, claim, and compensation, affirmative ethics rests on the notion of the random access to the phenomena that cause pain (or pleasure). This is not fatalism, and even less resignation, but rather *amor fati*. This is a crucial difference: we have to be worthy of what happens to us and rework it within an ethics of relation. Of course, repugnant and unbearable events do happen. Ethics consists, however, in reworking these events in the direction of positive relations. This is not carelessness or lack of compassion, but rather a form of lucidity that acknowledges the impossibility of finding an adequate answer to the question about the source, the origin, the cause of the ill fate, the painful event, the violence suffered. Acknowledging the futility of even trying to answer that question is a starting point.

Edouard Glissant (1991) provides a perfect example of this productive ethics in his work on race and racism. An ethical relation cannot be based on resentment or resignation, but rather on the affirmation of positivity. Every event contains within it the potential for being overcome and overtaken; its negative charge can be transposed. The moment of the actualization is also the moment of its neutralization. 'Every event is like death, double and impersonal in its double,' argues Deleuze (1990, 152). The free subject, the ethical subject is the one with the ability to grasp the freedom to depersonalize the event and transform its negative charge. The focus thus shifts to asking the adequate questions. Adequateness, both the logic of claim and compensation, lies at the heart of the ethical stance. This requires a double shift: of the pain itself—from the frozen or reactive effect to proactive affirmation—and of the line of questioning—from the quest for the origin or source to a process of elaboration of the kind of questions that express and enhance a subject's capacity to achieve freedom through the understanding of its limitations.

What is an adequate ethical question? One that is capable of sustaining the subject in his/her quest for more interrelations with others, that is, more Life, motion, change, transformation, and *potentia*. The adequate ethical question provides the subject with a frame for interaction and change, growth, and movement. It affirms life as difference-at-work. An ethical question had to be adequate in relation to how much a body can take, which is the notion of sustainability. How much can an embodied entity take in the mode of interrelations and connections, that is, how much freedom of action can we endure? That is the question. It assumes, following Nietzsche, that humanity does not stem from freedom, but rather that freedom is extracted out of the awareness of limitations.

Ethics is about freedom from the weight of negativity, freedom through the understanding of our bondage. A certain amount of pain, the knowledge about vulnerability and pain, is actually useful. It forces one to think about the actual material conditions of being interconnected and thus being in the world. It frees one from the stupidity of perfect health, and the full-blown sense of existential entitlement that comes with it. Paradoxically, it is those who have already cracked up a bit, those who have suffered pain and injury, who are better placed to take the lead in the process of ethical transformation. Because they are already on the other side of some existential divide, they are anomalous in some way—but in a positive way, for Deleuze. Their anomaly deterritorializes the force of habit and introduces a powerful element of productive difference. They know about endurance, adequate forces, and the importance of Relations.

Marxist epistemology and feminist standpoint theory have always acknowledged the privileged knowing position of those in the 'margins.' Postcolonial theory displaces the dialectics of center-margin and locates the force of discursive production. Affirmative ethics is on the same wavelength: only those who have been hurt are in a position not to return the violence and hence make a positive difference. In order to do so, however, they have to become-minoritarian, that is, transcend the logic of negativity (claim and compensation) and transform the negative affect into something active and productive. The center being dead and empty of active force, it is on the margins that the processes of becoming can be initiated. It is also crowded on the margins.

The figure of Nelson Mandela—a contemporary secular saint—comes to mind, as does the world-historical phenomenon that is the Truth and Reconciliation Commission in post-apartheid South Africa. This is a case of repetition that engenders difference and does not install the eternal return of revenge and negative affects, a massive exercise in transformation of negativity into something more livable, more life-enhancing. Christianity has tried to be here before. It has had an important input in the work of Cornell West, bell hooks, and other spiritually-minded activists today, especially in reconstituting a sense of community and mutual responsibility in places devastated by hatred and mutual suspicion. Affirmative nomadic ethics is profoundly secular and it refuses simply to turn the other cheek. It proclaims the need to construct collectively positions of active, positive interconnections and relations that can sustain a web of mutual dependence, an ecology of multiple belongings.

It is a case of extracting freedom from the awareness of limits. For the affirmative ethics of sustainability, it is always already a question of life and death. Being on the edge of too-muchness, or of unsustainability, surfing on the borders of the intolerable is another way of describing the process of becoming. Becoming marks a qualitative leap in the transformation of subjectivity and of its constitutive affects. It is a trip across different fields of perception, different spatio-temporal coordinates. Mostly it transforms negativity into affirmative affects: pain into compassion, loss into a sense of bonding, isolation into care. It is simultaneously a slowing down of the rhythm of daily frenzy and an acceleration of awareness, connection to others, self-knowledge and sensorial perception.

Ethics includes the acknowledgment of and compassion for pain, as well as the activity of working through it. Any process of change must do some sort of violence to deeply engrained habits and dispositions which got consolidated in time. Overcoming these engrained habits is a necessary disruption, without which there is no ethical awakening. Consciousness-raising is not free of pain. The utterance: 'I can't take it anymore!' far from being an admission of defeat, marks the threshold and hence the condition of possibility for creative encounters and productive changes. This is how the ethical dimension appears through the mass of fragments and shreds of discarded habits that are characteristic of our times. The ethical project is not the same as the implementation of ruling standards of morality. It rather concerns the norms and values, the standards and criteria that can be applied to the quest for sustainable, that is to say for newly negotiated limits. Limits are to be rethought in terms of an ethics of becoming, through a non-Hegelian notion of limits as thresholds, that is to say points of encounter and not of closure, living boundaries and not fixed walls.

The joint necessity for both the pursuit of social change and in-depth transformation, as well as for an ethics of endurance and sustainability, is important to stress because critical and creative thinkers and activists who pursue change have often experienced the limits or the boundaries like open wounds or scars. The generation that came of age politically in the 1970s has taken enormous risks and has enjoyed the challenges they entailed. A lot was demanded and expected from life and most ended up getting it, but it was not only a joy ride. An ethical evaluation of the costs involved in pursuing alternative visions, norms, and values is important in the present context where the alleged 'end of ideology' is used as a pretext for neoliberal restoration that terminates all social experiments. It is necessary to find a way to combine transformative politics with affirmative ethics so as to confront the conceptual and social contradictions of our times. Sustainable affirmative ethics allows us to contain the risks while pursuing the original project of transformation. This is a way to resist the dominant ethos of our conservative times that idolizes the new as a consumerist trend while thundering against those who believe in change. Cultivating the ethics of living intensely in the pursuit of change is a political act.

Bibliography

Agamben, G. (1998), *Homo Sacer: Sovereign Power and Bare Life* (Palo Alto, CA: Stanford University Press).

Ansell Pearson, K. (1997), *Viroid Life: Perspectives on Nietzsche and the Transhuman Condition* (New York: Routledge).

—(1999), *Germinal Life: The Difference and Repetition of Deleuze* (New York: Routledge).

Arendt, H. (1963), *Eichmann in Jerusalem* (New York: Viking Press).

Balibar, É. (2002), *Politics and the Other Scene* (London: Verso).

Bauman, Z. (1993), *Postmodern Ethics* (Oxford: Blackwell).

—(1998), *Globalization: The Human Consequences* (Cambridge: Polity Press.)

Benhabib, S. (2002), *The Claims of Culture. Equality and Diversity in the Global Era* (Princeton: Princeton University Press).

Benjamin, J. (1988), *The Books of Love: Psychoanalysis, Feminism and the Problem of Domination* (New York: Pantheon Books).

Bhabha, H. K. (1996), 'Unpacking My Library . . . Again,' in Ian Chamber and Lidia Curti (eds), *The Post-Colonial Question: Common Skies, Divided Horizons* (New York: Routledge).

Braidotti, R. (2002), *Metamorphoses: Towards a Materialist Theory of Becoming* (Cambridge: Polity Press).

Buchanan, I. and C. Colebrook, eds. (2000), *Deleuze and Feminist Theory* (Edinburgh: Edinburgh University Press).

Butler, J. (2004), *Precarious Life* (London: Verso).

Critchley, S. (1992), *The Ethics of Deconstruction* (Edinburgh: Edinburgh University Press).

Deleuze, G. (1968), *Spinoza et le problème de l'expression* (Paris: Minuit). English translation: (1990) *Expressionism in Philosophy: Spinoza*. trans. M. Joughin (New York: Zone Books).

—(1969), *Logique du sens* (Paris: Minuit). English translation: (1990) *The Logic of Sense*. trans. M. Lester and C. Stivale (New York: Columbia University Press).

—(1995), 'L'immanence: une vie . . .,' *Philosophie* 47.

Deleuze, G. and F. Guattari (1980), *Mille plateaux. Capitalisme et schizophrénie II* (Paris: Minuit). English translation: (1987) *A Thousand Plateaus: Capitalism and Schizophrenia*, trans. Brian Massumi (Minneapolis: University of Minnesota Press).

Fraser, Nancy (1996), 'Multiculturalism and gender equity: The US "Difference"' Debates Revisited,' *Constellations* 1.

Gatens, M. and G. Lloyd (1999), *Collective Imaginings: Spinoza, Past and Present* (New York: Routledge).

Gilroy, P. (2000), *Against Race: Imaging Political Culture Beyond the Color Line* (Cambridge: Harvard University Press).

Glissant, E. (1991), *Poetique de la Relation* (Paris: Gallimard). English translation: (1997) *Poetics of Relation*, trans. Betsy Wing (Ann Arbor: University of Michigan Press).

Griffin, G. and Braidotti, R. (eds) (2002), *Thinking Differently: A Reader in European Women's Studies* (Zed Books).

Grosz, E. (2004), *The Nick of Time* (Durham: Duke University Press).

Guattari, F. (1995), *Chaosmosis: An Ethico-Aesthetic Paradigm* (Sydney: Power Publications).

Habermas, J. (2003), *The Future of Human Nature*, trans. Hella Berster and William Rehg (Cambridge: Polity Press).

Haraway, D. (1997), *Modest Witness* (New York: Routledge).

Hardt, M. and A. Negri (2000), *Empire* (Cambridge: Harvard University Press).

Hill Collins, P. (1999), *Black Feminist Thought. Knowledge, Consciousness and the Politics of Empowerment*, 2nd edn (London: Routledge).

Irigaray, L. (1984), *L'éthique de la différence sexuelle* (Paris: Minuit). English translation: (1993) *An Ethics of Sexual Difference*, trans. Carolyn Burke and Gillian Gill (Ithaca: Cornell University Press).

Kristeva, J. (1980), *Pouvoirs de l'horreur* (Paris: Seuil). English translation: (1982) *Powers of Horror*, trans. Leon Roudiez (New York: Colombia University Press).

Laplanche, J. (1976), *Life and Death in Psychoanalysis* (Baltimore: Johns Hopkins University Press).

Lloyd, G. (1994), *Part of Nature: Self-knowledge in Spinoza's Ethic* (Ithaca: Cornell University Press).

—(1996), *Spinoza and the Ethics* (London: Routledge).

Lovibond, S. (1994), 'The end of morality,' in K. Lenno and M. Whitford (eds), *Knowing the Difference: Feminist Perspectives in Epistemology* (New York: Routledge).

Lyotard, J. F. (1983), *Le Différend* (Paris: Minuit).

May, T. (1995), *The Moral Theory of Poststructuralism* (University Park: Pennsylvania State University Press).

Morin, E. (1996), *Penser l'Europe* (Paris: Gallimard).

Nussbaum, M. (1999), *Cultivating Humanity: A Classical Defense of Reform in Liberal Education* (Cambridge: Harvard University Press).

Rabinow, P. (2003), *Anthropos Today* (Princeton: Princeton University Press).

Rose, N. (2001), 'The politics of life itself,' *Theory, Culture and Society* 18(6).

Chapter 12

From First Sparks to Local Clashes
Which Politics Today?*

Philippe Mengue

The grandeur of Deleuze's work is recognized today as an established fact, witnessed by its global reception[1]—and this is as it should be. But this fancy could also be dangerous, if it consists in the repetition of terms (nomadism, lines of flight) that have become empty of their spirit and ambiguous. It is dangerous if it serves to cover up the real problems that are our problems today, with scintillating and stylish formulas of the latest international intellectual fashion, and to mask the difficulties internal to the Deleuzian doctrine. With respect to the political dimension of Deleuze's philosophy, I think that we must undertake an in-depth reflection, if we want to continue to think inside the lines that he traced for us.[2]

The triumphal reception of *Anti-Oedipus*, which was linked to the critique of powers that Foucault had undertaken, gave birth to various very concrete and very active struggles. In the wake of May 1968, a renewal of politics was achieved and another kind of militantism was born. But, above all, there appeared a new style of life and a new mode of becoming subject (*subjectivation*). Deleuze and Guattari together with Foucault are at the source of the theoretical work of those who were called 'analysts of power' (like Toni Negri, Michael Hardt, Giorgio Agamben, Paul Virilio and more recently Manola Antonioli, Peter Sloterdijk, etc.). The most serious problem to be raised about this current—a problem that is well understood in the world of the intellectual avant gardes—is the relation between this tendency and present day politics. It seems to me that Deleuzian micropolitics has become in essence a collective ethics and a mode of subjectivation that understands itself as 'anticapitalist.' Will it be able to reach this self-proclaimed target? Would this anticapitalist ethics be able to endow itself with a really political translation?

One does not diminish the political influence of 'Deleuzism' (Deleuze + Foucault) if one says that it is felt solely inside the world of the intellectuals of the avant-guard and the latest artistic circles, and that it does not generate regroupings and new collectives. Rather, it satisfies itself, on the practical level, with the creation of 'resonances' with the forms of sensibility and thought that can bring about a new style of nomad life—an alternative life. Deleuze's work, with its indissociable link with the work of Foucault, exerts its influence today only through some kind of osmosis and intellectual impregnation on revolutionary movements, which are very heterogeneous (and even occasionally really antinomic to the true sense of his thought)—for example, the movements involved in the defense of the third world, the struggle for an other world, or the pro-Palestinian resistance.

Now, this undoubtful success at the ethical level (subjective as well as political, in the good sense), and the cultural level as well, may also be the reason for its handicap at the strictly political level. In the larger world of politics, on the left or on the right, and more generally, in the practical world as well as the world of theoretical reflection, Deleuze's political thought has been met with indifference or even forgetting. What is the meaning of this bifurcation—of this break? Is it enough to invoke as it often happens in these cases, the two fronts, conservative/revolutionary, and the partiality of repression and censorship perpetrated by the 'powers' and the institutions in place? Is it enough to invoke the unlimited capacity of the media for the 'recuperation' and defusion of every subversive and emancipatory thought? Or, rather, as I am inclined to think, should we not see in this partition the sign of a discomfort internal to the Deleuzian conception of the political?

Deleuzian politics wants to be a 'micropolitics' and it aspires explicitly to the abandonment of the so-called 'majoritarian' politics—macropolitics. It wants to be groupuscular: 'We are all groupuscules'—he used to say in 1972.[3] Should we understand by this that micropolitics would rather fight somehow for a reduced role—a minor role—an all-too-small (micro) role? Could this account for its small audience in the political space? But to accept this conception of the minor and the micro would be to commit a serious countersense because, in the case of Deleuze, 'minor' never means small number and amplitude. Deleuzian politics has never—it is very clear—desired to be a politics of small significance and little influence—this would be ridiculous!

Rather, the question is this: is micropolitics today able to put together—as it pretends to—an authentic politics? Shall we accept as necessary the *political* dead end attached to the nomadic errance and the micropolitical subversion? Or would it be possible instead, on the basis of a less literal but still faithful reading of the texts, to propose a political reading of Deleuze that would be less tense and less fixated on an arrogant position toward democracy, and the reality of the world and of today's cultures?

For the changes we are witnessing (which have become much more dramatic ever since he disappeared—there are now more than ten years since then) Deleuze's philosophy is still the one most important to meditate. The fundamental concepts that he created brought a radical novelty to political thought. However, the important question is to find out what we can do with them today, what concrete application we can give them, which political sense we can attribute them in the situation which is ours today and which is no longer the situation of the 1970s.

A lot of important facts beckon us, in my opinion, in the direction of a new political and intellectual situation. First of all, the fact that liberal societies allowed a theory like Deleuze's, which is supposed to be so radical and so subversive of them, to see the light of the day and to reach the success that we know—this fact cannot be overlooked the way that it is often overlooked among the currents of thought that resonate with his. In fact, it shows the total impertinence of the Deleuzian 'prediction' regarding the inevitable becoming-fascist of these societies and allows us to take a less hostile look at them.

On the other hand, our liberation from the caricatures of the cold war of a 'West' that is homogeneous and guilty of all evils permits us to better discern its layered, pluralist, and discontinuous character. It is now possible to be more sensitive and critical toward the sites of rebirth of a real fascism, of new theocratic powers, of the Islamist religious intolerance and of the totalitarian repression that is occurring in many Muslim countries. Finally, the new situation generated by the internal failure of communism, by the globalization of the economy and technologies, by the economic getting unstuck of many third world countries, by the democratization of the Euro-American countries, and by the importance attributed to human rights, does not allow any longer the insistence on a clear-cut confrontation between proletariat and bourgeoisie, in line with a reading inspired by the dogmatics of the class war (which was still intractable during the 1970s when the political doctrine of Deleuze was being elaborated).

In my opinion, these different elements prompt a renewed reception of Gilles Deleuze's political philosophy. Deleuze, thanks to his concrete engagements, gave us a political reading—with the accompanying political commitments—of his own theoretical principles that we could roughly call gauchiste and marxisant.[4] With Guattari, he undertook to think the event May 1968 and he got engaged in the kind of struggles that characterized that period. No doubt about all this. But the question addressed to him now is whether this posture and this kind of militancy are still politically sufficient (were they sufficient even then?).

I maintain that it is possible to stay faithful to the spirit of the system and to have a more 'liberal' reading (in the classical, both economic and political, sense) or, at least—the malfeasant connotations of the term in France not withstanding—a reading that would be less spiteful and more reconciliatory toward the form that democracy has taken in the contemporary Euro-American societies. Such a tendency to a reading that allows for some distance strikes me as more promising than the tentative of 'resistance' incited by the so-called revolutionary or simply the anti-liberal parties, taken as they are inside the dead ends and the twirlings of an already too old underlying Marxism. The fact is that in the face of the world-wide situation called 'globalization,' the thought of anti-liberal resistance tends to rejuvenate itself, with the help of heteroclitous borrowings from Deleuze and Foucault. This is what accounts for the relative success of Deleuzism in these milieus. But this use of Deleuzian notions is not the only one possible, nor is it the more pertinent one—this is what I want to try to show.

I have developed elsewhere the two major points of the Deleuzian politics— the distinction, history/becoming; and the primacy of the lines of flight. I will therefore go quickly over these points in order to spend more time on what I consider to be a real opening for our times.[5]

History, Becoming, Lines of Flight

For Deleuze, and this is an important thesis, becoming is not history, but rather what is torn off history and come to occupy a plane that cannot be reduced to facts or to conditions of actualization (inside history).[6] What is at stake is the very status of the revolution which, in its positivity, does not belong to the time of Chronos. 'They're constantly confusing two different things, the way revolutions turn out historically and people's revolutionary becoming' (N, 171).

What could the sense of political action be inside this ontological frame? We must invent it, Deleuze wrote, each time, we must disengage the sense of what does not happen (becoming or event) from that which happens and passes away—that which 'falls' into the past and never ceases to 'fall back again.' Inside this frame, the action has the sense of a permanent and endless recommencement (taking into consideration the inevitable deterioration) of subversion, of the harassment of the powers in place and the resistance to oppression. To the extent that what is at stake is waging war for the sake of the actualization of becomings or for the sake of the establishment and preservation of the sense that is already actual in the state of things, we can define with precision this politics as a guerrilla war. Guerrilla war is the essence of Deleuzian politics.[7] It gives its sense to revolutionary becoming. Hence the question: the revolutionary becoming of people—under which conditions can it be translated into politics? In other words, is it possible for this resistance and this guerrilla war to find an external expression at the level of collective action instead of being sequestered inside the subjective sphere of feeling (even if it is collective) and in actions that would stay dispersed and quasi-private?

I think that micropolitics has little to say *politically* because deep down it is an *ethics* of becomings—despite its intended objective. Its political sense is indirect. It counts on the effects that it induces to the political sphere, through the engagements, the individual or collective actions and the groups that occur because of it. It places itself deliberately outside the order that commands public decision for the sake of the common good and refuses or is contemptuous of rules constitutive of this space—both of the majority and those resulting from the struggle of opinions inside the public space. This principled hostile position toward the political space does no longer strike me as pertinent. I am convinced that micropolitics, the way that Deleuze and his successors came to think of it within the post-1968 frame of reference, is only one of its possible faces. I defend the idea that there is another possible reading of 'micropolitics'—one that begins with the idea that micropolitics is the external border of politics, that it is in a relation of 'internal exclusion' with respect to politics—in a situation of 'extimacy.'[8] In other words, I search for a reading that would maintain a close and deep link between a certain Deleuzian politics and actual liberal democracy—because it would be unreasonable to overlook the new monsters knocking at the door (world terrorism, green or Islamist fascism, inter-cultural tensions, etc.). What is happening to the revolution, inside this frame?

Deleuze's original idea is that it is becoming ('the revolutionary becoming of people') and not a set of realities that can be inscribed in history. People take for granted as self-evident that 'revolutionary' has for Deleuze the meaning that it has in the common sense of modernity. But this is not at all the case. The meaning of 'revolutionary' when applied to becoming, to the extent that the latter carries with it an ahistorical sense, can, in the final analysis, only be *returning* (*revenir*). Return has nothing to do with the conservation or the protection of established situations nor does it stay unopposed to progressing, as the case is with historical, chronological time. Becoming is not, for Deleuze, changing form or identifying with a pre-existing model, making or imitating someone or something. But then the term 'becoming' is not an end to attain in the future of chronological time. Becoming is *immobile*. It is a movement on the same spot, which includes a time that cannot move and has been waiting for us for ever, for the sake of something that is too big for us. This is why becoming has more to do with returning (*revenir*). To return is the essence of what is revolutionary.

Let us say that being revolutionary is to want to begin an altogether different thing, on new bases, 'from scratch'—that it is the idea of an absolute beginning. But by the same token it is also to begin again and to come back to the point of departure, to the 'roots' or to the 'bases.' To the bases of what? Indisputably, to the bases of the human condition. An ahistorical revolutionary becoming—what else could it mean but the 'becoming' in which everyone is implicated thanks to his or her ontological condition? This is the condition of having to live with other people, having to struggle, to be wounded, to suffer, to desire, to love, and to die. Becoming is returning. He is revolutionary who takes the tour, the revolution around his or her condition, becomes in it who *s/he* is and comes back to who s/he is: s/he becomes a being taken inside the event, *to die*; s/he becomes a being taken inside the event, *to desire*; s/he becomes a being taken in the event, *to work, to be with other people*, and so on. Every becoming is like death—becoming infinite: one does not come closer and closer to death in the sense of the decomposition of the body (being dead)—this is getting old. Rather, one is given (*voué*) to death, a pure 'to die,' as an always past and future event, different from the actual states of the body, its wounds, accidents, and illnesses. Becoming then is a verb, to return. This is the ingenious lesson of *The Logic of Sense*.

With reference to the political field, we must understand once and for all that there is no special becoming-revolutionary, next to other becomings; rather, it is becoming pure and simple that *is in itself revolutionary*. Given this push that Deleuze gives us, it is possible to maintain that what makes the 'revolutionary' of the revolution is the climbing back or the coming back— the rememoration of the condition of being together with people to the very void of knowing what society should be, to the very void of knowing the good and the just. Democracy centers around this void at which men and women, as speaking beings, gather together and propose precarious, imperfect, mobile, always unsatisfactory institutions, and, in the best of circumstances, open, not closed, and subject to public discussion. The revolutionary of return is s/he who returns to this departure point, re-memorates and brings back to the edge of this gaping hole in order to build around it a few precarious walls against the always present and contained violence, against destruction and death.

However, this moment of *anamnesis*, internal to the volte of the revolt and the revolution, is not a simple one. It involves tensions between two contrary movements. Nietzsche showed in his second *Untimely Meditation* that modern man is being consumed by an excess of historical knowledge and, as a result, a sprinkle of forgetting—of anti-historical ferment—is required for every firm, solid, and great thought. Forgetting what? Mostly, forgetting the immense suffering stemming from the fact of being—simply being, that is, being 'a little vortex of life in a dead sea of darkness and oblivion.'[9] It follows that the ahistorical thought of the human condition and its becomings, the function of which is to plunge us inside the ocean of the gaping hole must itself return, if we are to act anew and to recommence. Nietzsche describes this non-historical, and yet not eternal element as a state of being enveloped by an ahistorical cloud or fog.[10] The desire to recommence on new bases implies that becoming is a forgetful souvenir and a re-memorating forgetting—a becoming-return that sharpens up the revolutionary.

If we now exchange the guidance of *The Logic of Sense* for that of *A Thousand Plateaus*, what does Deleuze have to offer us on top of the wound and the battle as becoming-events? The examples he gives now confirm the reading that I am proposing. In *Kafka: Toward a Minor Literature*, he listed, for the first time, the variety of becomings: animals, children, woman, and, finally, becoming indiscernible. And the same thing happens in *A Thousand Plateaus*. We seem to be far from the work, desire, death, and solitude that we counted under the becomings of the human condition. But this is not the case.

The nearly invariable Deleuzian list is not arbitrary. Certainly, his entries are not models to copy or objects of identification; they are poles that mark the limits of the human condition in its universality. They are encounters that create the incalculable and unforeseeable 'events' that no one can avoid. In all of them, there is the separation, the wound of failure or exclusion, as *The Logic of Sense* had already shown. I speak of becomings and events in the plural. But on the surface of sense (or the plane of thought) there is definitely only one event. This Event is of the kind, death-wound[11] or rather and better, of the kind, 'crack.' '*Eventum tantum*' (LS, 151). It refers to something essential to the human condition—not an essence or nature—but an 'event in the precise sense, the groove of pure 'crack.' If we know how to reach the core of the pure event we are going to find there the wound, the crack and death—the Event of all events that is always *too big* for us. *This event is in all events or in all becomings.*

Indeed, to encounter ourselves as *animal* or in the animal is to be what we never stop, at the level of phylogenesis, recommencing to quit, or to be torn away from, and, as a result, remaining for ever attached to. To encounter ourselves as *child* is, at the ontogenetic level, to become, to become again what we never stop recommencing to quit and to carry along with us in every step we take. To encounter ourselves as *woman*, whether we are men or not, is to become what sexuation as a cut of the sexes makes us be at the level of the gender: beings of the fissure which are never definitely clear-cut (sectioned)— beings which carry the other inside the same. Finally, becoming *indiscernible*, this mysterious Deleuzian becoming—what else could it be other than a permanent becoming-return to the Nietzschean nothing, the little plug brought to the Ocean of night and forgetting turning everybody into a nothing, a nothing in particular, an anonymous one just like everybody else, lost inside the immensity of time, a pure point of flight, evanescence, the Event of the wound and 'crack'? This is then what lies under the 'bands,' the 'n-sexes,' and the becoming of little Hans.[12]

We see the close relationship that this ahistorical conception of becomings maintains with majoritarian politics. The becomings carry along with them a function of dissolution, of molecularization of all forms, and of rendering fluid all established codes. They are essentially deterritorializing because they are all in communication with the indiscernibility of nothing, which is the intensity internal to all becoming. The indiscernible nothing is therefore the *point of flight* of every becoming. Man has no *proprium*, his own is to have nothing of his own, standing always out of the way of every property and propriety—a being of flight, pure line of flight.[13]

Now, to determine becoming as becoming nothing, to posit the end (*terme*) of the human as indiscernible, unassignable, asignifying, and so on—is it not to recognize the very power of the universal as a power to flee determinations? The line of flight is an 'abstract line' and it is in being abstract, like the 'abstract machine' to which it is linked, that it is positive, that it generates breakaways, opens up flights, fissures the blocs, masterminds ways out of dualisms, and releases pure abstract lines that run. The power of deterritorialization being another name for human freedom has the positivity of the negative as its obverse side—the abstract universal as the nihilation of the particularities which code, territorialize, and confine us inside identificatory forms. It follows, in my opinion, that human rights, properly understood, are nothing but the practical universal, which as such permits the deterritorialization of all the concrete territories, wherein our egos, our desires, and our powers of emancipation, whether individual or collective, find themselves trapped, coded, and sequestered.

We can therefore conclude that people's revolutionary becoming is *internal* to democracy as a space of human relations marked by the abstraction of the universality of rights and by the endless becoming-return to the constitutive dimensions of our condition. It problematizes, puts into question, and deterritorializes whatever constitutes our being together. This deterritorializing slide opens the gaping hole or the void where the principles and the institutions of being together are floating. Deleuze and the Deleuzians often entertain the illusion of a *position of extra-territoriality* with respect to what they call pejoratively 'the West,' 'the liberal democracies,' and so on. But for the critical philosopher or intellectual of today, there can be no position of exteriority, especially not, if s/he swears on the word 'immanence.' Being internal or (even worse, in their opinion) 'integrated' to the project of permanent self-criticism of democracy, Deleuzian politics perfects (and legitimates) one of the essential functions of the liberal societies of Western Europe. This idea, which is decisive because it implies a change of mind toward democracy, will be confirmed through a discussion of multiplicities and nomadism.

The second central point that I want to put forward concerns the unity of the multiple. Deleuze's philosophy defines itself as a theory of multiplicities, a system of the multiple.[14] 'Multiplicities are reality itself'.[15] The multiple is not reduced to the plural; it can neither be counted nor totalized nor divisible, without changing nature.[16] A multiplicity or a rhizome is the joint functioning of heterogeneous elements (different from a structure) and has as an essential property the fact that any of its points or elements can be connected with any other.

Now, contrary to what one could come to believe given the *doxa* surrounding Deleuzism, the major problem of the multiple is the problem of unity: how is all that *being held* together? Indeed, if the multiple is not made by the assemblage of antecedent, stable units—if it is not an infinitely divisible extensity that would remain homogeneous, how can it form a whole? Unless we have recourse to the One as that which divides and differentiates itself and stands for the origin of diversity or to the All as that which, being in a central and hegemonic position, gathers under its law the diverse, how can the unity, the coherence, or the cohesion of the multiple be created? After all, the multiple possesses necessarily its own proper and specific form of unity or of totality that give it *consistency,* without which it would immediately dissolve. As far as Deleuze is concerned, this unification—and this is his fundamental thesis—comes from the *line of flight* that carries along with it, in its groove, the elements of the rhizome giving them consistency. The unification takes place *inside* the multiplicity, it does not preexist it. It is therefore inseparable from a plane of consistency, which, being a plane immanent to the lines and elements that compose the rhizome, does not supervise or overhang them by means of a supplementary dimension or a dimension external to the plane where these lines are deployed. 'It is deterritorialization that makes the aggregate of the molecular components "hold together"' (MP, 294). 'Multiplicities are defined by the outside: by the abstract line, the line of flight or deterritorialization according to which they change in nature and connect with other multiplicities. The plane of consistency (grid) is the outside of all multiplicities' (MP, 9).

This is then the principle of principles of the Deleuzian ontology. Deleuze will bring it to bear on the social and the political to such an extent that his major thesis in this domain will be the idea that a society being a multiplicity, 'leaks on all sides.'[17] 'A society, a social field does not contradict itself, but first and foremost, it leaks out on all sides. The first thing it does is escape in all directions. These lines of flight are what comes first (even if first is not chronological) (TRM, 127). 'For me, a society is something that is constantly escaping in every direction. . . . It is really made up of lines of flight. So much so that the problem for a society is how to stop it from flowing. For me, the powers come later . . . Society is a fluid, or even worse, a gas' (TRM, 280).

Starting from these two principles—from this ingenious intuition that definitely 'liquidates' every substantialism of the people and every organicism of the political (still present in Marx, at least in the state of nostalgia)—the major political problem of the plane of consistency and its nature is reached. If the unity of the connection of the heterogeneous is a unity of flight, of openness and deterritorialization (since the lines of flight come *first*[18]) how are multiple flights coordinated, how can they prevent their dispersal or their dissolution through scattering and their molecularization through crumbling? In sum, how is this thing *being held* together?

We could expect that Deleuze would appeal to the State, to the powers to be, and so on. But this, for him, would be a contradiction. Besides the fact that, from that point on, the State would be attributed a positive and legitimate role, it would also be acquiring an 'ontological' status in direct contradiction to the status that it must maintain within an ontology of lines of flight. Power, the State, and the entire plane of organization come 'second' in comparison with the powers of deterritorialization. It is desire and the lines of flight that assemble the social field. The fact that 'everything escapes' is the first given of a society (TRM, 128). The multiple that comes 'first' cannot, in its positivity, owe its consistency to that which is (a) external or transcendent to it; or (b) ontologically 'posterior' and derived from it—a kind of 'fallout' or necessary evil.[19] The apparatuses of power are the result of reterritorialization. They come 'second' as components of every arrangement, being neither constituents nor at the source of the arrangement itself. The latter, as we saw, is formed mainly by means of the powers of deterritorialization and the lines of flight (DRF, 125–6).

The multiple, therefore, must have a mode of unification that is proper and internal (immanent) to it. Specific unification: the micro-apparatuses or arrangements internal to multiplicities cannot be conceived as miniaturizations of State power or of Power full stop or any other global concept.[20] But what would the alternative be?

On the other hand, the mode of political unification cannot be conceived in the form of totalization—for example, the 'Party'—because this mode of totalization would reintroduce right away both 'representation' and hierarchy, namely, centralizations which are modes of the transcendent One. This postulate, bearing on the mode of the unity of struggles and multiplicities the axis of which is the refusal of representation (the intellectual no longer functions as a representative consciousness), has been raised ever since the famous interview of *L'Arc*, 'The Intellectuals and Power' (March 1972).[21] We are facing 'the indignity of speaking for others . . . those involved [must] finally have their say' (DI, 208). It is power that globalizes and totalizes and this is the reason for the critique 'of the so-called representative authorities of the French Communist Party or the French Trade Unions' (TRM, 210). Indeed, it would be bizarre, as Deleuze writes, 'to count on a party or on a state apparatus to liberate desires.'

Hence, the general problem of micropolitics—whether Foucaldian or Deleuzian—is this one: to find a kind of a principle of unification that would not be of the type 'State,' 'party,' totalization or representation.[22]

Deleuze's response is double. First, he will count on a form of spontaneous diffusion—a contamination of the struggles that would find themselves carried ahead by the one that is the stronger and the more deterritorializing; a kind of resonance at a distance, a kind of an echo able to jump over and to straddle the national borders or the borders of the sectors of production or even of life territories at a distance from each other. 'The most important thing is not authoritarian unification, but a kind of infinite swarming' (DI, 267). He will count on a kind of 'crystallization' that would be occurring throughout an entire society, just like the 'explosion' of May 1968, which was not decided by political or union organizations (themselves having been caught in the upheaval). 'In May '68, *from the first sparks to the local clashes*, the upheaval was brutally transmitted to the whole society' (DI, 266).

Is not there any collective means to reinforce, accelerate this spreading, this dissemination? This becomes the object of the second response, which is very equivocal and arguably abstract. Beginning with *A Thousand Plateaus*, Deleuze was going to count on what he called, '*war machine*' (DI, 267). What should we understand by this, given that, contrary to its name, it does not have the war for its object; it does not at all constitute a State apparatus, despite the fact that it does take the war as its object as soon as the State appropriates it? (MP, 420–1). The function, we are reminded, of the war machine is to trace 'a creative line of flight' (MP, 422). That is fine. But our question was about the 'how': how to link up and to connect the different lines of desire or flight? To this question, no answer is given. The destiny of the concepts of nomadism, war machine, smooth space, and so on should better be reserved for the aesthetic domain, where everything can be connected with everything without loss, where fluidity and abstraction represent eminent values of style and art, and where creation presupposes a certain spontaneity that does not tolerate planification. Their direct translation into politics has never been satisfactory. We find, therefore, intact once again the problem that was raised in 1972—the central *problem* of micropolitics: how can we, from a political point of view, bring about creative connections between lines of flight? We know that Deleuze never answered this question, not even in the 1990s, after *A Thousand Plateaus*, except in taking cognizance of the existence of 'minorities' that he called 'nationalitarian' and interpreted as the 'conditions for a worldwide movement' (MP, 470). He then made the anticipatory announcement (anticipatory, because this is not the case, for the moment) that 'they promote compositions that do not pass by way of the capitalist economy any more than they do the State-form. Obviously the minorities have not kept their promise. Where could we find today an important 'revolutionary movement'? Incantation? *Wishful thinking*?

Conclusion: We are brought back to the first kind of response and, we are therefore condemned to wage on possibilities of unexpected ripostes (against world capitalism), 'the unassignable material Saboteur or human deserter.'[23] The war machine sends us over, not to the war, but rather to the *guerrilla war*, to people's *becoming revolutionary*. As for the latter, it cannot be inscribed in history but only by means of a negative critique and a harassment of the powers in place. This, albeit often necessary, is nevertheless very unsatisfactory for the kind of politics that wants to be affirmative, in the Nietzschean sense, instead of being reactive, and beyond *ressentiment*.

The Doxic Plane of Immanence

To the extent that the destiny of micropolitics is then promised to a nomad guerrilla war, we can, at least, slide, under this concept anticipations of war (or terror) and to think that micropolitics is nothing but the external border of democracy (in the strong and current sense of the term, having become integrated in it and being ready to be summoned by it). This soft and weak— Gianni Vattimo would say, '*debole*'—reading, of a liberal and libertarian inspiration—a reading that is opposed to Toni Negri's otherworldly and marxisant reading—carries along with it two consequences: the revalorization and reactivation of the doxic plane and the reconsideration of tradition and of its role in the heterogenesis of cultures or civilizations. Despite its importance, I will move over the first point quickly (I have developed it thoroughly elsewhere) in order to insist on the analytic character (in Freud's sense of the word) of the doxic plane.[24]

We saw that Deleuze counts on a war machine that would be neither a State apparatus nor a mode of authoritarian unification (the Party as the avantguard of the proletariat), but rather one that would be capable of 'spreading' desires and struggles ad infinitum. But what he is looking for already exists, although he wants to know nothing of it. If we examine the public space of discussion and reflection internal to all democracies, we are going to see that this plane does not crown or totalize opinions, desires, struggles, and the like, but, rather, it constitutes a plane upon which a multitude of opinions, hopes, fears, affects, representations, struggles, appeals, and declarations find themselves toppled and grafted. This is a veritable plane of immanence and it is doxic because it is made of opinions. The immanent connection of the lines of flight is achieved upon this doxic plane of immanence (which functions as a veritable body without organs, thanks to its own void (*vide*)). It is a virtual plane that traverses the chaos.[25] As a result, it retains the three characteristics (connectivity, virtuality, and the attribute of traversing the chaos) that Deleuze expects from all planes of immanence.[26] It is in it, upon it, and through it that powers intervene, as do political organizations, unions, associations, and groupuscules. And it is by means of this plane that the indispensable powers of organization and decision are validated and legitimized in view of common action.

What is the big difficulty of micropolitics? It is that it refuses all mediation and all representation. It pretends to be capable of doing it, but—letting aside, for a moment, the problem of the theoretical or speculative validity of such a thesis—experience has shown that this refusal is absolutely impossible and not even desirable. Indeed, politics is by its nature linked to the function of mediation and representation—the doxic plane of immanence guarantees it. In the absence of this function, there could be no common action, which is the essential center of all political activity. Opinion is at the heart of politics.

Remark. This thesis changes drastically the relations between people and intellectuals and intellectuals and common sense. Micropolitics, to be sure, registers this result in part—but only in part. Everyone is taken up and confronts other people inside the doxic plane: all social categories on any subject whatsoever. Thanks to the insistence of the plane of immanence, opinions let their brutality and their unreflected spontaneity go and assume the obligation to justify themselves in front of the many adversary and rival opinions. The intellectual when s/he intervenes does it without any special privilege or authority—s/he is one voice among other voices. This is the reason for the feeling of not being understood that s/he harbors and for the constant temptation to be contemptuous of the 'democracy of the media,' of the 'masses,' of 'opinion' and to abandon the political field. When it came to *Groupe d'Informations sur les Prisons'* failure and to their own action, Deleuze stated that 'Foucault said it was not repression but worse: someone speaks but it is as if nothing was said. Three or four years later, things returned to exactly the way they were' (TRM, 277). This remark clearly shows what Foucault and Deleuze never did suspect: the break that for ever cleaves the thought of the thinkers of practical activity, which, as Hanna Arendt showed it so magnificently, grounds the autonomy of the political and renders it a sphere totally distinct from the theoretical and the philosophical. What is relevant in the case of thought and the verities of reason finds no possible application in the case of action. Deleuze and Foucault found that out at their expense in the case of GIP. But the common sense of the people has always known this gaping abyss and this explains their justified mistrust of pure thinkers and 'intellectuals.' Hanna Arendt wrote this about the political powerlessness of the truths of reason: 'The philosophical truth concerns man in his singularity—it is by nature non-political, However, if he philosopher wishes to see his truth prevail over the opinions of the multitude, he will be defeated.'[27]

As One/the Common (*Le comme un*)

In order to show the movement of the Deleuzian conceptualization and zero in on its take on actual political reality, I must take recourse to new conceptual levers. These, I hope, are going to allow me to justify and expand the idea of the doxic plane as constitutive of Western (Euro-American) politics. I group the main points of my reading under the following three entries:

1. There can be nothing common unless it has been represented (figured, fictionalized) in advance in discourse 'as one' (*comme un*). We must be able to represent the different antagonistic interests, along with their consequences, in order to compare them, hierarchize them according to their importance, decide, and also define the means for putting them into action. This kind of representation elaborates the interests through a discourse that should be able to command adherence inside the public space of the debate. What is required for the formation of common action? Given that the common does not belong to the objective order (see the permanence of conflict in human societies), but rather derives from its capacity to be taken as such, the conditions of the possibility of the political action necessarily include an element of consent to semblance. 'Praxis' is then the action that must be considered 'as one/common.' There is no human society, as Bergson maintained, deprived of the function

of fabulation (which is not an illusion, a lure or a 'mask')—fabulation without simulacra.[28] In other words, the consensus required to sustain the action 'as one/common' is possible only for as long as there is consensus for the existence, in all consensus, of semblance and fabulation. The acceptance of an element of semblance is an indissociable part of democracy.[29]

2. Every body politics involves a field of immanence on the surface of which the lines of flight of desire are connected. But this 'body' politics—as we understand it from the necessity of semblance—is not an organic or a chemical body, despite its 'molecular' aspects. The diffusion, contamination, and spreading, on which Deleuze counts so much, pass—and this is important— through speech and discourse. As a result, they are not, as Deleuze wrongly maintains, purely automatic chemical and organic processes, as if the term 'microphysics' (borrowed from Foucault) could be taken literally, in the sense that the physicists give it. The movement of liberation in this case would only be in a 'materialist' theory taken as the outcome of objective social phenomena and their contradictions. We would be confronted with some kind of 'machinic' movement—the result of social 'physics' or physiology—despite the fact that 'dialectics' would still have to be integrated in it, in order to compensate for the 'mechanist' aspect of the theory. This materialist model of objective processes collapses as soon as one insists on the principle (that this so-called 'materialism' considers to be 'idealist') that emancipation requires the raise of consciousness and the taking hold of speech (*prise de parole*). And this is because emancipation stems from a collective will—one that may still be implicit, confused, and unorganized. Yet, at the same time, this collective 'will' which, by itself, is silent most of the time, implies a space of discussion and consultation, and this is the only thing capable of opposing efficiently the annexation of the sense of this will by a Party or by a popular leader. By definition, the doxic plane allows for the possibility of the event, that is, of a change that cannot be deduced from an objective process and cannot be absorbed into the laws of history. The body politic is a fragmented body with multiple voices. Underneath these crying, diverging, resonating, and calling voices belonging to multiple language games,[30] a virtual space of reception—a plane of immanence—is already stretched and open. Without it, nothing would be held together and we would be sent over, no longer to a guerrilla war, but rather to the war of all against all that would be frightful because of the pure danger of violent death inhabiting it (Hobbes, Spinoza). Without it, there would be no possibility of preventing a decision—necessarily one—from turning into a motive for social rupture, given the inevitable exclusion of other opinions that it implies. The plane of immanence brings therefore an '*entente*'—in the second degree—an acceptance of the triumph and the enactment of a proposition contrary to our reasons and our interests. We are faced with a mode of unification, which by being transversal to the multitude of opinions does not at all muffle the multiple. The one exists as a decision, 'as one/common' (no

body politic can do without it); there is no totalization brought about by this field. The unification is merely *transversal*—I would say, tolerant; in matters of religion it presupposes secularism—because this is the way proper to the political multiplicity, the multitude, *to help the heterogeneous function*. Deleuze refuses to see this subtle play of democracies and crashes it under the term (infamous, for him), 'majoritarian.' His misunderstanding is really regrettable, because his theory of the multiple is the only one capable today of understanding post-modern democracies.

It does not seem to me out of place to say that Deleuze and Foucault, despite the affair GIP, did not bring the principle of micropolitics (that 'the prisoners speak') to the doxic plane—the unique place and the proper space for such taking of discourse. The doxic plane of immanence is the 'milieu'—the sought after IN-BETWEEN—because it is in-between the diverse opinions, in-between the multitude, the rhizomatic multiple and the plane of State power. *There is then no other war machine in the proper Deleuzian sense than the doxic plane of immanence.*

3. However, it is not my intention to restitute, under the name of doxic plane, a pure plane of argumentation that would allow 'communication without domination,' as Habermas and various forms of republicanism inspired by Kant's cosmopolitanism want it. I must therefore show that the doxic plane is irreducible to a plane of communication and rationalization based on universalizable 'reasons,' and that it releases the primordial importance of affects for the functioning of a democratic politics.

(a) A consensus obtained through pure argumentation purified of prejudices, traditional habits, and the influence of particular interests cannot exist for a variety of reasons, the most important of which is the one that I have already revealed: in the domain of the political and collective life, illusions are inevitable and desirable, even from the perspective of emancipation.[31] The indispensable role of utopias, of 'progressive' collective values and of the 'legitimacy' of grand institutions rests on the power of narration and fabulation, which is irreducible to a purely rational argument. Inside the doxic plane, rationality is always already distorted, as long as public opinion—the real base of consent to collective power—is always a more or less reasonable mixture of representation and affect. Such a mixture is not very stable, prone to change, and always under the obligation of having to adapt to the respect of the grand universal democratic principles.

(b) But the main reason for the irreducibility of the doxic plane to a rational space of argumentation comes from the fact that opinion is always anchored in the basic affects of the collective. Spinoza, in his *Political Treatise*, has shown that the multitude is not formed through the adoption of a contract, but rather through the validation of the State power in a game—in a permanently renewed quest—the affective bloc of which made of fear and hope is both constitutive and indispensable. Sovereign power rests on a consent that legitimates it and this consent is always to a great extent of an affective order. And since, as Spinoza showed, the affective reality of the political is a bloc made of fear and hope, we cannot blame the Western democracies for making use of fear and of a feeling of insecurity because this feeling is constitutive of the political. Everyone exploits it—especially those who oppose democracies—witness the way they wage the fear of capitalism, globalization, the degradation of the environment, and on and on. Indeed, fear is the principal political affect (Hobbes, Spinoza), despite the fact that democracy has to do its best in order that hope prevail over fear (the hope of improving one's life, Spinoza said).

Nevertheless, the doxic plane is not exhausted with the management of fears and hopes. It is also a real plane of *analysis*, in Freud's sense of the term. The plane relates opinions to the gaping hole of nonknowledge (of the just) and to the grand democratic principles, which, in being purely formal and by themselves empty of all content, frame, inside democracy, the work of opinion and form, in a sense, the attributes of the *plane of immanence*. To the extent that the doxic plane shows clearly and above everything else its function as autoreflexion of opinions, we should not cut off this function from its cathartic and really analytic dimension—'the analysis of the desires of the masses.'[32] This is the importance of Deleuze who, beginning with *Anti-Oedipus*, put forward this function, inherent in politics, and knew how to link up with the political genius of Spinoza in underscoring the conscious investments of desire and their priority over the conscious investments of interest (the object of schizoanalysis).

However, in the interest of the goal and the means of such an 'analysis,' it seems to me that we must today emancipate ourselves from the Deleuzian position. Contrary to what Deleuze thought, it seems very difficult, for the analytic work, to avoid bringing opinions face to face with the 'hole' of the political—and this is precisely what Deleuze refuses to do (as he does with everything that, as he says, would lead him back to 'castration' to Freud or to Lacan). The doxic plane of immanence, as it reflects on itself and on the plurality of opinions, cannot fail to uncover the void in the foundation of democracy. This inescapable void is the real that grounds political realism and that *phronesis* must confront. The analytic function of the plane has as its object *to lead* opinion *back again* to its void—to bring the most solid opinion back to the underlying gaping hole of the political that would dissolve its compactness. This is the source of the values of equality (in the *taking hold of speech* in the face of the void of the political), the values of tolerance (in the void of savoir) and of solidarity (in our originary nakedness and non-transcendable precariousness stemming from our condition of being in time). The multitude is not a 'natural' given, but it is an exactly symmetrical response to the hole that has no response. The doxic plane of immanence traverses chaos—the gaping hole—insofar as the knowledge of what is just is politically lacking. And it is in view of this absence of knowledge (*savoir*) that we are all gathered together around the hole, and equal in our capacity to offer opinions. Power is in the center but in the center is void. The analytic labor of the plane of immanence—the cathartic effect intrinsically linked with it—is to steer cathartically the collective affects, upon which every politics is based, in their operation of this new kind of transversality in the direction of the constitutive void.

It is not then the division in antagonistic social classes because of economic interests, as Marx thought, that is at the foundation of the historical human societies. If this were the case, the conflict could be resolved. Putting forth these struggles of interests—which of course exist—is to misunderstand the ultimate division that hollows humanity without remedy, no matter what its social system might be. To center entirely upon the struggle of interests, power, or class is still a way of fantasizing a possible unity—a possible way of filling the hole of history and the political, that is, the wound of humanity that has no healing. As long as we fight, we put out of our sight the ultimate and tragic division. Aggressiveness masks anxiety. The hole of the political is delimited by the *awareness of the impossibility of a truly human community* having the kind of social unity where all divisions would be healed. There is an irremediable lacuna or gaping hole in the heart of humanity that every society has endeavored to hide. This void, upon which all human institutions rest, without finding a ground, is called 'chaos' in Greek. To think, Deleuze says, is to confront the chaos. It is this confrontation to which the Western postmodern democracies are being promised, and it is this that gives them their great dignity, despite the imperfections and injustices that people like to blame them for, without noticing that with this critique we do nothing else but to maintain the gaping hole, ground and legitimate them.

Conclusion: This is the direction that the renewal of democracy asks for today. It is, I think, much more fecund than otherworldly nomadism and the communicative ethics of Habermas. The multitude does not exist in its unification but only in and through the doxic plane of immanence. Without it, it is only a 'mass' or rather atomized and disseminated individuals, deprived even of the consistency that a 'gas' has. The sought after unification, the war machine, is no other than this virtual plane of immanence because it is the only thing capable of assuring us of the consistency and the internal unity proper to the multiple.

Toward a Cultural Heterogenesis

In the hour of globalization, what can Deleuze's political philosophy offer? Its practical bearing is very ambiguous. Politically, it is possible to interpret it as a cosmopolitan nomadism without borders, in the way that Hardt and Negri made possible with their theory of multitude;[33] or, obversely, it is possible to interpret it as an opposition to all forms of globalization and cosmopolitanism. And here we reach the heart and the essence of politics. How is political activity actualized—how does it exist? What is an occurrence/taking place (*avoir lieu*) for the political? And is it possible for this occurrence/taking place not to be connected to the question of place (locus, *topos*), namely, to the question of a specific place on the earth—a particular territory—and, therefore, to the question as to who 'inhabits' this place and who is called a 'people'? A dislocated people, one in a state of pure dislocation and deterritorialization—can it have a political dimension, possess a reality, or a being that is political?

Brought back to the Deleuzian theme, these questions open up a questioning decisive for our time. The Deleuzian philosophy defines itself as a *philosophy of difference* and is suspicious both of universals and identity.[34] On the political plane of the relationship between cultures, nations, and civilizations, it does not fit a rationalist project of a 'cosmopolitan' project embodied today by Habermas, in his explicit allegiance to Kant and to practical juridical reason.[35] Cosmopolitanism of a Kantian inspiration always goes together with an overbid of integration and association inside larger and larger units, more global or even *globalizing* for the time being, accompanied by the Idea of a universal Republic, or even, according to some, by the Idea of a world State. It would then be absurd, for Deleuze, to think of such a unification, at the world level, since nothing could strike him as more frightening.

At any rate, on this international plane, we encounter, as an indubitable fact, the diversity of cultures and civilizations. Within each cultural ensemble, what, in the first instance, unites people is something like a 'common sense.' Being a contingent empirical formation, purely factual and even fictitious, it bears the traces of the violence of history and the relations of force. From these it acquires the ability to be recognized right away, to have its own (regional or national) style made of its particular collective tonalities, the expression of which is, in part, found condensed in its common convictions and the grand symbols transmitted from generation to generation—its common memory, its holidays, commemorations, and so on. As Hanna Arendt[36] has shown, common sense—tradition as the heritage that the past transmits—is the ground and *Ariane's thread*, which, in politics, serves as a line of orientation.[37] And here, we rediscover the primordial question—on an other plane, to be sure, under a different light, but one nonetheless that the actuality of the contemporary world compels us to raise—the question of the relations between deterritorialization and territorialization. As we saw, there is primacy of the lines of flight, but normally this fact should not lead to a politics of systematic rupture with the old—a politics of *tabula rasa* (or rather more subtly to the prejudice of the absence of prejudice). It should not lead to the contempt for traditions, considered to be folklore, exotic patterns, odds and ends of used codes and of obsolete and bygone rules.

The first reason for a prudent relation with the tradition is the one that Deleuze himself suggests, although, in his case, it remains negative. He warns us that deterritorialization and reterritorialization have dangers that are proper to each one, that neither is good in itself (MP, 277). Although distinct, they are inseparable (MP, 260, 268). But from the fact that the value of each process is relative and conditional we should not conclude that they are of equal value. Deterritorialization is primary because it is the one that holds together the molecular constituents, it is the one that makes history, it is upon its own trajectory that reterritorialization occurs (MP, 269, 360, 415). Territorialization is indispensable, even incontestable, if we want to escape the danger of abolition and collapse inside the black holes, which are the dangers proper to the lines of flight. Territorialization then possesses the status of a safeguard. It is an indispensable 'necessary evil.' Its ontological status of depot, of fallout and fossilization does not prevent it from playing the role of a necessary obstacle or of a protective rampart; and yet, it does not earn the status of a true positivity; it remains a useful negative, something relative to circumstances.

It is difficult, however, to be satisfied with the status of such a function. Being confronted more than ever before by the erosion of differences inside a technical and economic uniformity and by the peril of the collapse of the diversity of peoples and nations, we are becoming aware of the fact that lines of flight are not traced miraculously and abstractly, but rather that they are drawn from the profound and well understood wealth of tradition. Would the thinker, Deleuze, be possible without Spinoza, Nietzsche, and Bergson? The most innovative line of flight does not reject tradition to an out of date past that one lets unceremoniously fall behind him like a cast off, dead skin, the way a positivist and technologizing modernism would have wanted it. The traditions that carry cultures in their difference are not at all of the order of inalienable and quasi-sacred goods, with a content that has to be maintained as such, no matter what the price is. A tradition cannot be reduced to the conservation of a common patrimony; it does not consist in protecting and holding intact from any modification that which is transmitted. What is transmitted—the gift or the legacy—belongs to the order of a *differenciating openness.* Tradition and the past are the necessary conditions for the auto-reflection of the self and of the actual world, and, therefore, the condition of a *comprehensive openness.*

The second reason for according a real positivity to the collective tradition is the most important one. It lies in the fact that the line of deterritorialization, in its most advanced and intense point, comes always from afar to find a way to renew and take up again a deep fault, dried up for the moment and silenced— one which, like a spring, begins to speak again. It is the future that illuminates the present, but it is the past that sketches the future inside the present and causes the really emancipatory deterritorializations to occur. What shall we do in order to prevent the flight from turning into a *stampede*—a flight of the self and the world? In order for the outside with its appeal not to turn to resignation and forgetting in an intensification of struggles and an activist violence pretending to be directed toward a messianic future, we must think of ways to trace the line of flight that would allow the common cultural past to become the object of a *critical and re-interpretive* re-appropriation.

The fecundity and subtlety of Deleuze's thought seems to permit the refusal of the alternative between the cosmopolitan conception of Habermas and the pseudo-nomadic conception of 'those without borders' espoused by Hardt and Negri. Habermas bets on 'constitutional patriotism.'[38] And by this he means the fidelity, not to a fatherland understood as a nation—a homogeneous ethnic group—but rather a fidelity to universal principles of the democratic type, especially to human rights. He thinks that this kind of fidelity would be enough to legitimize a post-national political power, for example, a common European political power. The beauty—very Kantian—of this conception has the disadvantage of forgetting that authority is never grounded on the will alone, pure and enlightened by mere practical reason, and armed with its grand moral and juridical principles. The reality of the base of the political is that the legitimacy of power is always and for the most part of an affective origin. And the feelings of belonging to a common identity, far from being purely volatile and arbitrary, are anchored in the force of a tradition, of a shared culture, and of a civilization that is transmitted from one generation to the next. Identity cannot be the result only of identification with abstract, empty, impersonal, and general principles. Moreover, constitutional patriotism is as a matter of principle or virtually without borders. The political cannot take place (without place or people) or be defined (as the question of Europe shows it today) unless a common power is able to operate within finite limits or borders. Without this, constitutional patriotism will be, in the best of cases, the patriotism of a place called 'Europe' (determined territory) and of a 'people' (the European) in gestation. The frontiers of the same sentiment of belonging are always mythical and fabled, relative, arbitrary, revisable, and artificially constructed—this is certain—but the problem is that, whatever they may be, they are needed, under the penalty of political failure.

To be sure, there is no 'people' (one and substantial); there has never been and there will never be one. There are only always more or less fleeing multitudes (Spinoza's thesis). But, at the same time, these 'multitudes' are not entirely dispersed and totally dislocated, eternal wanderers on the surface of the sphere. In fact, they are always de facto linked with one another, inside and by means of particular cultural traditions, which give them a relative, precarious, in gestation identity, always under question, tugged at, fissured, yet being the basis for a collective affect of belonging, and rendering possible projects and willings that are being accepted as if they were 'common.' In this basis of the sentiment of belonging, one always finds, next to ideals and principles, a semblance—a tradition that is in part the result of fabulation. Being fictitious and invented, it carries nevertheless affective weight, comparable to the force of the myth. It is this dimension and this massive fact that postmodern nomadism with its vision of the abolition of all borders seems today to forget.

The defence of a distance between cultures, necessary for them to be able to retain their singularity and to be recreated, is the condition of *cultural heterogenesis*. Hardt and Negri do not seem to distrust enough the apology of hybridization and interbreeding, even when it is cultural.[39] Often, this is the shortest route to sub-cultures and to market-induced 'uniformization,' and the prostitution of whatever can be bought, commercialized, and exchanged. A real opening presupposes that the other is other and, therefore, a stranger to the culture welcoming him or her. And for this interaction to be fecund, the one who welcomes must be able to re-elaborate the gift in accordance with its own cultural resources. This is re-interpretive appropriation, especially in the light of the grand democratic principles. It is the condition of one's own enrichment, the result neither of a simple handing down nor of servile imitation. Recreation and differenciation presuppose the independence and distance of cultures instead of their being co-mingled in a mad whole, dislocated, and without specific contours and borders.

The tradition at the heart of the cultural and civilizational fact is not reduced to the conservation of a common patrimony; it does not require holding intact, in the face of all modifications, what is transmitted. To stress the weight of culture is not *a neo-conservative or traditionalist* argument. What is transmitted—whether gift or legacy—is of the order of an opening. It is a setting upon in the direction that gives a specific possibility of access to the world and to being. These settings upon are plural, co-present, and heterogeneous; they are not totalizable inside a unity and they are called civilizations. Such openings call us to a re-interpretation of the past, to a retrieval that is both critical and open. Without therefore presupposing any ethnic homogeneity, they sketch out an immediately recognizable style of existence, and a manner of thinking and relating to the world, which is unique, precious, and fragile in equal measures. This is the case for the Asiatic, Indian, and Arab-Muslim civilizations as much as it is the case for the European. It makes them be relatives and communicating with one another, as much as it makes them different and distant. Each of them is taken up in a *cultural heterogeneity* where it never stops to differentiate itself by itself, despite the fact that the forces of the first stratum—those of eco-techno-science—tend to make them more and more resemble one another. Given that the eco-techno-science is, by vocation, without borders and *globalizing*, its stratum enters into a conflict with political power, which cannot operate without frontiers, nor without a dominant orientation in the direction of a *singularizing distance* and, therefore, in the direction of cultural heterogeneity.

Unlike the abstract universality of the juridical legality, which concerns every one in the same space and at the same moment, and which is imposed from the outside as transcendent to the territorialities and cultures, the potential universality of a culture is immanent and the result of having gained in depth in the course of its own tradition. And this internalization is also encountered in the other cultures existing side by side during the same historical epoch. The universal is an affair of being a relative or being proximate. Without being identical or the result of rubbing off the universal on the particularity of cultures, the universal is what inspires or sets upon different ways to say or to live something.

Cultural heterogeneity because it occurs inside the work of internal consistency does not abolish the possibility of establishing correspondences and, therefore, forms of a specific universality. Virtual universality among cultures belongs to the order of a universality without transcendence or abstraction, and without a political community that would be unique, integrating, and totalizing. It operates from the distance and the difference of cultures; it sketches out a horizon of entente and tolerance that makes civilization a 'value,' albeit this value does not coincide with any particular civilization. Rather, it is found in all civilizations, working and orienting them from the inside toward their proper excellence. The more a culture accedes to its proper 'consistency,' the more different it is, nearer and in resonance with the others, helping us to see relativism as the result of a very strong fascination with the titillations of appearance and of an intense forgetting of what links together in virtual transversality.

If the philosophy of Deleuze represents a great gift, it is because it has the tools for thinking one of the most important problems of present time, offering them to us who can no longer count on practical a priori or on dialectical totalizations in process. How can we think of new forms of unity and universality, without resurrecting the one, the All, and the community?

It seems to me that Gilles Deleuze offers us the possibility to exit this *aporia*. I would say in order to conclude, as I use his work as a trampoline, that the really immanent form of universality generates a lateral and horizontal line, which traverses the multiple of each territoriality, ethnic group, people, or nation and allows it to resonate from one soil to the other, in and through their differences. One could say in the case of this transversal universality that we are faced with the *as one/common (comme un) without community*. Transversality—a concept dear to Guattari—does not bring about a human community. The latter, more so today than ever before, does not exist but only in semblance. We have equivalences, analogues of rules, and common conventions—a universality of transversality and of semblance, which is not to be confused with falsehood. It is the 'as' (*comme*) that makes the common of the (for ever absent) community. Neither the shimmering of difference nor the wild nomadism or the generosity of the universal rules of our humanitarian charts suffice to create a politics measuring up to the stakes of our times.

Notes

* Translated by Constantin V. Boundas and Crina Bondre Ardelean.

1 His books have been translated in many languages and his philosophy is being taught in the most prestigious universities of North America. See Cusset F. (2003), *The French Theory* (Paris: La Découverte).

2 With the exception of Manola Antonioli's *Géopolitique*, few French works focus on this important dimension of Deleuze's work. See also my book, *Deleuze et la question de la démocratie* (Paris: L'Harmattan, 2003). In English, on the other hand, there are many publications. See Patton P. (2000), *Deleuze and the Political* (London: Routledge); Holland E. (1999), *Deleuze and Guattari's Anti-Oedipus* (London: Routledge); Protevi, J. (2001), *Political Physics: Deleuze, Derrida and the Body Politic* (New York: Athlone).

3 See for example Deleuze G. (2002), *Desert Island and Other Texts, 1953–74* (New York: Semiotext(e)), 206–7; hereafter referred to as DI.

4 Despite Deleuze's reworkings, criticisms, relegations, and adjunctions of concepts (pick-up method and collage), especially with respect to the Leninist position, this qualification fits very well the political doctrine of Deleuze and Guattari, as long as the meaning of the term is brought to bear on the analysis of the new forms of capital and State power. It is in this very narrow sense that Deleuze, in one of his last interviews with Toni Negri (1990), was able to state: 'I think that Félix Guattari and I have remained Marxists.' Deleuze, G. (1995), *Negotiations*, trans. M. Joughin (New York: Columbia University Press), 171; hereafter referred to as N.

5 See Mengue, P. (1994), *Gilles Deleuze ou le système du multiple* (Paris: Kimé); and *Deleuze et la question de la démocratie*. On this reading of political philosophy, see Mengue, P. (2004), *La philosophie au piège de l'histoire* (Paris: La Différence).

6 'Becoming isn't part of history; history amounts only to the set of preconditions, however recent, that one leaves behind in order to "become" that is, to create something new' (N, 171). See also Deleuze, G. and Guattari, F. (1994), *What is Philosophy?* trans. H. Tomlinson and G. Burchell, G. (New York: Columbia University Press), 96 and 111–12, hereafter referred to as WiPh. History, therefore, is nothing but the history of 'what goes down in it: 'It always goes down in History, but never comes from it.' Deleuze, G. and Guattari, F. (1987), *A Thousand Plateaus: Capitalism and Schizophrenia*, trans. B. Massumi (Minneapolis: University of Minnesota Press), 296; hereafter referred to as MP.

7 See the magnificent exergue of *Negotiations*.

8 I borrow this term from Lacan to indicate that micropolitics can be, at one and the same time, inside and outside of politics (Deleuze calls the latter 'macropolitics' or 'majoritarian' politics—always in a pejorative way).

9 Nietzsche, F. (1983), *On the Uses and Disadvantages of History for Life, Untimely Meditations*, trans. R. J. Holingdale (Cambridge: Cambridge University Press), 64

10 What is necessary, therefore, is forgetting the ontological forgetting or the forgetting of a major indifference, inherent in Being or Becoming (a very un-Heideggerean theme). For the 'unhistorical fog' in Deleuze, see WiPh, 96, 111–12.

[11] Deleuze, G. (1990), *The Logic of Sense*, trans. M. Lester with Ch. Stivale, ed. C. V. Boundas (New York: Columbia University Press), 151–2 ; hereafter referred to as LS.

[12] The dot, dot, dot (*points de suspension*) is very appropriate to the indefinite flight that constitutes the affective intensity of Deleuze's thought—although never used by him. We may find it amusing to say (and I see again, in his effort to refer to the abstract line, his long and sharp nails clawing the air) that Deleuze's thought is intensified, neither when facing the question mark, as it is with Sartre, nor when facing the exclamation, as it is with Sade or with the Kant of the sublime, but rather, in front of the points/dots (multiplicities) of suspension (indefinite line of flight).

[13] Finally, what did Lacan mean by *objet a*? If we bracket the altogether legitimate critique of 'familialism' to which Lacan totally subscribes, what is it that separates Deleuze's conception from Lacan's, given that, on the essential point of the *objet a*, they both agree in thinking it as a shooting point—as the vanishing point of desire and sense? However, Deleuze and Guattari wrongly think (they stay for ever with the ideology of 'repression' and 'oppression') that this point of flight is constituted against the signifying 'chains' (a term that they take literally, as an instrument of social and political power) and that the Freudian unconscious legitimizes oppression and the 'despotism of the signifier.'

[14] This is the main and dominant concept. 'The notion "multiplicity" is for me important,' wrote Deleuze in his 'Letter-Preface' to Martin J.-C. (1993) *Variations* (Paris: Payot). 8. See also *Negotiations*; Deleuze, G. and Parnet, C. (1987), 'The Actual and the Virtual,' in *Dialogues*, trans. H. Tomlinson and B. Habberjam (New York: Columbia University Press); *A Thousand Plateaus*, chaps. 'Introduction' and 'Rhizome.' See also my *Gilles Deleuze ou le système du multiplicité*.

[15] Preface to the Italian translation of *A Thousand Plateaus*, reprinted in *Two Regimes of Madness: Textes and Interviews 1975–1995*, trans. Anne Hodges and Mike Taormina (New York: Semiotext(e), 2006).

[16] Following Bergson, Deleuze talks of two kinds of multiplicity: the quantitative and spatial, which is divisible, denumerable and definable in terms of its elements and the qualitative whose properties are to be continuous, heterogeneous, and simple.

[17] See the many references in *A Thousand Plateaus*: 'a society is defined by its lines of flight, which are molecular'—the opposite is true in Marxism where society is characterized by its contradictions. 'There is always something that flows or flees' (MT, 216, 142, 204, 205 etc.).

[18] Many references in *A Thousand Plateaus*. See MT, 56: 'In fact what is primary is an absolute deterritorialization, an absolute line of flight.' See especially MT, 140–1 for the important note on Deleuze's difference from Foucault, and 108–10, 204–5, etc. Deterritorialization and reterritorialization are distinct, yet inseparable, 213, 217, 269–70, 303–4 etc. but deterritorialization is always primary.

[19] Powers are the products of lines of flight and, by turning and falling back on them, they are responsible for crashing and stifling them (DRF, 118).

[20] See the critique of Foucault in the 1986 essay, 'Desire or pleasure,' reproduced in DRF, 114.

21 Reprinted in *Desert Islands*, 206–13.

22 DRF, 121. The problem was raised in 1972, but five years later (1977) it had not made any progress. It will be the same twenty years later (1994) when this article appeared in the *Magazine Littéraire*. Here is the question: 'Has Michel made progress with the issue under consideration: how can one uphold the rights of a micro-analysis (diffusion, heterogeneity, fragmentary character) and still allow for some kind of principle of unification . . .?' (DRF, 132).

23 MT, 422. Notice the 'Unspecified enemy.' Should we today include those that we call 'terrorists' in the service of a radical and warlike Islamism? We must admit that the equivocation is serious and difficult to accept.

24 See Mengue, P., *Deleuze et la question de la démocratie.*

25 We mean 'chaos' here in the fundamental sense, the gap of nonknowledge, the nothing we are within the void of time.

26 This concept leads us to the idea that democracy is not practiced first and foremost inside the Parliament and through the legitimate games of the parties or national representation. Democracy is always one of opinion and the multitude. The doxic plane is located nowhere in particular; it traverses all institutions, all parties, every association—even those who play boules. It is a virtual plane, not being anchored in networks or media, despite the fact that these are finding a place in it. It is a *transversal* plane. Given that it intersects and traverses opinions, it puts them in a situation of critical self-reflection, which is not the prerogative of intellectuals and the media. The latter was clearly shown in France with the vote for the European constitution that defeated the 'yes,' supported nonetheless by the majority of the media, journalists, intellectuals, and prominent political figures.

27 Arendt, H. (1989), *La crise dela culture* (Paris: Gallimard), 313.

28 On the notion, simulacrum, that Deleuze abandoned later on, see 'Klossowski or Bodies-Language,' in *The Logic of Sense.*

29 See Machiavelli and especially Spinoza (more acceptable to revolutionary Deleuzians). Spinoza dares to make his own the ruse of semblance and manipulation and to recommend a purely pragmatic use as a warranty of internal peace and social cohesion—both being supreme goals of the State. See among other passages the magnificent and explicit passage of his *Political Treatise* (X, # 8): 'But men are so to be led, that they may think that they are not led, but living after their own mind, and according to their free decision.' See also Leo Strauss, 'L'Etat et la function sociale de la religion,' in *La Critique de la religion chez Spinoza* (Paris: Cerf, 1996).

30 Jean-François Lyotard (1988), *The Differend*, trans. George Van Den Abeele (Minneapolis: Minnesota University Press) has successfully uncovered this essential aspect of postmodern politics.

31 Is the critique of illusions and of all powers to be that involve an external authority politically—not theoretically—reasonable? Can they occur without triggering a political catastrophe and a grievous attack against 'the spiritual patrimony of civilization'? (See Freud, S., *Civilization and Its Discontents*). Freud, who, on the collective practical plane, had made certain 'illusions' exempt of criticism, showed that the fact that these illusions were deeply rooted suggested the greatest possible prudence in the pursuit of emancipation.

[32] DI, 267. Schizoanalysis is being defined in *Anti-Oedipus*.

[33] Provided, of course, that Toni Negri's theory, with its concepts, empire, and multitude, can still be assimilated to a 'cosmopolitan' thought.

[34] See 'Introduction,' in DR.

[35] See Habermas, J. (1998), *L'Intégration républicaine* (Paris: Fayard).

[36] Deleuze has nothing to say about Arendt's work, which nevertheless is very important for the question of cultures and traditions and for their relations in a global perspective. The late translation of her work in French did not permit any confrontation. But, in my opinion, the problematics of her work destabilize the sense of micropolitics and reveals its shortcomings—and this accounts for the silence.

[37] See 'Compréhension et politique,' in *La Nature du totalitarisme* (Paris: Payot), 44. This principle frontally opposes the rejection of common sense already present in 'The Image of Thought' of *Difference and Repetition*. But this opposition must be qualified by the consideration that Deleuze's position is purely speculative, while Arendt's is essentially 'political,' in other words, it is a position that has accepted the fault that separates the philosophico-political from the political in the case of practice, and the acting in 'human affairs.'

[38] Habermas, J. *L'Intégration républicaine*, 124; see also p. 85: 'a European constitutional patriotism.'

[39] See, for example, in *Empire* (Harvard: Harvard University Press, 2000) the apology of the 'mixture,' which is not a warranty for the rhizomatic phenomenon (13 and 456). Lévi-Strauss, in his second UNESCO speech, adopted a position which is critical of interbreeding. See 'Race et culture' in *Le Regard éloigné* (Paris: Plon, 1983), 46.

Chapter 13

Deleuze's Practical Philosophy*

Paul Patton

Deleuze has always described his work alone and with Guattari as 'philosophy, nothing but philosophy, in the traditional sense of the word' (Deleuze 1980, 99).[1] *What is Philosophy?* distinguishes philosophy, science, and art as three distinct modalities of thought in terms of their different methods and products: science aims at the representation of states of affairs by means of mathematical or propositional functions, while art aims at the capture and expression of the objective content of particular sensations—affects and percepts—in a given medium. Philosophy is different in that it does not seek to represent independently existing objects or states of affairs or to express particular affects and percepts. It produces concepts, where these are a certain kind of representation distinct from those produced by the arts or the sciences.

Philosophical concepts are not referential but expressive.[2] According to Deleuze and Guattari, they express 'pure events': to become, to deterritorialize, to capture, and so on. For this reason, they are not assessed in terms of their truth or falsity but according to the degree to which they are 'Interesting, Remarkable or Important' (Deleuze and Guattari 1994, 82). Expression is not representation in the sense that science represents physical bodies and states of affairs by recreating their 'actualization' in thought. Rather, the expression of events in philosophical concepts is the counter-actualization of bodies and states of affairs by presenting them as determinate forms or 'incarnations' of a given event: becoming, deterritorialization, capture, and so on.

Deleuze also describes his work with Guattari as political philosophy, even though political thought does not appear as a distinct modality in this account (Deleuze 1995, 36, 170–1). The absence of any account of specifically political reason is one of the reasons for Philippe Mengue arguing in his recent *Deleuze et la démocratie* (Mengue 2003) that Deleuzian political thought is fundamentally hostile toward democracy.[3] Despite this absence, it is clear that for Deleuze and Guattari philosophy has a political vocation. On their account, the purpose of the philosophical creation of concepts is essentially pragmatic. The aim is not merely to recognize or reconstruct how things are but to transform existing forms of thought and practice. Philosophy is 'utopian' in the sense that it carries the criticism of its own time to its highest point and, in doing so, 'summons forth' a new earth and a new people (Deleuze and Guattari 1994, 99).

What kind of political philosophy is this and what purpose does it serve? However much they borrow from Marx's analysis of capitalism and however much they embrace the utopian idea of a philosophy that calls for new earths and new peoples their work does not sit comfortably alongside traditional Marxist concepts of society, history, and politics. But nor does their work employ the language or methods of contemporary liberal political philosophy. Unlike Rawls, they do not engage in the systematic reconstruction of our considered opinions on the nature of justice, freedom, and political organization. Unlike Habermas, they do not seek to provide clear and unambiguous normative standards for the evaluation of political institutions or society. In some respects, as I will argue, their approach is closer to a deconstructive rather than a reconstructive political philosophy.

Perhaps a useful way to approach the problem concerning the kind of political philosophy Deleuze and Guattari provide is to return to the tripartite division of thought outlined in *What is Philosophy?* In some respects, this resembles the division found in Kant's three Critiques: science, philosophy, and art as distinct modalities of thought correspond to the Kantian domains of theoretical, practical, and teleological reason. Kant distinguishes theoretical and practical reason by suggesting that theoretical reason is concerned with the knowledge of objects that are given to us by means of the senses, whereas practical reason is concerned with objects that we produce by means of action in accordance with certain principles. The reason for this, according to Kant, is that when we are concerned with the practical use of reason we consider it in relation to the determination of the will, which he defines as 'a faculty either of producing objects corresponding to representations or of determining itself to effect such objects' (Kant 1996, 148). Deleuze and Guattari do not rely upon a concept of the will, or indeed a concept of human nature as defined by the freedom of the will and the faculty of reason. However, they do rely upon a constructivist conception of philosophy as the creation of concepts, where these are not supposed to represent pre-given objects but rather assist in bringing about new configurations of bodies and states of affairs (new peoples and new earths). In this sense, they suggest that 'the concept is the contour, the configuration, the constellation of an event to come' (Deleuze and Guattari 1994, 32–3).

It is for this reason I suggest that we should conclude that Deleuze and Guattari's philosophy must be considered a form of practical reason. This is the hypothesis I propose to examine in this chapter. I want to explore some of the ways in which their conception of philosophy might be consistent with a broadly Kantian conception of practical reason, while also noting their differences. My interest in pursuing this idea is not to undertake a systematic survey of their relationship to Kant but rather to ask whether this comparison helps to answer the question raised earlier about the nature of their political philosophy and to explore ways in which Deleuze and Guattari's political philosophy might be developed and brought into contact with other forms of contemporary normative political philosophy. For example, does it help us to see in what sense Deleuzian philosophical concepts are intended to be action guiding rather than or perhaps as well as descriptive of past or present events? Does the distinction between actualization and counter-actualization of states of affairs correspond to the Kantian difference between representation of given objects and the production of objects (or events and states of affairs) not given in experience? Finally, with reference to Mengue's criticism, what is the relation of Deleuze's political philosophy to liberal democratic institutions and practices?

Ontology and Ethics of Deterritorialization

One obvious difference from Kant is that Deleuze and Guattari do not derive practical principles on the basis of an ontology of free and rational individual subjects. Instead they present an ontology of *assemblages* which encompasses both the assemblages of desire, language, knowledge, and affect which produce certain kinds of subject and the assemblages of social relations, equipment, and populations which produce certain kinds of society. The successive plateaus within *A Thousand Plateaus* describe many different kinds of assemblage with reference to different empirical domains: machinic assemblages of desire, collective assemblages of enunciation, nomadic assemblages and apparatuses of capture, as well as ideational, pictorial, and musical assemblages. They provide a series of new vocabularies in terms of which we can describe aspects of the natural and social world. These include the terminology used to describe different kinds of social, linguistic, and affective assemblages (strata, content and expression, territories, lines of flight, or deterritorialization); the terminology employed to outline a micro- as opposed to macro-politics (body without organs, intensities, molar, and molecular segmentarities, the different kinds of line of which we are composed); and the terminology employed to describe capitalism as a non-territorially based *axiomatic* of flows (of materials, labor and information) as opposed to a territorial system of overcoding. They include a concept of the State as an apparatus of capture which, in the forms of its present actualization, is increasingly subordinated to the requirements of the capitalist axiomatic, and a concept of abstract machines of metamorphosis (nomadic war-machines) which are the agents of social and political transformation.

Deleuze and Guattari do not provide any explicit defense or justification of normative principles. Rather, the elaboration of their ontology of assemblages provides a demonstration of such principles (in the sense of presenting or showing rather than deducing these principles). The successive accounts of the different kinds of assemblage describe a world which accords systematic priority to certain kinds of movement: to becoming-minor as a process of deviation from a standard, to lines of flight or deterritorialization, to nomadic machines of metamorphosis rather than apparatuses of capture, to smooth rather than striated space, and so on. In this sense, their ontology of assemblages is also an ethics or an ethology. This ethics might be characterized in the language of one or other of the plateaux as an ethics of becoming, of flows or lines of flight, or as an ethics and a politics of deterritorialization. I argued in *Deleuze and the Political* that the concept of deterritorialization best expresses the ethico-political sense of this ontology (Patton 2000, 9, 136). How does it work?

In the concluding statement of rules governing some of their most important concepts at the end of *A Thousand Plateaus,* deterritorialization is defined as the movement or process by which something escapes or departs from a given territory (Deleuze and Guattari 1987, 508), where a territory can be a system of any kind: conceptual, linguistic, social, or affective. By contrast, reterritorialization refers to the ways in which deterritorialized elements recombine and enter into new relations in the constitution of a new assemblage or the modification of the old. On their account, systems of any kind always include 'vectors of deterritorialization,' while deterritorialization is always 'inseparable from correlative reterritorializations' (Deleuze and Guattari 1987, 509).

Deterritorialization can take either a negative or a positive form: it is negative when the deterritorialized element is subjected to reterritorialization that obstructs or limits its line of flight. It is positive when the line of flight prevails over the forms of reterritorialization and manages to connect with other deterritorialized elements in a manner that extends its trajectory or even leads to reterritorialization in an entirely new assemblage. As well as distinguishing negative and positive deterritorialization, Deleuze and Guattari further distinguish between an absolute and a relative form of each of these processes. This corresponds to the ontological distinction they draw between a virtual and an actual order of things: absolute deterritorialization takes place in the virtual realm while relative deterritorialization concerns only movements within the actual. In the terms of their ontology of assemblages, it is the virtual order of becoming that governs the fate of any actual assemblage. Absolute deterritorialization is the underlying condition of all forms of relative deterritorialization. It is the immanent source of transformation, the reserve of freedom or movement in reality that is activated whenever relative deterritorialization occurs. This is a Bergsonian concept of freedom in the world rather than a Kantian concept of freedom of the will. The sense in which it amounts to an ethical principle embedded within a conception of the world becomes clear when Deleuze and Guattari describe absolute deterritorialization as 'the deeper movement . . . identical to the earth itself' (Deleuze and Guattari 1987, 143). Finally, in accordance with their method of specification of concepts by proliferating distinctions, they distinguish between the connection and conjugation of deterritorialized elements in the construction of a new assemblage.

The effective transformation of a given field of reality (actuality) requires the recombination of deterritorialized elements in mutually supportive and productive ways to form assemblages of connection rather than conjugation. Absolute and relative deterritorialization will both be positive when they involve the construction of '*revolutionary connections* in opposition to *the conjugations of the axiomatic*' (Deleuze and Guattari 1987, 473). Under these conditions, absolute deterritorialization 'connects lines of flight, raises them to the power of an abstract vital line or draws a plane of consistency' (Deleuze and Guattari 1987, 510).

Absolute deterritorialization expresses the normative ideal at the heart of Deleuze and Guattari's ethics: it is a concept of abstract, non-organic and creative life which underwrites both the deterritorialization of existing assemblages and the connection of deterritorialized elements and their reconfiguration into new assemblages. It is the freedom expressed in the creative transformation of what is, but at the same time a concept of freedom that is incompatible with liberal concepts predicated upon the continued existence of the stable subject of freedom.[4] The molecular as opposed to the molar line of which individual and collective subjects are composed already constitutes a mortal threat to the integrity of such a subject. It is along this line that the subject undergoes 'molecular changes, redistributions of desire such that when something occurs, the self that awaited it is already dead, or the one that would await it has not yet arrived' (Deleuze and Guattari 1987, 199). The freedom expressed in Deleuze and Guattari's third line, the line of flight or absolute deterritorialization, is positively monstrous from the point of view of the subject. Once embarked on this line, 'One has become imperceptible and clandestine in motionless voyage. Nothing can happen, or can have happened, any longer . . . Now one is no more than an abstract line, like an arrow crossing the void. Absolute deterritorialization' (Deleuze and Guattari 1987, 199–200).

Paradoxical Normativity

Deleuze and Guattari's concepts are normative, not merely in the sense that any concept is normative by virtue of the manner in which it enables some inferences and disables others, but in the sense that they are the elements of a form of practical rather than theoretical reason.[5] They provide a framework within which to evaluate the character of particular events and processes. They enable us to pose question such as: is this negative or positive reterritorialization? Is this a genuine line of flight? Will it lead to a revolutionary new assemblage in which there is an increase of freedom or will it lead to a new form of capture or worse? (Deleuze and Parnet 1987, 143–4).

Several consequences follow from the normativity of Deleuze and Guattari's concepts. First, we can appreciate why a representationalist or empirical reading does not do justice to their analyses. The descriptive character of much of their work, along with the wealth of empirical material employed in the presentation of their concepts, creates a temptation to read them as proposing an empirical account of the affective, linguistic, and social world that we inhabit. In this manner, for example, Hardt and Negri take Deleuze and Guattari's account of capitalism as control by means of an axiomatic or set of variable relationships between the elements of production of surplus value as the basis for their understanding of contemporary society. In the same way, they take their analysis of the real subsumption of labor to capital and Deleuze's concept of 'control society' as the basis for their analysis of the 'material transformation' of the means of production of social reality under late capitalism (Hardt and Negri 2000, 22–5, 325–7). Thus, in relation to their analysis of the biopolitical production of subjectivity they comment that 'We are indebted to Deleuze and Guattari and their *A Thousand Plateaus* for the most fully elaborated phenomenological description of this industrial-monetary-world-nature, which constitutes the first level of the world order' (Hardt and Negri 2000, 424 n. 23).[6]

To be fair to Hardt and Negri, they do recognize that the concept of nomads is a normative rather than an empirical concept, the primary function of which is to express forces of resistance to the mechanisms of control which are 'capable of not only organizing the destructive power of the multitude, but also constituting through the desires of the multitude an alternative' (Hardt and Negri 2000, 214). Nor are they alone in succumbing to the temptation to assume that Deleuze and Guattari are engaged in a form of social science. Critics such as Christopher L. Miller rely on this assumption in criticizing the empirical bases of their concepts. Miller argues that their reliance upon anthropological sources in their discussion of nomadism commits them to an 'anthropological referentiality' which is compromised by the primitivist and colonialist character of those sources.[7]

Second, even though the basis of the framework of evaluation is assemblages rather than individuals, it does carry implications for how individuals should act. Foucault drew attention to this dimension of Deleuze and Guattari's machinic ontology when he famously compared *Anti-Oedipus* to St Francis de Sales' *Introduction to the Devout Life*: 'I would say that *Anti-Oedipus* (may its authors forgive me) is a book of ethics, the first book of ethics to be written in France in quite a long time' (Foucault 1977, xiii). Foucault went on to suggest that *Anti-Oedipus* could be taken to offer individual guidance in identifying and avoiding all the varieties of 'fascism' that entrap our desires and bind us to the forms of power that maintain systems of exploitation and domination. In this sense, he suggested, Deleuze and Guattari provide rules for the conduct of a non-fascist life: pursue thought and action by proliferation, juxtaposition, and disjunction rather than by hierarchization and subdivision; prefer positivity over negativity, difference over uniformity, nomadic or mobile assemblages over sedentary systems and so on (Foucault 1977, xiii–viv).

At several points in *A Thousand Plateaus*, as though in response to Foucault's provocation, Deleuze and Guattari assume the speaking position of this kind of practical ethicist. For example, when they offer guidance in the construction of a 'body without organs' (BwO):

> You don't do it with a sledgehammer, you use a very fine file. You invent self-destructions that have nothing to do with the death drive. Dismantling the organism has never meant killing yourself, but rather opening the body to connections that presuppose an entire assemblage, circuits, conjunctions, levels and thresholds, passages and distributions of intensity, and territories and deterritorializations measured with the craft of a surveyor . . . You have to keep enough of the organism for it to reform each dawn; and you have to keep small supplies of significance and subjectification, if only to turn them against their own systems when the circumstances demand it, when things, persons, even situations force you to; and you have to keep small rations of subjectivity in sufficient quantity to enable you to respond to the dominant reality. . . . (Deleuze and Guattari 1987, 160)[8]

Immediately after setting out such rules of conduct, however, Deleuze and Guattari go on to caution the reader of the dangers these carry and the need for further discrimination. In other words, they confound the suggestion that there are straightforward, unequivocal criteria by which one can lead a nonfascist life or construct one's own body without organs. The reason is that BwO's come in many guises; they exist already in the strata as well as in the destratified planes of consistency on which BwOs are formed, while the BwO formed on a plane of consistency can easily turn cancerous. The problem of evaluation and discrimination re-emerges at every stage: How can we fabricate a BwO for ourselves without its being the cancerous BwO of a fascist inside us, or the empty BwO of a drug addict, paranoiac, or hypochondriac? (Deleuze and Guattari 1987, 161).

For Deleuze and Guattari, this kind of ambivalence inheres in all of their concepts of life, creativity, and transformation. Consider the lines of flight along which individual or collective assemblages break down or become transformed. On the one hand, in so far as we are interested in bringing about change we cannot avoid experimentation with such lines because 'it is always on a line of flight that we create' (Deleuze and Parnet 1987, 135). In this sense, lines of flight are potential pathways of mutation in an individual or social fabric and sources of the affect associated with the passage from a lower to a higher state of power, namely joy. On the other hand, lines of flight have their own dangers. The danger is that, once having broken out of the limits imposed by the molar forms of segmentarity and subjectivity, a line of flight may fail to connect with the necessary conditions of creative development or be incapable of so connecting and turn instead into a line of destruction. When this happens, lines of flight or deterritorialization are a path to the most extreme failure and the affect associated with this passage to a lower state. They can become the source of 'a strange despair, like an odor of death and immolation, a state of war from which one returns broken' (Deleuze and Guattari 1987, 229).

Finally, we can draw a number of conclusions with regard to the kind of evaluation sustained by Deleuze and Guattari's practical philosophy: first, that it will be endless since one can never be certain about the final or true character of a given event or process. Kantian evaluation of the moral character of actions is also endless, but for a different reason. For Kant, we can never be entirely sure that we have acted out of duty and not out of some self-interested motive. This is an epistemological problem rather than a consequence of the equivocal character of the actions as it is for Deleuze and Guattari. In the evaluative schema of *A Thousand Plateaus*, nothing is unambiguously good or bad.

> Nothing's good in itself, it all depends on a careful systematic use. In *A Thousand Plateaus* we're trying to say you can never guarantee a good outcome (it's not enough just to have a *smooth space*, for example, to overcome striations and coercion, or a *body without organs* to overcome organizations). (Deleuze 1995, 32)

The potential danger and uncertainty associated with lines of flight is the primary justification for the essential prudence of Deleuzian politics. It is because we never know in advance which way a line of flight will turn, or whether a given set of heterogeneous elements will be able to form a consistent and functional multiplicity, that caution is necessary.

Second, evaluation will always be contextual or responsive to the character of the events and processes involved. It is for this reason that Deleuze and Guattari invoke Artaud's hostility to the judgment of God: the judgment of God stratifies the BwO of the body and makes it into an organism. It makes the BwO of desire into a subject. It implies a single unilateral frame of evaluation such as we find in Kant. Actions, in the end, fall either on the side of good or evil. For Deleuze, following Nietzsche and Artaud, things are never so simple. Actions take place between finite beings in particular circumstances. They are the outcome of a specific play of forces rather than universal requirements of rationality or freedom. They give rise to specific and local forms of obligation, antipathy, or attraction.

Third, the conditions of evaluation will lead to paradox. In this sense, even though they do not dwell on the aporetic character of the extreme form of the concepts outlined in *A Thousand Plateaus,* Deleuze and Guattari's practical philosophy resembles Derrida's deconstructive analysis of determinations of the will in general (decision). It is not difficult to find the elements of paradox in their characterization of the ambivalence of their concepts.[9] Consider the ambiguous status of relative deterritorialization which can be either positive or negative. It is negative when the deterritorialized element is immediately subjected to forms of reterritorialization that enclose or obstruct its line of flight. It is positive when the line of flight prevails over secondary reterritorializations, even though it may still fail to connect with other deterritorialized elements or enter into a new assemblage. Relative deterritorialization therefore can lead either to effective change or transformation within a given territory or system or to defeat and immediate reterritorialization. Since absolute deterritorialization is the underlying condition of relative deterritorialization in all its forms, it follows that it is both the condition of possibility of change and the condition of its impossibility.

This affinity with Derridean aporia is not unrelated to the contextual character of Deleuzian evaluation. They share an ethical orientation toward the event or the emergence of the new, where this implies a rupture with present actuality and its possible future forms. As Kant showed in his analysis of genius in art, the advent of the genuinely new implies the reorganization of rules for the production and evaluation of the work in question. By definition, we cannot know in advance what form this will take. This is why Deleuzian principles of evaluation are equivocal and open-ended: they are rules for the creation of the new. If they eschew general prescription this is because they answer to a pragmatic aim altogether different from that of universalizing judgment: 'to bring into existence and not to judge . . . What expert judgment, in art, could ever bear on the work to come?' (Deleuze 1997, 135).[10]

Toward a Deleuzian Theory of Right?

Within the domain of practical reason, Kant distinguishes between the ethical, in which the incentive to act in accordance with the moral law is bound up with the very idea of such a law, and the juridical, in which external incentives are attached to publicly promulgated laws. The theory of those laws for which only external incentives such as coercion by force or the threat of punishment is possible is what he calls the Doctrine of Right. It deals with the sum of the conditions under which the actions of individuals can be correlated in accordance with the freedom of each: 'Any action is right if it can coexist with everyone's freedom in accordance with a universal law . . .' (Kant 1996, 387). In turn, the theory of right may be divided into private right, which encompasses the laws regarding the behavior of individuals, which apply even in the absence of any public political authority, and which are necessary if their actions are to remain consistent with the freedom of others; and public right, which encompasses the system of laws needed in order that a multitude of human beings may live together in a civil condition (Kant 1996, 455).

In *Anti-Oedipus* and *A Thousand Plateaus*, Deleuze and Guattari do not directly address the political domain of public right. They consider the different forms of modern government only from the Marxist perspective of their subordination to the axioms of capitalist production. From this point of view, authoritarian, socialist, and liberal democratic states are considered equivalent to one another insofar as they function as models of realization of the global axiomatic of capital. They allow that there are important differences between the various modern forms of state, but provide little discussion of these differences. Equally, they point to the importance of the changes to the majoritarian order or public right that come about through struggles for civil and political rights, for equality of economic condition and opportunity, for regional and national autonomy and so on, but offer no normative theory of the basis of such rights or the kinds and degrees of equality that should prevail.

Instead, they focus on the minoritarian becomings that provide the affective impetus for such struggles (Deleuze and Guattari 1987, 470–1). On their view, the source of political creativity must always be traced back to subterranean shifts in allegiance, attitude, sensibility, and belief on the part of individuals and groups. These give expression to the multitude of ways in which people deviate from the majoritarian standard against which their rights and duties as citizens are measured. At the same time, the significance of such minoritarian becomings for public political right depends on their being translated into new forms of right and different statuses for individuals and groups: 'molecular escapes and movements would be nothing if they did not return to the molar organizations to reshuffle their segments, their binary distributions of sexes, classes and parties' (Deleuze and Guattari 1987, 216–17).

Under the influence of Marxist approaches to politics, they focus on the conditions of revolutionary social change rather than the conditions of maintaining political society as a fair system of cooperation between its members. At the same time, they reject key tenets of Marxist social and political theory. They insist that social change is brought about by movements of deterritorialization and lines of flight rather than class contradictions. Their rejection of the organizational and tactical forms of traditional Marxist politics is definitively expressed at the end of *Dialogues* when Deleuze and Parnet abandon the concept of revolution defined by the capture of State power in favor of a new concept of *revolutionary-becoming* (Deleuze and Parnet 1987, 147). Revolutionary-becoming must be understood in the light of Deleuze and Guattari's concern with the emergence of the new or the advent of the truly Other as Derrida would say. This Other is irreducible to the possible future forms of the actual present. Becoming revolutionary is therefore a matter of finding the lines of flight that undermine the existing order and trace the outlines of the new.[11]

In this manner, even though they offer neither descriptive nor normative accounts of macro-political institutions and procedures, Deleuze and Guattari provide a language in which to describe micro-political movements and infra-political processes that give rise to new forms of constitutional and legal order. The concepts they invent thus bear indirectly upon the forms of public right. Concepts such as becoming-minor, nomadism, smooth space, and lines of flight or deterritorialization are not meant as substitutes for existing concepts of freedom, equality, or justice but they are intended to assist the emergence of another justice, new kinds of equality and freedom as well as new kinds of political differentiation and constraint.

From the point of view of political evaluation, we find in relation to these movements of becoming, deterritorialization, or the production of smooth space the same kind of indeterminacy and ambivalence that arises in relation to the ethical judgment of individual transformations. Smooth spaces are like lines of flight or deterritorialization in that, although they do not amount to spaces of pure freedom, they are nevertheless the kind of space that can lead to the transformation of existing institutions or the displacement of the goals of political conflict. Emergences of smooth spaces are conditions under which 'life reconstitutes its stakes, confronts new obstacles, invents new paces, switches adversaries' (Deleuze and Guattari 1987, 500). However, in accordance with the ambivalence which is always present in Deleuzian evaluation, we must always assess what kind of smooth space we are dealing with: is it one which has been captured by State forces or one which results from the dissolution of a striated space? Does it allow more or less freedom of movement? Above all, we should never believe 'that a smooth space will suffice to save us' (Deleuze and Guattari 1987, 500).[12]

Becoming-Democratic

What is Philosophy? offers no more direct account of principles of public right. The focus in this book is on the political vocation of philosophy, where this is aligned with the struggle against capitalism: 'Philosophy takes the relative deterritorialization of capital to the absolute; it makes it pass over the plane of immanence as movement of the infinite and suppresses it as internal limit, *turns it back against itself so as to summon forth a new earth, a new people*' (Deleuze and Guattari 1994, 99). Elements of Deleuze and Guattari's Marxism remain in their diagnosis of the present, for example their analysis of the isomorphic but heterogeneous character of all states with regard to the global capitalist axiomatic. From this perspective, they suggest that even the most democratic states are compromised by their role in the production of human misery alongside great wealth: 'What social democracy has not given the order to fire when the poor come out of their territory or ghetto?' (Deleuze and Guattari 1994, 107). They maintain their commitment to the revolutionary-becoming of people rather than the traditional Marxist concept of revolution, even as they point out that the concept of revolution is itself a philosophical creation.

However, at this point, something new appears in Deleuze and Guattari's political lexicon. On the one hand, the concept of becoming-revolutionary is defined in terms of people's relationship to a philosophical concept, where the primary example is not drawn from Lenin but from Kant's distinction between the bloody events which took place in Paris in 1789 and people's enthusiasm for the idea of a constitutional state which enshrined the equal rights of men and citizens.[13] On the other hand, they contrast the actual universality of the market with the virtual universality of a global democratic state and call for resistance to the present in the name of a 'becoming-democratic that is not to be confused with present constitutional states' (Deleuze and Guattari 1994, 113; translation modified). They describe their own political philosophy as reterritorialized on a new earth and a people to come, unlike those found in actually existing democracies. The many critical remarks about actually existing democracies in this book leave open the possibility that other actualizations of the concept of democracy might be possible. In this sense, Deleuze's later political thought explicitly presupposes a concept of becoming-democratic or democracy to come.

But what does this mean and what role does this concept play? One way in which philosophy's task of counter-actualizing the world might be achieved is through the invention or reinvention of concepts such as revolution and democracy. *What is Philosophy?* does not offer a renewed concept of democracy in the light of which we might point out the ways in which present incarnations are inadequate to the pure event of democracy. However, it does suggest other ways in which a Deleuzian practice of philosophy might assist a becoming-democratic, for example through the account that it gives of the relationship between philosophy and opinion.

One of the elements of a theory of public right according to contemporary democratic theorists is a theory of public reason. Given that the goal of political association is to determine a collective will as the basis for laws and public policy, then these principles will govern public debate with a view to such collective decisions.[14] Where do these principles come from? One answer, given by John Rawls, is to say that the ultimate foundation for such principles lies in the considered judgments or opinions of the people concerned (Rawls 1985). For Rawls, the theory of justice and the conditions of a well-ordered society must be tested against the considered judgments of the society. These judgments are not reducible to the day-to-day opinions of citizens. They are expressed in the institutions and in the constitutional and legal settlements of the society. They set limits to the conduct of public debate and provide the normative framework within which disagreements can be settled, or at least kept within reasonable bounds so as not to threaten the political order.

Rawls' liberal conception of democratic politics therefore implies a distinction between two kinds or levels of opinion: considered judgments about right ways of acting, as embodied in institutions and historical documents, and everyday opinions on matters of current concern or public policy. Deleuze and Guattari also draw a distinction between everyday opinions on matters of current concern and the opinions embedded in the national characteristics of a people, their conceptions of right, and their practical philosophy as this is expressed in political and legal institutions. In the context of their all too brief account of what they call 'geophilosophy,' they ask at one point whether philosophy in its present critical form is closely aligned with 'the modern democratic state and human rights' (Deleuze and Guattari 1994, 102). In reply, they point out that there is no universal democratic state since the market is the only thing that is universal under capitalism. There are only particular 'nationalitarian' philosophies reterritorialized on particular forms of democratic state, the contours of which are determined in part by the philosophical 'opinions' of the peoples concerned (Deleuze and Guattari 1994, 102–4). These 'nationalitarian' opinions about what is right, fair, and just will constrain the institutional and legal actualization of democratic ideals in a given society. It follows that the form in which modern democratic states appear will be determined in part by the philosophical opinions of the people or peoples concerned. In addition, to the extent that modern democratic states function as models of realization of the immanent axiomatic of global capitalism, they will be constrained by their subordination to the requirements of this system. That is an important part of the reason why 'our democracies' do not provide optimum conditions for resistance to the present or the constitution of new earths and new peoples. The consensus of opinions in these societies all too often reflects 'the cynical perceptions and affections of the capitalist' (Deleuze and Guattari 1994, 108, 146).

The task of political philosophy is defined by Deleuze and Rawls alike in terms of its relationship with philosophical or considered opinion. However, the important question is what kind of relationship philosophy has to opinion understood in this way? One model of critical engagement with *doxa* is provided by classical Greek philosophy. Deleuze and Guattari describe this as a dialectic that constructs an ideal or tribunal before which the truth-value of different opinions can be assessed. They suggest that while this dialectic purports to extract a form of knowledge from opinions, opinion continually breaks through so that in the end 'philosophy remains a doxography' (Deleuze and Guattari 1994, 80). Rawls' political liberalism provides another model of engagement with opinion, one that does not attempt to gauge the truth or falsity of opinions but rather seeks to reconstruct the considered opinions of an historically specific form of society in order to render them systematic and coherent. In this way, it produces a concept of a fair and just society, subject to the qualification that this concept might change as the considered opinions of the society change.[15]

Deleuze and Guattari's 'utopian' conception of philosophy implies a more critical relation to opinion. Their conception of the political vocation of philosophy as helping to bring about 'new earths and new peoples' suggests more extravagant ambitions than Rawls' realistic utopianism. It points to their focus on critical engagement with and transformation of considered opinions rather than their systematic reconstruction. That is why, in the brief exergue to *Negotiations*, Deleuze presents philosophy as engaged in a 'guerilla campaign' against public opinion and other powers that be such as religions and laws (Deleuze 1995). Success in this kind of political philosophy is not measured by the test of reflective equilibrium or by the capacity to maintain a well-ordered society but by the capacity of its concepts to engage with and assist movements of deterritorialization in the present. Deleuze's criticisms of the inequalities produced by capitalism might be understood in this light. They challenge existing opinions about what is acceptable with the aim of extending and developing equality of condition within contemporary societies. Such criticism must engage with forms of becoming-revolutionary that are immanent and active in present social and political life if they are to assist in opening up paths to the invention of new forms of individual and collective life.

The concepts of becoming-revolutionary and becoming-democratic together define the novel normativity of Deleuze's later political philosophy. Deleuze's support for 'jurisprudence,' understood as the invention of new rights, indicates how these two becomings might converge in effective political change: revolutionary-becomings provide the micro-political basis on which new rights may emerge. In turn, these become incorporated into the moral and legal order of existing democracies, thereby extending their responsiveness to the will of individuals and groups affected by new technologies, new therapeutic and other practices (Deleuze 1995, 169–70). Becoming-revolutionary and becoming-democratic do not specify a determinate state of affairs that we should strive to bring about, like the 'just constitutional regime' which Rawls takes to be the object of political endeavor (Rawls 1993, 93). Like all the concepts that philosophy invents or reinvents in order to counter-actualize the present, these do not simply represent an actual state of affairs. They are nevertheless concepts of practical reason in the sense that they give expression to a pure event of revolution and a pure event of democracy. The 'pure event' of democracy points toward future as yet unrealized forms of democracy, but also reminds us that there is no definitive form that will ever arrive. In the same way, the pure event of revolution is not reducible to the events of actual historical uprisings. In each case, it is not the concept of an actual or potential existing democracy or revolutions but rather 'the contour' or 'the configuration' of an event that remains perpetually to come (Deleuze and Guattari 1994, 32–3).

Notes

* This paper was presented at 'The Living Thought of Gilles Deleuze' International Conference, Copenhagen, November 3–5, 2005. It has benefited from discussions with many of the participants but in particular Gene Holland, Dan Smith, and Ken Surin.

1 'A philosophy is what Félix and I tried to produce in *Anti-Oedipus* and *A Thousand Plateaus*, especially in *A Thousand Plateaus*, which is a long book putting forward many concepts' (Deleuze 1995, 136).

2 Deleuze and Guattari argue that the concept 'has no *reference*: it is self-referential, it posits itself and its object at the same time as it is created' (Deleuze and Guattari 1994, 22).

3 For detailed rebuttal of Mengue's charge of anti-democratic tendencies in Deleuze and Guattari, see Patton 2005*a*, 2005*b*.

4 In *Deleuze and the Political*, I call this 'critical freedom' in order to distinguish it from liberal concepts of positive and negative freedom (Patton 2000, 83–7).

5 On the normativity of concepts, see Brandom.

6 Similarly, Negri's review of *A Thousand Plateaus* described this book as offering 'a perfectly operational phenomenology of the present' (Negri 1995, 108).

7 See Miller (1988), 'Beyond identity: The postidentitarian predicament in *A Thousand Plateaus*,' in *Nationalists and Nomads: Essays on Francophone African Literature and Culture* (Chicago and London: The University of Chicago Press), 171–244. This chapter is a slightly revised version of 'The postidentitarian predicament in the footnotes of *A Thousand Plateaus*: Nomadology, anthropology, and authority,' *Diacritics* 23(3), 1993, 6–35. See also the exchange between Miller and Eugene Holland over the question of the referential status of Deleuze and Guattari's concepts in *Research in African Literatures* 34(1), Spring 2003, 159–73; 34(3), Fall 2003, 129–41; 34(4), Winter 2003, 187–90.

8 See May (2005), 151–3.

9 At one point, they refer to the 'paradox' of fascism understood in terms of the ambiguity of the line of flight (Deleuze and Guattari 1987, 230).

10 For further discussion of similarities between the political philosophies of Deleuze and Derrida, see Patton 2003*a*, 2003*b*.

11 Kenneth Surin elaborates on the difference between the question of revolution posed in terms of the actual and the question of becoming-revolutionary posed in terms of the virtual in commenting on Deleuze's 'Immanence: A life' (Surin 2005). He suggests that the question whether revolution is possible is uninteresting when posed in terms of the actual because it cannot encompass the truly revolutionary break with the actual. Only the question posed in terms of the virtual can encompass the conditions under which absolute deterritorialization is manifest in positive form, leading to new kinds of social assemblage, new earths, and new peoples.

12 Eyal Weizman provides a striking example of the political polyvalence of the concept of smooth space in his paper 'Walking through Walls' (Weizmann 2005). He describes the Israeli military tactic of literally walking through walls and presents evidence in the forms of interviews with IDF officers to show that

they draw upon Deleuze and Guattari's concepts of smooth and striated space in order to theorize this tactic.

¹³ Deleuze and Guattari refer to Kant's discussion of this in *The Contest of Faculties* Part 2 section 6 and to commentaries on this text by Foucault, Habermas, and Lyotard (Deleuze and Guattari 1994, 224 n.13).

¹⁴ Mengue is undoubtedly correct to point out that this amounts to a properly political or 'doxological' plane of immanence on which it is not concepts, percepts, or affects that are produced but 'solidarity and consensus regarding what is to be done here and now' (Mengue 2003, 52). He is also correct to suggest that the absence of any account of specifically political reason is a shortcoming of the tripartite division of thought outline in *What is Philosophy?*, and to point out that this absence is not necessary: Deleuzian concepts readily lend themselves to at least a descriptive account of public reason. The formation of consensus or 'right opinion' can be understood as the outcome of a specific and rhizomatic play of opinions, expert advice, interests, and values such that it 'operates a veritable deterritorialization of opinion' (Mengue 2003, 53). Such collective decision-making involves the reterritorialization of opinion on an idea or set of ideas of the public good.

¹⁵ Rawls admits this dependency of the principles of justice on current knowledge and the existing scientific consensus and concedes that 'as established beliefs change, it is possible that the principles of justice which it seems rational to choose may likewise change' (Rawls 1973, 548).

References

Brandom, R. (2001), 'Reason, Expression and the Philosophic Enterprise,' in C. P. Ragland and S. Heidt (eds), *What is Philosophy?* (New Haven and London: Yale University Press), 74–95.

Deleuze, G. (1980), Interview with Catherine Clement, 'Entretien 1980,' L'Arc no. 49, rev. edn, pp. 99–102.

—(1995), *Negotiations 1972–1990*, trans. Martin Joughin (Columbia: University of Columbia Press).

—(1997), *Essays Critical and Clinical*, trans. Daniel W. Smith and Michael A. Greco (Minneapolis: University of Minnesota Press).

Deleuze, G. and Guattari, F. (1987), *A Thousand Plateaus: Capitalism and Schizophrenia*, trans. Brian Massumi (Minneapolis: University of Minnesota Press).

—(1994), *What is Philosophy?*, trans. Hugh Tomlinson and Graham Burchell (New York: Columbia University Press).

Deleuze, G. and Parnet, C. (1987), *Dialogues*, trans. Hugh Tomlinson and Barbara Habberjam (London: Athlone Press).

Foucault, M. (1977), 'Preface', *Deleuze and Guattari, Anti-Oedipus: Capitalism and Schizophrenia*, trans. Robert Hurley, Mark Seem and Helen R. Lane (New York: Viking Press).

Hardt, M. and Negri, A. (2000), *Empire* (Harvard: Harvard University Press).

Kant, I. (1996), *Practical Philosophy*, Cambridge Edition of the Works of Immanuel Kant,translated and edited by Mary J. Gregor (Cambridge: Cambridge University Press).

May, T. (2005), *Gilles Deleuze: An Introduction* (Cambridge: Cambridge University Press).

Mengue, P. (2003), *Deleuze et la question de la démocratie* (Paris: L'Harmattan).

Negri, A. (1995), 'On Gilles Deleuze and Félix Guattari's *A Thousand Plateaus.* *Chimères* 17 (Fall 1995).

Patton, P. (2000), *Deleuze and the Political* (London and New York: Routledge).

—(2003*a*), 'Future Politics' in Patton and Protevi (eds), *Between Deleuze and Derrida* (London and New York: Continuum), 15–29.

—(2003*b*), 'Concept and politics in Derrida and Deleuze,' *Critical Horizons* 4(2), October, 157–75.

—(2005*a*), 'Deleuze and Democratic Politics,' in Lars Tønder and Lasse Thomassen (eds), *On Radical Democracy: Politics Between Abundance and Lack* (Manchester: Manchester University Press).

—(2005*b*), 'Deleuze and democracy,' *Contemporary Political Theory* 4(4), December, 400–13.

Rawls, J. (1971), *A Theory of Justice* (Cambridge, MA: Harvard University Press).

—(1985), 'Justice as fairness: political and metaphysical,' *Philosophy and Public Affairs* 14, 223–57.

—(1993), *Political Liberalism* (Columbia University Press).

Surin, K. (2005), 'The Socius and Life,' paper presented at 'The Living Thought of Gilles Deleuze' International Conference, Copenhagen, November 3–5.

Weizman, E. (2005), 'Walking Through Walls,' paper presented at 'Cosmopolitanism and Design' Conference, University of Technology, Sydney, October 21–22.

Chapter 14

Gilles Deleuze's Politics
From Marxism to the Missing People

Alain Beaulieu

Deleuze imbues his entire body of work with a political character, without ever synthesizing his political thought in any one specific work. We propose to bridge this gap by clarifying the nature of the Marxist orientation of Deleuze's thought, showing how capitalism acts as an apparatus of repression on the 'desiring machines,' examining the reasons that led Deleuze to declare war on the state, and commenting on the statement according to which 'the people are missing.'

Marxist Without Being Marxist

Deleuze is among the fiercest opponents of the globalization of Capitalism and the democratic state. His criticism is a continuous resistance to Neo-Liberal invasion, but also denounces any form of political organization, whether this organization is intended to form absolutist and totalitarian, universal democratic, or reactively anarchic power. Deleuze never presented his political thinking succinctly in any specific work, though he always considered that politics covered his entire body of work. Unlike the majority of the French intelligentsia in the 1950s and 1960s, he never joined the Communist party. In the twilight of his life, he was nonetheless planning a book on the 'Greatness of Marx.'[1]

This paradox—which makes Deleuze a 'Marxist without being Marxist'—illustrates the singular direction of the political orientation of Deleuze's thinking. In an article cosigned by a group of activist-intellectuals, Deleuze states his support for certain actions of the militant Left while denouncing terrorism led by the Italian Left in the mid-1970s and the repression exercised on this same Italian Left by the government in power.[2] This position loses its contradiction if we consider Deleuze's critique of Marxism. Deleuze refuses to believe that noisy revolutions or 'great events' are necessary to emancipate those whose rights have been curbed by dominant thinking. The great revolutions have often turned to catastrophes, he reasons: The English Revolution sparked fanatic wars led by Cromwell, the French Revolution caused the excess of the Terror regime, the Russian Revolution created goulags, the American Revolution globalized the economy, and so on. Deleuze condemns these great liberation movements that, more often that not, lead to systems of power worse than those that preceded them.

If Deleuze wanted to create his own 'line of flight' out of the cycle of revolution, it is not because he refused to struggle. On the contrary, his entire philosophy can be seen as a continuous fight led by 'war machines.' What kind of revolutionary movement did Deleuze encourage? The leftist agitations Deleuze supported are those that promoted a notion of power (*puissance/potentia*) independent from any will of domination (*pouvoir/potestas*). This follows the distinction we find in Latin—a language from which Spinoza drew the most fascinating consequences—between *potestas*, understood as a way to exercise control over individuals, and *potentia*, understood as a desire to be affected in various ways.[3] The goal of the Deleuzian insurrection against the state is not that of bringing an ideal power into the hands of the dominated, but rather that of situating political debate in the process of creating a yet inexistent nation-state and an unconstituted people.

The flattening of desire into an appetite for consumption stems from massive adhesion to the Neo-Liberal regime that conditions our democracy. Deleuze denounces this desire to consume the market's objects as one of the most degrading inventions and shameful and incessant compromises that humanity created. This test of shame is the engine behind Deleuze's political thinking: '[The feeling of shame] is one of the most powerful incentives toward philosophy, and it's what makes all philosophy political.'[4] As we will see, art is a privileged ally in confronting this feeling of shame for Deleuze, who developed his political thinking not only through philosophy (Spinoza, Nietzsche) and various resistance movements (mental illness, nomads, Palestine, etc.), but most especially from writers and filmmakers. Deleuze places Kafka, Straub, Perrault, and Godard with those who best succeed in thinking about the *malaise* in contemporary politics; in other words, democracy itself as a neutralization of the *potentia*. Real leftist agitations pass through art.

Capitalism and Schizophrenia

In *Anti-Œdipus*, Deleuze and Guattari orient their attacks simultaneously against psychoanalysis and Capitalism. They criticize psychoanalysis for not taking the investment of desire in the social field into account. The 'family novel,' or 'familialism,' of psychoanalysis never ceases to direct the desire of the Œdipian triangle to lower personal issues by connecting them to harmful liaisons with the father or mother. This personalist vision of desire is no longer applicable to a thinking in the case of which the desiring and delirious energy

occurs in the social fields from the start. We desire the construction of collective arrangements of enunciation, Deleuze maintains, long before we come
to desire our parents: *'Délire* is world-historical, nothing to do with the family.
It fastens on the Chinese, the Germans, Joan of Arc and the Great Mogul,
Aryans and Jews, money, power, and production. Not on mommy and daddy
at all' (N, 23). Deleuze and Guattari recognize the merit of Capitalism, which
favors society's economic values, in articulating the desire of the social field.
However, they also denounce the despotic organization by which Capitalism
administers the flow of monetary and material desires. Of course, desire flows
in the Capitalist regime: there are deposits and withdrawals of money, loans
and reimbursements, investments, production and sales, and so on. But this
monetary fluctuation is always focused on the desire of more value.

Psychoanalysis ignores the social nature of desire while Neo-Liberalism
makes capital the only possible means of investing desire. At first, these two
critiques seem independent. However, Deleuze and Guattari are denouncing
one single misunderstanding of desire. Indeed, psychoanalysis and Capitalism
both play exemplary parts in the universal history of the repression of desire.
Psychoanalysis and Capitalism have little nuance, as they are shameful and predefined means of channeling desire. Psychoanalytic therapy asks the patient
to confess a pre-existing Œdipal complex, whereas Capitalism 'pre-orients'
desire to profit and consumption. Besides, we clearly recognize the defense of
individualist values, which appear simultaneously in Capitalism's praise of personal affairs and the intimacy of the Freudian Œdipus. Capitalism produces
many Œdipus who, in turn, feed Capitalism. This is why we cannot speak of
the repression of desire by one of these elements without also mentioning the
crushing of desire by the other.

How can this repression be countered? This is one of the core questions
Deleuze and Guattari ask in *Anti-Œdipus*. And this is their answer: To free
desire/*potentia*, one has to identify the dark common denominator of psychoanalysis and Capitalism. And this common denominator, which Freud
and Neo-Liberals have hid, is schizophrenia. Indeed, the schizophrenic is
excluded from the Capitalist system and this also indicates the limitations of
psychoanalysis. Par excellence, the schizophrenic is unable to find a place in
the market economy and has an unconscious that is unknown to psychoanalytic theories. In other words, schizophrenic thought as a conceptual persona
is not profitable for business and its delirium exceeds the scope of couch therapy. The schizophrenic persona corresponds perfectly to the untimely figure
that Deleuze and Guattari needed in order to develop a theory of the functioning of desire that doubles as political thought.

Many interpretations stumble into nonsense by presenting schizophrenic
desire—neutralized by Capitalism and psychoanalysis—as a clinical reality. This mistake can be avoided if we consider the Deleuzo-Guattarian

schizophrenization of desire not as a medical state (the 'hospital schizo'), but rather as a process. In the *Abécédaire* (Letter D), Deleuze reminds the reader that he never encouraged the production of 'shadow men.' What interested Deleuze and Guattari is the way by which the schizophrenic persona experiments with the intensity and *potentia* of desire. Like a machine, the schizophrenic functioning of desire can fail and break down at any time. Mechanized desire takes into account this discontinuity of desire, which flows without any predefined form of organization. Mechanized desire is disjunctive by its leaps and unexpected and sudden ruptures. Thus, it is a vital force that does not heed any law of predefined meaning, including Œdipal signification and maximized profits, of course. This conception of desire involves an absolute deterritorialization that escapes the structuring and counter-productive repression that is characteristic of the psychoanalytic and Capitalistic representations of desire. Yet a danger remains: the reterritorialization of desire with the creation of a political state (i.e. the transformation of *potentia* into *potestas*).

Struggle Against the State

Deleuze's condemnation of the Capitalist and democratic state is an extension of Marx's and Nietzsche's anti-state visions. From a Marxist standpoint, the state must be abolished because it only serves the interests of the bourgeois who wish to keep the proletarian class in chains.[5] Nietzsche breaks with the democratic regime because of its decadent Egalitarian ideal and dismissal of an emerging Superman able to create a new system of values.[6]

According to the universal history presented in *Anti-Œdipus*, the state, dominated by a sovereign, belongs to the past. This type of state does not have to be abolished simply because its end has already occurred. The Capitalist age gives way to an era of despotic regimes unified by a monarch figure. The universal is no longer represented by a supreme chief; it is now the market and its rules that dominate the universal (N, 172; WiPh, 106). However, the desire for the state does not disappear completely from Neo-Liberal regimes. It simply takes a new form, leaving room for something even worse than a sovereign-dominated state. This most fearful something is the democratization of a despotism, the norms of which are dictated by the market. The sole tyrant of the former despotic regime now leaves room for a multiplicity of despotic entrepreneurs. Deleuze and Guattari see here the resurgence of the old desire of *Urstaat*, the supreme state: 'Decoded flows strike the despotic State with latency; they submerge the tyrant, but they also cause him to return in unexpected forms; they democratize him, oligarchize him, segmentalize him, monarchize him, and always internalize and spiritualize him, while on the horizon there is the latent Urstaat, for the loss of which there is no consolation.'[7] The struggle has to be led against each and every *Urstaat*, including its new globalized and democratized form, which Deleuze characterizes as Neo-Fascism:

> The new fascism is not the politics and the economy of war. It is global agreement on security, on the maintenance of a 'peace' just as terrifying as war. All our petty fears will be organized in concert, all our petty anxieties will be harnessed to make micro-fascists of us; we will be called upon to stifle every little thing, every suspicious face, every dissonant voice, in our streets, in our neighborhoods, in our local theaters.[8]

In *A Thousand Plateaus*, this discourse of struggle against the *Urstaat* becomes more specific and intense. *Anti-Œdipus'* struggle against Capitalism and psychoanalysis expands in such a way that the notion of the state now covers all organizational forms surrounding any particular figure. Thus, Husserl becomes the state leader of phenomenology, Freud becomes the state leader of psychoanalysis, and so on. As soon as an immovable structure is put into place (scholar hierarchy, desire for capital, border limits, etc.), a sedentarization occurs or the limits of a territory are drawn and one faces a state apparatus. Deleuze and Guattari are not merely struggling against the specific apparatus of Capitalism, they are also and most especially developing a real and effective model of struggle that is able to counter the various forms of hierarchized organization that block the unpredictable movement of vital *potentia*.

   A Thousand Plateaus' anti-state struggle offers a complex network of conceptual ramifications. Let us concentrate on the distinction between two types of space: smooth and striated. This opposition is part of the broader inquiry of spatiality, which is a way of denouncing the inflation of time and history that has governed philosophy from Hegelian idealism to the Hermeneutic thought, by way of Heideggerian ontology. Deleuze and Guattari side with the second of Nietzsche's *Untimely Meditations*. 'The history is one with the triumph of States.'[9] Indeed, History is more willing to describe the triumph of those who have imposed their law than those who were able to struggle in the shadows. The 'resistors' or—in keeping with the glossary of *A Thousand Plateaus*—the 'nomads' are living in a smooth space without borders. On the other hand, the state stratifies and divides its territory not only to impose external limits, but to rule over interior movement and thus better control it. There is constant rivalry between state administrators and nomads. The former try to control migration while the latter follow their stateless instinct:

> One of the fundamental task of the State, write Deleuze and Guattari, is to striate the space over which it reigns, or to utilize smooth spaces as a means of communication in the service of striated space. It is a vital concern of every State not only to vanquish nomadism but to control migrations and,

more generally, to establish a zone of rights over an entire 'exterior,' over all of the flows traversing the ecumenon. (TP, 385)

Nomads must fight the state apparatus of capture and sedentarization; they must create war machines as tools in the struggle against territorialization. The war machine is to the nomad as the striating state is to the despot (TP, chap. 12). He who says nomad also says nomadic people. Nomads share gregarious instinct. And what of the group of nomads? We know that it is a group of resistors. As Neo-Liberal ideology becomes more and more dominant, where does this group of stateless nomads hide? Deleuze's answer: This people is missing; it is even what is missing the most.

The Missing People

Deleuze frequently returns to the theme of a people that does not yet exist. Is this a hope or an announcement? A utopic dream or a prophesy? Deleuze does not pretend to invent the idea of a missing people. All those who have been sensitive to the people's absence—a group to which Deleuze belongs—come from the world of the arts: the poet Mallarmé and the painter Klee,[10] the dramaturge Carmelo Bene[11] and several post-war filmmakers (C2, 215–24). But it is first and foremost from Kafka that the Deleuzian analysis of the missing people stems. Both modest office worker and real visionary situated at the crossroads of Czech, German, and Yiddish cultures, Kafka is one of the twentieth-century writers who shook political consciousness with the most endurance. Some analysts even saw one of the causes of the Spring of Prague[12] in two conference series organized in the 1960s in Eastern Europe to liberate Kafka from his anti-Socialist interpretation.

It is from a note in Kafka's journal that Deleuze explains his concept of a missing people:

> . . . literature is less a concern of literary history than of the people [. . .] Even though the personal affair (*einzelne Angelegenheit*) is often thought calmly, one still does not reach the boundary where it connects up with similar affairs, one reaches this boundary soonest in politics, indeed, one even strives to see it before it is there, and often sees this limiting boundary everywhere. [. . .] What in great literature goes on down below, constituting a not indispensable cellar of the structure, here takes place in the full light of the day, what is there a matter of passing interest for a few, here absorbs everyone no less than as a matter of life and death.[13]

For Kafka, literature, which is able to go beyond individual expression by taking the affairs of a stateless people in hand, is the surest way of going about

politics. Such literature is no longer the work of one person, Deleuze and
Guattari comment, but that of a collectivity. It expresses the 'collective assemblage of enunciations.'[14] Kafka qualifies this literature of a forming people as
minor.[15] 'Collective assemblage of enunciations' is therefore not the result of
deliberation. It goes beyond the private without, however, falling back on the
public sphere. The problem with the public arena is not only that it is not open
to all and excludes some groups; it is rather that it denies or ignores the pre-
language stage of experimenting with deterritorializing powers that naturally
elude discursive rationality. Deleuze does not believe that a model should be
developed that is institutionalized and continually better at 'bracketing' social
inequalities and developing, for public discourse, inclusive structures more apt
at defining the common good. The public sphere remains a dominated space.
The use of a public 'counter-space'—a parallel space for discussion—must face
the same insufficiencies. Public or counter-public, rational discourse seeks
to transcend the immanence (law, order, norm, constitution, etc.) and fails
the immanent experiment of the impersonal powers of deterritorialization.
'Collective assemblage of enunciations' eludes the insufficiencies associated
with the private sphere's egoism and the public sphere's transcendency, speaking not in the name of, but for, a people of nomads who are destined to never
constitute a nation-state.

The relationships Kafka established between politics and literature provide
the primary motivation for a missing people to exist; they must invent a minor
language able to resist the dominant language. The major language organizes this evolution by launching orders, imposing borders on a territory, and
smothering all present capacity of resistance. And today the language of the
democratic regime plays the role of the major language. It is democratic declarations with universal pretensions that must be resisted.

> *We lack resistance to the present.* [. . .] Art and philosophy converge at this point:
> the constitution of an earth and a people that are lacking as the correlate of
> creation. [. . .] Democracies are majorities, but a becoming is by nature that
> which always eludes the majority. (WiPh, 108)

In a pragmatic way, Kafka incarnates the idea of resistance in the present
moment, through a literature that is stripped of all desire for domination.
He does not call for the coming of a people made up of revolutionaries able
to overturn the huge social and diabolical machines that were multiplying
at the dawn of the twentieth century: the Capitalistic American, the bureaucratic Russian, and the Nazi German. If Kafka did not adopt a fundamentally
destructive tone regarding the realities he described, it is because he did not
believe in the idea of new beginnings. In his short stories and novels, Kafka
does not identify with any party that exists or is being formed, and he shows
no revolutionary desire founded in predetermined ideology. Precisely, therein

lies the strength of commitment of Kafka, who was aware of the emerging political trends of his time and predicted the totalitarian aspect of each one. He denounces the repressive nature of the great ideological innovations of his century to better hear the voice of a missing people, a collectivity whose greatness lay precisely in its incapacity to partake in mass politics. It is as if the only worthy politics could spring from the excluded margins, from which real emancipation—a liberation of powers—becomes possible.

Following Benjamin and Adorno, Deleuze criticized the lack of creation in the resistance to the present and saw a need for politicizing art.[16] Deleuze was fascinated by artists when they establish a connection between art and politics, while maintaining their distance from the widely held opinions of their era: 'For the race summoned forth by art or philosophy is not the one that claims to be pure but rather an oppressed, bastard, lower, anarchical, nomadic, and irremediably minor race' (WiPh, 109). It is no surprise then if Deleuze shows such great admiration for the Palestinians, a stateless people deprived of a territory.[17] Nor is it a surprise when Deleuze condemns the ideology of human rights, which he feels is ultimately the protection of the rights of Western entrepreneurs without regard for singular creations: 'Rights save neither men nor a philosophy that is reterritorialized on the democratic State. Human rights will not make us bless capitalism [. . .] Human rights say nothing about the immanent modes of existence of people provided with rights' (WiPh, 107).[18] It is precisely to these exceptions that the minor language attempts to bestow rights.

When it becomes political, modern cinema also has the capacity to show us a missing people of unique resistors (C2). One of the primary differences between classic cinema of the first half of the century and modern cinema is its political nature. Eisenstein's films show a people in the heights of revolution. Assemblies, coups d'état, political overthrows, hostage taking of presidential palace, and the like. These actions are at the very core of Eisenstein's revolutionary cinema. The first American cinema, through Griffith's works and the Western, also filmed the constitution of a new society. This cinema is in contrast to the militant cinema of the post-war era when the people had disappeared. Filmmakers like Straub, Godard, and Quebecer Pierre Perrault no longer show people in action; rather, they portray isolated individuals for whom, a bit like Kafka, the line has been smudged between the political and the private. They no longer act collectively; they experiment individually with the absence of any institutionalized, nationalized, or static sense of the collective. Modern political cinema no longer shows the revolution at work, but rather the impossibility of giving life to an identity-based and homogenous nation.

For Deleuze, 'great politics'—to borrow Nietzsche's expression—only occur when singularities, unorganized as a people, find themselves in the middle of a creative process. In this context, political desire persists while revolutions and the quest for a new order work inevitability to form despotic states. It is in the assumption of this tension between desire for the creation of a people and the danger of the establishment of a state that the greatest challenge posed by Deleuzian political thought resides: 'As we know, the revolutionary problem today is to find some unity in our various struggles without falling back on the despotic and bureaucratic organization of the party or State apparatus.'[19]

No dream of absolute emancipation underlies Deleuze's political ideas. Like philosophy, politics is a process of creation that is exempt from any finality. In reading Foucault, Deleuze retained that the machines of power constantly change shape while always pursuing the same repressive aims.[20] The apparatus of sovereignty (*dispositifs de souveraineté*) of the eighteenth century were fought to give birth to the disciplinary apparatus (*dispositifs disciplinaires*) of the nineteenth century and their mechanisms of penal, institutionalized, and hospitalized repression. These means of exercising power have mutated to societies of control that are adapted to the population's threshold of tolerance.[21] Today, Man is the subject of constant surveillance: by his banker, who knows at every moment the state of his debt, by his employer, who ensures the profitability of his company by managing employee training programs intended to increase productivity, and marketing agencies who spy on the public's littlest habits to better craft new consumer needs. To this, we could add the new avenues offered to insurance companies by the decoding of the human genome and interactive publicity that is broadcast onto small screens according to consumer patterns. Today under permanent control, the Deleuzian people is nonetheless one of the creators that currently resist and that continue to face new situations that are as shameful as they are sources of indignation. When it creates a new language for an unformed people, political art becomes a testimonial to this resistance in addition to sketching out new possibilities for ways of living independently from institutionalized majority thought. In contrast to bloody revolutions and the formation of even more pathetic states, especially in societies favorable to globalization of the democratic state, Deleuzian political art—the art best able to generate a 'possible universal figure of minoritary consciousness'[22]—never makes shedding men's blood the price to be paid for its right to exist.

Do mediatized objectors belong to just such a minority consciousness? If so, visionary activists and other visible resistors of the globalized market economy (Human Rights Watch, Amnesty International, etc., which often select their interventions according to media presence) do not make up a real minority for Deleuze, and this is because their existence is determined by their relationship to majority standards set by the dominant power. Deleuze distinguishes the minority as a state-of-being (*état de fait*) and the minoritary becoming (*devenir minoritaire*) (DR, 204–24). Unlike the established and visible minority, the minoritary becoming is always in the process of becoming. The media simplify the reality of social struggles by opposing North and South, the Third World and rich countries, terrorists and democrats, and so on. For Deleuze each one of us has a South and a Third World (DR, 204–24). Of course, this is imperceptible and escapes the cameras and discussions of minority states-of-being.

Deleuze's militantism without party affiliation not only takes the opposite direction of power state training, it also preserves his independence vis-à-vis organized militant resistance and parallel organizations, the avatars of identitary ideals. The figure of the deserter of the state, free to express non-dominating powers and oppose all desire for control to which Deleuzian micropolitics attempt to bestow rights, find legitimacy in a world where the option of violence against the established order or compromise with the powers-that-be are just as unconvincing. The styles of existence of micropolitical actors rise above the mayhem; they work on particular acts that never correspond with known programs and commitments. This is therefore a position that is as demanding as it is original, and to which we look to Deleuze in an era when international summits and the often brutal and bloody protests that accompany them multiply. Such actions, led by parties generally in the perimeter of security, are unable to persuade others of the necessity of (re)defining the democracy that all blindly trust. Deleuze is not looking for a way to unify the missing people in the power of a *demos*. Rather, he wonders if leaders and resistors (the minoritary states-of-being) are ready to trade their desire for power and domination for a desire for imminent strength.

From a Deleuzian point of view, political decisions and mediatized resistance are prisoners of a system of representation where the normalized scenario is predictable: Some try to impose their laws while others come together to better protest the established order. Affective bodies reach their full capacity of expression by eluding recognized values and removing themselves from all defined form of organization to experiment with the potentialities of desire and build a continuum of affective variations independent of systems of power. Thus, Deleuze's particular militantism brings about general theories of state toward ethics as an experimentation of particular lifestyles.[23] This reconfigures solidarities where minoritary becomings fight *with* the irreducible vital forces of all known political parties, whether that of democrats, organized resistance, or anarchists.

We would be tempted to believe that Deleuzian politics do not form a relationship with the reality of present parties. Indeed, many texts lead us to think that Deleuze believes political reality is only a kind of work of art that is in constant formation and where the existence of the collectivity is sublimated in order to better allow creators to speak and act. However, this abrupt aesthetization of Deleuzian politics hides a deeper and more authentic motivation connected to the *polis*. Deleuzian politics resist all empires, refuse to encourage organized activism, show distaste for individual 'egocultric' liberties and denigrate the society of universal laws of cosmopolitan pretension. Does this position join that of the defenders of the collectivity of differences? Here, we think of Maurice Blanchot who sees community in terms of a 'non-reciprocal

relationship,' of Jean-Luc Nancy who thinks community is made up of 'dispar-
ate singularities,' and of Giorgio Agamben whose community consists of 'singularities without predefined identities.'[24] But what of the Deleuzian nomads?
It would not seem that here it is a question of living in community units that
are ideally respectful of all differences. Deleuze distinguishes himself from
the new ideology of the community 'united in difference' by according—again
in a typically Nietzschean gesture—greater value to exceptional beings than to
defenders of ultimate tolerance. Cynical in many ways,[25] these singular beings,
who seek neither to know the truth (knowledge) nor to exercise domination
(power), are completely emancipated from the romantic dream of recompos-
ing unity by welding heterogenous parts:

> We live today in the age of partial objects, bricks that have been shattered to
> bits, and leftovers. We no longer believe in the myth of the existence of frag-
> ments that, like pieces of an antique statue, are merely waiting for the last
> one to be turned up, so that they may all be glued back together to create a
> unity that is precisely the same as the original unity. We no longer believe in
> a primordial totality that once existed, or in a final totality that awaits us at
> some future date. We no longer believe in the dull grey outlines of a dreary,
> colorless dialectic of evolution, aimed at forming a harmonious whole out of
> heterogeneous bits by rounding off their rough edges. (AO, 42)

It is easy to define negatively the fragmented people of whom Deleuze
speaks: This people is non-democratic, stands beyond good and evil, defends
no categorical imperative, has no constitutional plans, is not submitted to any
defined law, ignores consensus, common sense, the common good, virtue, com-
municational reason, and fair discussion as a means of resolving conflicts. Is it
then the law of 'each man for himself' that rules? Not exactly, since members
of the missing people are also able to form connections among themselves:
'Not even a puzzle, whose pieces when fitted together would constitute a whole,
but rather a wall of loose, uncemented stones, where every element has a value
in itself but also in relation to others.'[26] The untimeliness of the unformed
people expresses itself through the fact that it is singularities that make up
and maintain deep relationships without necessarily being contemporaries.
These singular beings appear at diverse eras and in often faraway lands, calling up sometimes virtual meetings through which the absence of predefined
norms and a universal system of values can be experienced. Deleuzian politics
is fundamentally untimely. Thus, Kafka, the deserter in Judaic and German
empires, takes his line of flight when Fascism, Stalinism, and Americanism
come knocking at the door (K, 41). Straub and Huilet defend a homemade
cinematographic writing intended for the forgotten people by the new market
economy;[27] and perhaps some among us come to give rise to some *potentia* that
is still absent and independent of the new globalized order and/or terrorist

organizations. This incalculable ensemble, this uncemented brick wall, is what the missing people might look like; a people who—luckily perhaps—are forever yet to be formed.

Notes

1. Deleuze, G. (1995), 'Je me souviens,' *Nouvel Observateur* Nov. 16–22, 115 (untranslated—according to the Revised Bibliography of the Works of Gilles Deleuze compiled by T. S. Murphy and available at <www.bibliothequedusaulchoir.org/activites/Deleuze/Deleuze%20Bibliogr.pdf>).

2. Deleuze, G. (1977), 'Nous croyons au caractère constructiviste de certaines agitations de gauche' (petition concerning the Italian left), *Recherches* 30, Nov., 149–50, (untranslated).

3. Deleuze, G. (1988), 'Power,' in *Spinoza. Practical Philosophy* (San Francisco: City Light Books), 97–104.

4. Deleuze, G. (1995), *Negotiations* (New York: Columbia University Press), 172; hereafter referred to as N. See also Deleuze, G. and Guattari, F. (1994), *What is Philosophy?* (New York: Columbia University Press), 107–8; hereafter referred to as WiPh.

5. Marx, K. and Engels, F. (1970), *The German Ideology*. Part One (New York: International Publishers), 85.

6. Nietzsche, F. (1996), *Human, all too Human*, Part I (Cambridge: Cambridge University Press), §472; Nietzsche, F. (2007), *The Dawn of Day* (Mineola: Dover Publications), §179.

7. Deleuze, G. and Guattari, F. (1983), *Anti-Œdipus: Capitalism and Schizophrenia* (Minneapolis: University of Minnesota Press), 222–3; hereafter referred to as AO.

8. Deleuze, G. (2007), 'The Rich Jew,' in *Two Regimes of Madness. Texts and Interviews 1975–1995* (New York: Semiotext(e)), 138.

9. Deleuze, G. and Guattari, F. (1987), *A Thousand Plateaus: Capitalism and Schizophrenia*, trans. B. Massumi (Minneapolis: University of Minnesota Press), 394; hereafter referred to as TP.

10. Deleuze, G. and Guattari, F. (1987), *A Thousand Plateaus*, 346; Deleuze, G. (1989), *Cinema 2. The Time-Image* (London: The Athlone Press), chap. 8, n. 41; hereafterr referred to as C2.

11. Deleuze, G. (1993), section 5: 'Theater and Politics of *One Manifesto Less*,' in C. V. Boundas (ed.), *The Deleuze Reader* (New York: Columbia University Press), 204–24; hereafter referred to as DR.

12. Deleuze, G. and Guattari, F. (1986), *Kafka. Toward a Minor Literature*, trans. D. Polan (Minneapolis: University of Minnesota Press), 96, n. 3, hereafter referred to as K.

13. Kafka, F. (1948), *The Diaries of Franz Kafka* (New York: Schocken Books), 193–4 (December 25, 1911; I modified the translation slightly), quoted in Deleuze, G. and Guattari, F. *Kafka. Toward a Minor Literature*, 17.

14. G. Deleuze and F. Guattari, *Kafka. Toward a Minor Literature* (Minneapolis: University of Minnesota Press, 1986), p. 18 and elsewhere; G. Deleuze and F.

Guattari, *A Thousand Plateaus* (Minneapolis: University of Minnesota Press), 7, 36, 79, 88, 130 and 145.

[15] Kafka, F. *The Diaries of Franz Kafka* (December 25, 1911).

[16] Deleuze considers some of the parallels established between Foucault and the Frankfurt School as a series of misunderstandings, which also is applicable to his own thought. See Deleuze, G. (2006), 'What is a Dispositif?,' in *Two Regimes of Madness* (New York: Semiotext(e)), 338–48. Deleuze and Foucault distrust the Frankfurt School representatives particularly when they assimilate individual creations to some general considerations linked to a global project of emancipation.

[17] Deleuze, G. (1998), 'The Indians of Palestine' and 'The Grandeur of Yasser Arafat,' *Discourse* 20(3), 25–9 and 30–3.

[18] Marx and Nietzsche had already taken a stand against the 1793 Universal Declaration of Human Rights. Similarly, Badiou denounces the general nature of human rights seeing that it does not take singular situations into consideration. See Badiou, A. (2001), *Ethics. An Essay on the Understanding of Evil* (London/New York: Verso). Elsewhere, Badiou presents a militant politics 'without party' that is similar to some of Deleuze's views. See Badiou, A. (2005), *Metapolitics* (London/New York: Verso), 122.

[19] Deleuze, G. (2004), 'Nomadic Thought,' in *Desert Islands and Other Texts. 1953–1974*, 260.

[20] Deleuze, G. (2006), 'What is a Dispositif?,' in *Two Regimes of Madness. 1975–1995*, 338–48; 'Control and becoming' and 'Postscript on control societies,' in *Negotiations*, 169–82; 'Desire and Pleasure,' in Davidson A. I. (ed.), (1997), *Foucault and his Interlocutors* (Chicago: Chicago University Press), 183–92.

[21] Kafka stands at the crossroad of these two kinds of society. See Deleuze, *Negotiations*, 179.

[22] Deleuze, G. (1978), 'Philosophie et minorité,' *Critique*, 369, Février, 154–5 (untranslated).

[23] See Mengue, P. (1999), 'Gilles Deleuze et la grandeur du mineur,' *Il Particolare*, 1, 41–74. Mengue criticizes the potentially tyrannical nature of Deleuze's micropolitics. In order to counter this danger and to create more 'social linkages,' he suggests reconnecting with the concepts of democracy and human rights, which were very quickly removed from the Deleuzian system. It would then be possible to map out a political plane of immanence based on an ideal of communication. Despite stating a certain disloyalty to the Deleuzian thought, this interpretation is hardly convincing. See also Mengue, P. (2003), *Deleuze et la question de la démocratie* (Paris: Harmattan).

[24] Blanchot, M. (1988), *The Unavowable Community* (Barrytown: Station Hill Press); Nancy, J.-L. (1991), *The Inoperative Community* (Minneapolis: University of Minnesota Press); Agamben, G. (1993), *The Coming Community* (Minneapolis: University of Minnesota Press).

[25] In reference to Husserl's *Krisis* (implicit), Foucault compares the Cynics to the 'functionaries of humanity.' See the 1983–84 lectures at Collège de France called *Le courage de la vérité* (unpublished); their audio version (document C-69) is available at *Institut Mémoires de l'édition contemporaine* (Abbaye d'Ardenne, France).

26 Deleuze, G. (1997), *Essays Critical and Clinical* (Minneapolis: University of Minnesota Press), 86.

27 In the same way J.-M. Straub supports the missing people against the new people; see *Rencontres avec Jean-Marie Straub et Danièle Huilet* (Le Mans: École régionale des beaux-arts), 46.

Chapter 15

Affirmative Nomadology and the War Machine

Eugene W. Holland

The question I want to raise here concerns the nature of the relations between nomadology and nomadism in the broad sense, on the one hand, and nomadic peoples, nomad warriors, and the war machine, on the other. Deleuze and Guattari are quite explicit that what they call the 'war machine' only has war as its object under certain conditions.[1] And just as Deleuze and Guattari insist that the war machine and war are not't the same thing—that the relation between the two is 'synthetic' (in the Kantian sense of the term (TP, 417))—I want to insist that nomadism and the war machine are not the same thing, that although the war machine is indeed a 'nomad invention,' (TP, 417) it is just one invention among many others. In much the same way, I will insist that the concept of nomadism cannot be limited to nomadic peoples: the 'nomad science' discussed in the treatise on nomadology, for example, does not belong only to nomad warriors—and the same is true for 'nomad games' such as the Chinese game of 'Go' contrasted with chess, for 'nomad sports' such as soccer contrasted with American football, and for 'nomad music' such as improvisational jazz contrasted with classical music. As Deleuze and Guattari affirm, nomads do not hold the key to nomadism: 'the nomads do not hold the secret: an "ideological," "scientific," or artistic movement can be a potential war machine, to the precise extent to which it draws, in relation to a *phylum*, a plane of consistency, a creative line of flight, a smooth space of displacement' (TP, 422–4).

Why insist on distinguishing between nomadism and the war machine? First of all, to avoid misunderstanding: why use the term 'war machine' if the machine does not always have war as its object?—if war only becomes the object of the machine under certain conditions?—if under other conditions, as Deleuze and Guattari themselves say, the machine can have as its objective 'building bridges or cathedrals or rendering judgments or making music or instituting a science, a technology . . .' (TP, 366). But beyond the interests of clarity, there are two other, more substantial reasons.

For one thing, the extreme elasticity of the concept of the war machine is such that it gets used to characterize two very different phenomena: the becoming-warrior of nomads confronting the State, and the total war of ecumenical capitalism. Now it is true that the war machine figures among a whole set of apparently outdated phenomena that come back to the fore, according to Deleuze and Guattari, after the passage through modernity—most notably machinic enslavement and smooth space itself, which tend to replace social subjugation and the striation of space operated by the modern State and capitalism. But the question is, in what respect do the war machine of nomadic peoples and global capitalism resemble one another? Are the features shared by a band of nomad warriors and ecumenical capitalism really pertinent features? For the nomad war machine, opposition to the State is all-determining; but ecumenical capitalism is not opposed to States at all: it engulfs them, and appropriates them as so many models of realization for its axioms.² Or one could say that the relevant similarity stems from the smooth space occupied by both machines. But even if we were to admit that ecumenical capitalism operates in smooth space, this space is a function of the world market, and the essence of capitalist operations is to control the flows circulating in this space so as to capture surplus value, not to prevent the capture of the space by a State, which is the essence of nomad-warrior operations. What is more, even if it is true that ecumenical capitalism launches its axioms on the world market largely in order to avoid and overcome State recoding and reterritorialization—and that is precisely the sense in which capitalism re-opens a smooth space vis-à-vis the striated space of the State, whereas nomad warriors strive to protect their smooth space from State striation to begin with—war has become *immanent* to globalizing capitalism; henceforth, global capitalism amounts to 'total war' (TP, 466–7): the relation of war to the capitalist war machine is analytic, whereas its relation to the nomad war machine was synthetic. The difference is crucial: whereas the nomad war machine has smooth space as its principal (or analytic) object and war as a secondary or supplementary (synthetic) object, the capitalist war machine has total war as its principal object, along with the appropriation of the entire world by means of axiomatic conjunctions, and only produces in a supplementary or secondary way the kinds of transversal or nomadic (deterritorializing) connections that run counter to its (reterritorializing) axioms of capture and domination.

It must be said that Deleuze and Guattari are perfectly explicit about the dual nature of the war machine: at the end of the treatise on nomadology, they acknowledge that there are in effect 'two kinds of war machine' (TP, 423), even though this duality ends up significantly complicating the relation between nomadism and the war machine. But there is another, more decisive reason why it is important to distinguish between nomadism and the war machine. It is, in short, that the war machine represents the patently *reactive* aspect of nomadism. For it is opposition that in effect transforms nomadism into a war machine, by assigning it the State as its enemy or obstacle and war as its (synthetic) object. It goes without saying—or almost does—that the reactive aspect of a phenomenon should be considered secondary to its positive or affirmative aspect; I suggest that this 'almost' goes without saying because Deleuze and Guattari themselves only say this in a footnote, and say it about Foucault's work, not their own.[3] In any case, the essential thing is to understand what the affirmative aspect of nomadism actually is, and on this, Deleuze and Guattari are definitive: '[if] the war machine was the invention of the nomad,' they insist, '[this] is because it is in its essence the constituent element of smooth space, the occupation of this space, displacement within this space, and the corresponding composition of people' (TP, 417). Similarly, in the conclusion of the treatise on nomadology, and on precisely the topic of the supplementarity of war vis-à-vis nomadism itself, they insist that even if nomads can make war, they do so 'only on the condition that they simultaneously create something else, if only new nonorganic social relations' (TP, 423). The principal and positive object of nomadism is therefore a distinctive composition of social relations occupying smooth space, not war. And so in order to save the concept of nomadism from its becoming-reactive in opposition to the State, we must understand just what this composition of nomad social relations in smooth space actually entails.

Are nomadic peoples always organized in a nomadic fashion? That is beside the point: for one thing, Deleuze and Guattari's concept of nomadism depends as much (if not more) on the term *nomos* in Greek philosophy (and on its differential relations with *polis* and *logos* (TP, 353, 369–73, 384–6)) as on nomadic peoples themselves—whence the importance of rigorously distinguishing between 'nomad' as an adjective referring to nomadism in the general sense, and 'nomads' as a noun referring to nomadic peoples; for another thing, Deleuze and Guattari say a lot more about the way nomads occupy and move around in smooth space than about the composition of their social relations. Hence the importance of the examples of nomad science, nomad sports, and nomad music mentioned above, which offer insights into this question of the composition of the nomad social field.

In this respect, what Deleuze and Guattari say about science is crucial: 'the way in which a science, or a conception of science, participates in the organization of the social field, and in particular induces a division of labor, is part of that science itself' (TP, 368–9). By way of illustration, the same can be said of music: the way in which a practice or a conception of music participates in the composition of the social field and induces a particular division of labor is part of the music itself. So just as Deleuze and Guattari differentiate nomad science from royal science, we can distinguish according to the same criteria a nomad music—that is to say, improvisational jazz—from royal or classical music. Briefly, the three basic criteria are as follows:

1. In nomad science, there is indeed a technical division of labor—the differentiation of activities, the specialization of functions—but there is no social

division of labor that would place certain positions or functions above others. Royal science, by contrast, entails a disqualification of manual labor in favor of intellectual labor, and thereby superimposes a social division of labor—hierarchy, power differentials, distinctions of prestige and remuneration—on the technical division of labor.

2. At the same time, royal science institutes a separation between conception and execution. With the emergence of royal science, an artisan class where conception and execution coincided in the same person gave way to a proletarian working class of unskilled labor faced with a scientific class holding a monopoly of knowledge and control. 'The State does not give power (*pouvoir*) to the intellectual or conceptual innovators; on the contrary, it makes them a strictly dependent organ with an autonomy that is only imagined yet is sufficient to divest those whose job it becomes simply to reproduce or implement of all of their power (*puissance*)' (TP, 368).

The same is true for music. In a symphony orchestra performing classical music, conception is sharply separated from execution: musicians merely reproduce a program created in advance by the genius-composer, and what's more, they play at the command of the orchestra conductor. In jazz improvisation, by contrast, conception and execution coincide in the same personnel and at the same time, and there is no need for a conductor.

3. Jazz improvisation perfectly illustrates a third criterion of nomad science and of the nomad body politic in general—the criterion Deleuze and Guattari adapt from Gilbert Simondon which distinguishes nomad composition from hylomorphic organization (TP, 555 n. 33). It is not only that nomad science and music operate by creative itineration rather than by reproductive repetition (of a score or an alleged law of nature), as we have seen; it is also that they remain sensitive to the singularities of sound-substance, physical substance, biological substance, and so on. Each musical key has a special tonality, and therefore presents distinctive possibilities for composition or improvisation. Moreover, a 'wrong note'—or rather, an unexpected note—played by a jazz musician is not necessarily a mistake—as it would most certainly be if it were played by a classical musician—inasmuch as the other musicians in the group can always incorporate it as a singularity into the piece they are improvising. In the smooth space of musical improvisation, it is never a question of imposing form on a passive, inert substance: neither the substance of sound nor of human beings, neither the musical key nor the musicians are passive. Instead, there is a process of spontaneous structuration where a certain singular coherence emerges which is not imposed by either a conductor or a score, but remains absolutely immanent to the creative activity of the group. A nomad body politic follows immanent rules (*nomoi*) which are for the most part implicit, rather than obeying laws (*logoi*) that are formulated and/or imposed explicitly by a transcendent agent or agency (TP, 369–74).

In this brief sketch of features characteristic of the nomad body politic, there are echoes of certain manifestly political notions such as self-management (*autogestion*), radical democracy, and direct democracy. It is no accident that Howard Brubeck, brother of the great jazz pianist, would have called jazz 'democracy in music,' which brings us back to the relations between affirmative nomadology and political philosophy, as these are developed in *What is Philosophy?*.

Philosophy becomes political, as we learn from this last collaborative work, as soon as the problems to which its concepts respond are no longer internal to philosophy—paradoxes, or problems that were badly posed by other philosophers—but rather link philosophy to what lies outside it, to its current milieu. Putting philosophy into contact with its outside is the function of 'utopia' according to Deleuze and Guattari: 'utopia is what links philosophy with its own epoch . . . The word utopia therefore designates that conjunction of philosophy, or of the concept, with the present milieu—political philosophy.'[4] But here again, as it was for nomadology, it is important to evaluate the positive and the negative aspects of this relation of philosophy to its milieu. Is philosophy work, or is it free action?—to invoke another important conceptual distinction made in the treatise on nomadology.[5] Most of the time, when Deleuze and Guattari address this relation explicitly, they do so in negative terms—and this despite the positive connotations of the term 'utopia': 'it is with utopia that philosophy becomes political and takes the criticism of its own time to the highest point'; or again: '[philosophical utopia] etymologically stands for absolute deterritorialization but always at the critical point at which it is connected with the present relative milieu, and especially with the forces stifled by this milieu'; worse yet: '[We] continue to undergo shameful compromises with our time. This feeling of shame is one of philosophy's most powerful motifs'; and again: 'books of philosophy and works of art . . . contain their sum of unimaginable sufferings. . . . They have resistance in common—their resistance to death, to servitude, to the intolerable, to shame, to the present'; and finally: 'revolution is itself utopia of immanence . . . inasmuch as [its] features connect up with what is real here and now in the struggle against capitalism' (TP, 99, 100, 108, 110, 100)—Compromise, critique, shame, suffering, resistance, struggling against capitalism: a whole litany of gripes and grievances that risks drowning philosophy in a tidal wave of *ressentiment*.

This having been said, it must also be said there is no question of completely eliminating critical or warfare nomadology in order to replace it with a purely positive nomadology: what living sentient being could possibly not be against suffering and against capitalism? Rather, it is a question of restoring affirmative political philosophy and affirmative nomadology to their rightful primacy of place vis-à-vis critique, shame, resistance, and all the rest. In particular, it is a question of finding alternatives to capitalism rather than struggling against, criticizing, or resisting it. Fortunately, Deleuze and Guattari themselves provide means for doing so.

For philosophy, as we know from their last collaborative work, was born and has flourished in milieus of deterritorialization—the Greek city-state, formerly; the world market these days—and political philosophy should be able to take advantage of the opportunities offered by deterritorialized social milieus. So what are the nomad alternatives to the forms of social organization generated by and in turn reinforcing the norms of the modern State? Nomad science? Nomad music? Why not a nomad justice?—a concept Deleuze and Guattari mention on several occasions in the treatise on nomadology, but without developing it (TP, 353, 355, 366). Why not a nomad citizenship?

It is true that we should avoid simply 'multiplying models,' as Deleuze and Guattari warn against toward the end of the last plateau of the book—after having presented at least six models of smooth and striated spaces! (TP, 499). But they are right: it is not a question of multiplying nomad models to adopt, but rather of bringing to light examples of nomadism in order to adapt them to various diverse circumstances—that is, of bringing to light actual instances of nomadism whose principles can be adapted to other fields of activity. And one of the prime functions of philosophical concepts is precisely to extract such principles from instances of real-life nomadism—such as nomad science, nomad music, and so on. Another function would be to create new concepts in light of such real-life examples.

Take the concept of nomad citizenship as an example of the creation of a new concept based on principles taken from instances of real-life nomadism. Now in the context of affirmative nomadology, the positive or utopian force of a philosophical concept can be measured along two axes:

1. Its capacity to intervene in and transform our habits of thought and desire.
2. Its capacity to give expression to a process of becoming or social movement and thus to prolong or increase the social force of that becoming, or even to enable it to propagate into other social fields so as to connect with other processes of becoming.

The concept of nomad citizenship is designed to overturn the commonplace conception of citizenship that links it exclusively to a closed and bounded space, that is, to the striated space of the State: nomad citizenship offers prospects for engagement and belonging on a variety of different scales, both smaller and larger than the scale of the State, as we shall see. This aspect of the concept plays on the common meaning or connotations of the word nomad: a refusal of borders, displacement in space, and the like. But more important, the engagements of nomad citizenship are horizontal, so to speak, in contrast with the vertical engagements of conventional citizenship: nomad citizens are directly involved with other people and other groups, instead of with the State. On a small scale, take as examples the cooperatives, mutual companies, associations, and foundations that already provide more than ten per cent of all employment in Europe;[6] consider also socially responsible investing, and the so-called 'Sociétés Coopératives d'Intérêt Collectif': in French, these are known as 'entreprises citoyennes' (the equivalent American expression being 'triple bottom-line enterprises') where emphasis is placed not just on strictly economic profitability, but also on the environmental impact of products and on the quality of work and of the social relations at work—relations composed in principle along the lines of direct democracy, self-organization, and self-management. On a larger scale, there is the important and expanding role played by worldwide nongovernmental organizations (NGOs) such as Doctors-without-Borders. These kinds of active engagement and feelings of responsibility toward others certainly suggest a mode of citizenship very different from the conventional citizenship monopolized by the State.

A last example, by way of conclusion. In the 1970s and 1980s, peasants in Bolivia were in dire straits, to say the least: not only was the Bolivian State— itself on the verge of bankruptcy—not helping them, it was in fact working in concert with McDonalds to appropriate peasants' fields and transform them into grazing land for cattle to make hamburgers. But by relying on long-standing traditions of self-sufficiency and self-governance, some peasants organized themselves into production cooperatives to grow coffee and chocolate (ER). Since it was not a question of regressing to subsistence agriculture, their products had to be put on the market—and it was there that they encountered the free trade movement, coming from the other side of the world (from Belgium, in fact). The encounter was a very fruitful one, whose success has since spread widely, to the point that Bolivian cooperatives now produce, in addition to coffee and chocolate, textiles and clothing for export, as well as meat for local (intra-national) consumption. So here are two movements involving engagement and taking responsibility—operating on two very different scales, it is true—that a single concept of citizenship adapted to contemporary circumstances should be able to comprehend: a concept such as nomad citizenship, which serves to highlight and affirm such social engagements undertaken outside the norms of the State and of capitalism.

To be sure, one could ask about this example whether it involves a struggle waged on the level of axioms or a struggle directed against the capitalism axiomatic itself—but it might also be considered a zone of indiscernability between the two. In any case, I hope to have demonstrated the significance of the concept of nomad citizenship—either to supplement standard State citizenship, or even to replace it—and especially to have demonstrated the importance of rigorously distinguishing between affirmative nomadology and the war machine.

Notes

1. *A Thousand Plateaus* (1987), (Minneapolis: University of Minnesota Press), '1227: Treatise on Nomadology—the War Machine,' especially pp. 415–23; hereafter referred to as TP.

2. *A Thousand Plateaus*, 'Apparatus of Capture,' especially pp. 448–73.

3. *A Thousand Plateaus*, 531 n. 39: 'Our only points of disagreement with Foucault are the following: (1) to us the assemblages seem fundamentally to be assemblages not of power but of desire (desire is always assembled), and power seems to be a stratified dimension of the assemblage; (2) the diagram and abstract machine have lines of flight *that are primary, which are not phenomena of resistance or counterattack in an assemblage, but cutting edges of creation and deterritorialization*' (emphasis added).

4. Deleuze G. and Guattari, F. (1994), *What is Philosophy?* (New York: Columbia University Press), 100

5. *A Thousand Plateaus*, 397: 'The two ideal models of the motor are those of work and free action. Work is a motor cause that meets resistances, operates upon the exterior, is consumed and spent in its effect, and must be renewed from one moment to the next. Free action is also a motor cause, but one that has no resistance to overcome, operates only upon the mobile body itself, is not consumed in its effect, and continues from one moment to the next. Whatever its measure or degree, speed is relative in the first case, absolute in the second.' Here again, it is not a question of denying any possibility of philosophy as work, but rather of restoring philosophy as free action to its rightful position.

6. See Rouillé d'Orfueil, H. (2002), *Economie, le réveil des citoyens* (Paris: La Découverte); hereafter referred to as ER.

Chapter 16

Deleuze and 'pairing at a distance'*

Arnaud Villani

In Deleuze's *Abécédaire,* one finds what looks like an intuition—or what would be even worse, a feeling—that relates to the definition of the Left as a 'sensibility to what is the furthest away.' In this chapter, I would like to examine whether this definition, which intersects the ideas of disparateness and divergence, could safeguard Deleuze's philosophy against all 'aristocratic' interpretations and also render manifest a principle that would sustain his system. I will pursue this examination through an analysis of Deleuze's politics respecting the principles that are central to his work. My analysis will not turn into an arbitrary reconstruction that starts with Deleuze as *pretext*, but rather it will be a precise deconstruction of the edifice of micropolitics that takes off from Deleuze as *text*.

In *Difference and Repetition* there is a memorable text, in which Deleuze shows that the road to the infinite, whether it goes by way of Leibniz's infinitely small or by way of Hegel's infinitely big, always comes down to the 'the atonement of difference,' bringing the latter time and again under an identitarian reference.[1] To those who like to follow the road of a more coherent Leibniz, without the facile introduction of a Grand Signifier full of goodwill that tends to assemble every possible contingency inside a very big Sense,[2] Deleuze gives a rather brusque nudge toward another direction. Could there be then an 'over there' in Deleuze and if so, of what kind would it be? Under which conditions would the neo-Platonic invitation, 'to flee over there, to flee,' still make sense? This can be reformulated as follows: What is this author's conception of utopia?[3]

Pairing at a Distance as an Explanation of Deleuze's Choice of Authors

Why does Deleuze write on Hume, Nietzsche, Spinoza, Kant, and Leibniz? Is this a series of chance encounters or shall we rather suspect that there is an intrinsic reason to the series, the coherence of which we cannot see right away? Is there something common between Kant and Nietzsche, Hume, and

Spinoza? And if it is true that Leibniz was able to challenge the propositions of a great empiricist like Locke almost point by point, would this not be true in the case of Hume also? I suggest that the guiding thread in his choice of authors is the problem of the 'distant.'

A remark in *Empiricism and Subjectivity* helps foreground the idea of an 'extension at a distance.' The question here is about the kind of 'extension' necessary to sympathy, given that the latter (which, in Hume, is the origin of morality) is naturally limited only to the family. In the same work, imagination, being the faculty of the most distant,[4] is supposed to be able to traverse the entire world in great speed. I do not think that these are haphazard remarks, given that, in his work with Cresson at a moment that clearly shows the point to be his own, Deleuze insists:

> Passions must extend to the furthest point . . . But, then, wouldn't the passion lose in vivacity whatever it gains in extensity? In order for passions to become interested in what is distant, in order to overcome their natural partiality, it is not enough that they extend themselves artificially; it is necessary that, in the extensity . . . they conserve their natural vigour. In other words, the more distant, the general interest, must become the most proximate and immediate.[5]

Kant, in his introduction to the *Critique of Judgement*, clearly showed the gap, in fact, the abyss, between nature and freedom and searched for a bridge between these two extremes. Similarly, we can find this 'pairing at a distance' in the imagination—the keystone of the Humean system (after all, the debt of the German to the Englishman is well known)—that would illustrate[6] the argument of the second synthesis of reproduction in the imagination *ab absurdo*, with its major leaps from summer to winter, snow to fruits, red and heavy to black and light, and man to animal. Kant's insistence on schematism—this 'art hidden in the depths of the human mind' also belongs here. And the same goes for the 'free play' of imagination and understanding—those two hardly compatible faculties that excite each other in order to get the upper hand as a result of their regulated struggle. Finally, pairing at a distance is also present in the effect that determines the imagination, as soon as it accepts its defeat at the hands of the sublime. In this case, the imagination has to accept the necessity of linking the sublime to the human mind and of passing over the task to Reason and its own faculty to go to the *extreme ends* of the series—in this particular case, to go from nature to liberty by means of a morally determined beautiful. All this 'enlarging' and 'giving a great deal to thought' cannot fail to give patents of nobility to a well 'tempered' distant. What is noticeable in Deleuze's presentation in *Kant's Critical Philosophy* is his admiration for the architectonic of Kant's work and its ability to create the largest possible space or to accommodate absolute contraries.[7]

In the case of Spinoza, the problem is more difficult. It could be focused on the idea of *expression* to which Deleuze dedicates an entire volume. The sense that 'expression' carries is clearly revealed the moment that Deleuze invokes a fundamental affinity between Spinoza and Leibniz in the context of this problem.

> For while the concept of expression adequately applies to real causality, in the sense that an effect expresses its cause, and knowledge of the effect expresses a knowledge of its cause, the concept nonetheless goes farther than causality, since it brings *a correspondence and a resonance into series that are altogether foreign to one another*. . . . This genus directly explains *the possibility of distinct and heterogeneous series (expressions) expressing the same invariant* (what is expressed) by establishing in each of the varying series the same concatenation of causes and effects. Expression takes its place at the heart of the individual. . . . And Leibniz by *monad* no less than Spinoza by *mode*, understands nothing other than an individual as an expressive center.[8]

In the expression, the relationship and the univocity of the substance that expresses itself, the attribute that expresses the substance and the essence that is being expressed (and also the relationship of substance, attribute, and mode) are all unveiled so that the expression is like a real relationship that makes the distant near.

On this point, Leibniz, the 'conciliator,' is more clear: the *petites perceptions* connecting us to the canon fire in China and the theme or the formula, 'over there just like here'[9] that accompanies them, as well as the fold that, in being a series, goes on to infinity,[10] manifest the same basic preoccupation. Finally, it will not be difficult to show, beginning with *The Birth of Tragedy*, the importance of the contraries in Nietzsche's work: one needs plenty of time to interpret them and to show them as a relationship of the kind, 'pathos of distance.'

Here, we must not forget the extent to which the history of philosophy has retained the trace of the syntonous and the similarly oriented. Consider, for example, Stoic philosophy (one of the abiding and recurring references of Deleuze), whether on the side of the sixteenth-century resemblances that Foucault analyzed in the beginning of *The Order of Things* (the image of the chord stretched throughout the universe) or whether on the side of differences turned toward the idea of a collection of contingent truths. The latter, without belonging to the order of reasons, demand that God, through sheer kindness, brings them back to the principle of sufficient reason, imposing to all differences, at one stroke, the pacification of a pyramidal vision, as Leibniz classically expressed it or, as Whitehead did it less classically, through the *tender care* of God, his *'creative advance'* and the *'pereunt et imputantur'* of time to which one must give sense at all costs.

It is not, therefore, only the Stoic logic of the event that influences Deleuze but, more deeply, the Stoics' theory of univocity and *amor fati*—in fact, the latter influence explains the former. Indeed, it is clear that the Stoic space of bodies as a space of the 'glittering' bodies of the mind is one of 'proximal distanciation' of the grand fraternity of beings. Whether in the case of the Stoics or whether in the case of Spinoza and Leibniz, we see in this kind of philosophy, which expresses itself willingly in circles and metamorphoses of circles, that centers and periphery are strictly the same—even those that are the most distanced (see Spinoza, *Ethics* 1, prop. 15: 'Whatsoever is, is in God, and without God nothing can be, or be conceived'; and prop. 18: 'God is the indwelling and not the transient cause of all things'). *Panta plērē theōn*, everything is full of Gods; 'Here too (*kai entautha*) there are Gods,' Heraclitus said standing at a baker's oven. Transitive is 'what never stops passing away.' Immanent, on the contrary, is what inhabits the smallest detail of its own production. This is the model of an *appropriation* of the real according to the mode of the proper (*proper/proprius*). The same thing can also be read within the order of time, ever since the statements of the wisdom of the Pharaohs and ever since Parmenides: past, present, future cannot be distinguished; they are altogether there (according to the definitive formula of the eighth fragment of Parmenides' poem: '*homou pan, hen, syneches.*'

How is this grand theme of philosophy manifested in Deleuze? In an identical and yet totally different manner. If everything is there at the same time and neither space nor time makes a difference, the problem is that everything will be gathered together inside the unity of Mind or absolute Reason. And of course, in this case, 'coming to be disappears and death is out of the question' (fourth fragment). But this is precisely what Deleuze does not want at any price. Nevertheless, his *aion* links together past and future while jumping over the present. It also conserves the 'center of infinite energy' as it takes chaos to be the origin of unforeseeable 'jets' which, thanks to their great speed, are imperceptible and useless. And as a result, the gigantic Stoic network of the *nexus causarum*, with its subtlety of *confatalia* and the subordinate networks of perfect causes (*the aition di ho* that the Stoics borrowed from *Phaedo*, 97) and auxiliary causes (material causes, the *aition hou oukh aneu* of the same *Phaedo*) strikingly anticipates that which, from one fold to another, is able to create the idea of a wave of resonance, where each fold is animated and expressed by all the others, for all infinity. This is what places everything in the proximity of a prominent singularity, an encounter or a joy.

To be sure, it is clear that immanence is not just a word for Deleuze; rather, it is a rule of construction. It is therefore not a question of giving permission to resorb what exists—the bodies, and the forms in general—back into the serenity of a Spirit. His solution consists in deploying, on the side of space and time, (both exclusive and *intolerant* because *they contain forms*) something intermediary—itself tolerant and *maintaining the in-between forms between form and the informal.* Virtual, continuous, and heterogeneous series spring out of chaos. The fact that they slow down, as they crystallize into actualities, makes them visible. But this should not be read as a catastrophic exhaustion. To a detached look, nothing ever is a catastrophe, except in the sense that the term acquires in Thom's mathematics. For a long time, Deleuze remained seduced by Riemann's topological constructions (layers), where the more distanced turns into the more near, and multiplicities/varieties, in the case of which one and the same value is in itself different, turned into absolute vicinity. The reason is that, as in Heidegger's *Entfernung,* space is *diastema* rather than distance.

This does not mean that we return to Crollius, Aldrovandi, Paracelsus, or Porta, or that stressing the resemblance between the aconite and the eyes, or between the nut and the brain, could ever produce anything but a 'pathetic philosophy.' But the problem becomes really serious when, in classical philosophy itself, we detect the risk of a gigantic repetition. This is the great debate that Jacobi launched in his *Letters to Mendelssohn on the Doctrine of Spinoza* that opened up the *Pantheismusstreit*: The grand rationalism that develops in every possible direction the formal paradigm of the logic of subject/predicate (Whitehead) and the *inest subjecto,* that is, the tautology of the *logic of* inherence—is it not simply a grand analytic judgment that adds nothing to knowledge? The conservation of proximal distancing, univocity, and the continuity of the heterogeneous cannot be established unless difference *is* in itself and for itself and a logic of the event is allowed to surge. The incorporeal verbal, the Spinozist expression and the Leibnizian fold, the modified imagination of Hume and Kant, the Kantian introduction of the negative magnitude with its 'turning point,' or Schopenhauer and Nietzsche's transition from representation to will, from form to force—all this preserves inherence and leads us to the real problem, namely, to consistency.

Deleuze has the immense merit of condensing in a single intuition all these innovations that have transformed philosophy: this is the *virtual.* The virtual is, in fact, a force; it puts on a form as it actualizes itself but also it re-virtualizes the actual, endowing it—given the great power of the center of energy from which the virtual is derived—with an impetus and a life that comes to define art. It is a factory segment, a passage, derailment, event, fold, constellation, encounter—the notorious invisible (*adelon*) that Plato, Plotinus, and the entire tradition of the Intelligible had been looking for, overlooking unfortunately both bodies and *physis.*

Hypothesis on the Origins of Pairing at a Distance

'Pairing at a distance' then is related to a philosophy of the leap. Inside the domain of creation, pairing explains why metaphor is radicalized and turned into metamorphosis while the poem is no longer a kind of handy comparison ('this golden sickle in the field of stars': the crescent of the moon) and turns into a surprising oxymoron (the earth, 'blue as an orange': the definition of the Beautiful in Lautréamont). Deleuze always quotes the verse of Sophocles: 'Which demon has leapt the greatest distance?' In fact, there is a way of interpreting the *line of flight* as another expression for the pairing at a distance.

That there is life in the philosophy of Deleuze is acknowledged by Deleuze himself—for example, in *Negotiations*: 'thought has never been the affair of theory. It is about the problems of life.' Everything I've written is vitalistic, at least I hope it is.'[11] But what kind of relation can there be between life and the leap; the coincidence of opposites in Nicolas of Cusa; the 'white chicken' of the Taoists 'that leaps over the gap'; or the eagles, these sons of the Alps that 'cross the abyss' in Hölderlin?

A genial trio of romantic philosophers from Tübingen took from the Greeks the formula, '*hen panta.*' To translate this formula as 'One/All' is sheer falsification because '*hen,*' 'the one,' is coupled here with '*panta,*' which does not mean whole, but rather 'all things,' that is, multiplicity. Life, for the Greeks, is the force that urges to be born and to appear—the force that interweaves the one and the multiple within the one *physis*. This explains why in an interview done through the mail, Deleuze responded negatively to my rather provocative question, whether *physis* had a place in his work. But his negative response should not confuse us. It is a fact that Deleuze does not really refer to the Greeks, with the exception of the Stoics. But this does not mean that when it comes to Deleuze and to the Greeks it is not in fact the same problem that is being played out.

It is indeed the problem of the coordination of univocity and multiplicities that preoccupied Deleuze fundamentally. We are going to see later on why he preferred 'univocity' to 'one' and 'multiplicities' to 'multiple.' But is it not also a maximal distension that governs, inside his *aion*, the couple past/future that leaps over the present as the two confront each other without any intermediate? And is it not also a rich 'couple of contraries' that juxtaposes the actual and the virtual? In other words, it is not absurd to meditate on what Deleuze owes to the 'symbolic machine' that never stops haunting philosophy: when pure logic throws it out of one door, it comes back again through another (the door of anthropology). Reflecting on the symbolic in Deleuze (something that right away would constitute a new symbol with the oldest philosophy coming suddenly to life under the same roof as the most contemporary one) would make possible for an entirely new interpretation of 'absolute speed' *to bring about the elimination of the distance between near and far* (to speak of 'deterritorialization,' in this case, would be pleonastic).

I feel compelled at this point to interject a constant preoccupation of my own research that has been an enigma: why, to put it directly, Parmenides and Deleuze? Why this great distance or this 'great passage' (I am reminded here of the title of Kenneth Roberts' fine work on the North-West passage) between

the extreme ancient and the extreme contemporary? To think of Deleuze
as a historian of ideas that the encounter with Guattari has debauched, or,
obversely, to think of a 'post-modern' Deleuze that quickly forgot the classi-
cism of his beginnings, allows one to babble a few neologisms, without ever
understanding what Deleuze accomplished in philosophy and for philosophy.

Let us then return anew to the origin of philosophy. The ease with which
philosophers take for granted the fable of the birth of philosophy in the pure
and simple substitution of *mythos* by the *logos* has always struck me as com-
ical, while at the same time it threw me in a great perplexity. Centuries of
propaganda must have been required to favor such a linear progress, such an
illusion of pre-formation or a 'retrograde movement of the true' for such an
enormity to be swallowed. And nothing really changes if, in order to mitigate
the claim, we pretend that this was not accomplished in the course of one day.
Humanity has not ceased to think and to live within the *encompassing cover of
myth* during the past millennia—within this *kratos* that initially signified the
myth's nourishing envelopment and only later on came to mean the leading
and dominant power that came to be related to a certain reasoned discourse.
If we come to think of it for a moment, we are going to admit that such a state
could not have suddenly disappeared and that, on the contrary, like the powerful and subtle civilizations of the Hittites and the Aratahs (patiently rediscov-
ered through a couple of stones or a tumbler as the only vestiges), it must have
left deep *traces*.

No matter how much *logos* attacked and corroded the myth, it never failed
to maintain deep relations with it. What does it then preserve of its ancestral
heritage, and why does this preservation interests philosophers, from the one
closest to the origin (the presocratics) to the one the farthest away from it
(Deleuze)? The answer is obvious, but if we consider it in itself it looks very difficult because it asks for a radical turn in our conception of the origin and the
continuity of Western philosophy. The tradition has never stopped repeating
that philosophy coincides with the advent of *logos* and its victory over *mythos*,
as another Saint Michael vanquishing the dragon, and this has always had an
element of truth: From then on, we stopped placing ourselves under a Said
which, foreign to human Reason, fell from the sky in order to solicit the critical
power of a properly human argumentative discourse (it does not take long of
course after that to incite *religions* of faith). Nevertheless, what remains unseen
in all this is that the myth does not abandon its place without leaving behind
its *globalizing* aspect that seizes everything in its strong 'hold.'

I assume, then, from the origins until now the presence of death within
philosophical *logos*, with its 'glorious body' and its pure form devoid of content. In a similar sense, Nancy spoke of 'divine places' that are left behind
after the disappearance of the gods. This 'form of hold' is not without consequence: it gives shape to the philosophy that follows. Whether in the countless
names of Greek thought (*harmonia, echein, amoibos, symbolon, holon, syneches,*

pan, hen panta, demas, sphairos, tonos, hen diapheromenon eautoi, meson, symp-noia, homonoia, dike, and on and on) or in the fortunes of the German term '*Zusammenhang*' in Dilthey and Marx, the term '*Mitte*' in Kant or Hölderlin, the notion '*Geviert*' in Hölderlin (the 'circle of effectivity') and Heidegger or again in the 'spinal chord' of Von Hofmannsthal—in all these, according to my hypothesis, 'the spirit of myth' is present—its *Geist* as *revenant* (returning/ghost) haunts philosophy.

We now know, thanks to Clastres and more recently thanks to Henaff,[12] that the entire life of traditional groups was governed by exchange, gift, and counter-gift—the return to equilibrium through the paying off of the 'debt,' sacrifice, and the refusal of all accumulation. With Bataille and Baudrillard, we call 'symbolic' this very strange dual machine where two elements placed in a situation of contrariety do not cease to exchange their places and their substance in order to create a real entity that philosophy has rightly named 'passage' 'interval' or 'between the two.' Inside this entity, the autonomous and stubborn presence of the two elements is being effaced, without either one disappearing; rather, the elements are in a state of becoming. But if the myth is the inadmissible ambiance that sustains the life and reality of all members of the society in which it survives, symbols, so frequent in traditional clans, are nothing else but the effects of myth. And as soon as *logos* makes its appearance, they persist in early philosophy and in the great tragedians (just like they do in China with the Taoists) because of the remanence and the *miniaturized figures* of the myth.

The myth as a 'statement of truth' leaves behind a special 'tone' that Nietzsche did not fail to notice in the loftiness and the allure of certain presocratics. Pythagoras, Empedocles, Anaxagoras would be specimens of this 'lordly' tone, that Kant later on denounced with justification. But the *legacy* of myth is not there—far from it. The myth is left behind as *the welcoming void of a totalizing form.* Confucius' utterance is very much to the point: 'a house is lived in what is empty in it.' In short, the positive side of chaos (the gaping hole) can not only be found in the totality of its possibles but also in the simple form of what offers *a* place (*lieu*). The myth—Griaule shows it with arresting truth in his *Dieu d'eau*[13]—never crashes the delicate particularities with its totality; on the contrary, it makes room for them. Similarly, the symbol will be the form of a failed (*faillé*) whole, being endlessly traversed by an exchange that plies the elements and gives them a place of power. The same thing must be said about forms related to the thought that *represents the myth* through the power that supports unity and multiplicity, total organism, and a well-sutured separation. Two elements chosen for their absolute distance constantly penetrate each other and are dissociated from one another. Being in a state of infinite exchange, they introduce the infinite inside and between themselves—in short, they find each other on the fringes of the universe—within reach. From this point of view, an entire new history of the first Greek philosophy waits to be written.

Deleuze's Link to Myth and Symbol

We understand that, when the essential disappears (and this makes a world be a world) no matter how strongly we believe in the intoxicating importance of determining ourselves as an adult in terms of what makes the specificity of being human, we do not neglect nonetheless to preserve a trace of the essential, just like Aeneas did when he carried the Manes and the Lares of his ancestors, on his way to establish a new city. We have seen that this trace, in the case of the symbol and of everything related to it (coincidence of opposites) mimes what is proper to the myth—the encompassing receptacle. We are given an element of the real (man), we are asked to imagine its extreme opposite (woman) and within the distention that separates and puts them in relation to each other, we try to introduce an image (a concept) of the world. Hence the burning zeal of the Pythagoreans and the men of the Academy for the representation of tables of symbols and lists of dichotomies. Deleuze often permitted us to see that the concern for pairing at a distance runs through his entire work; he showed this in crucial elements of the authors that he chose to write about, and in formulas and typical couples (past/future, actual/virtual. smooth/striated, territory/deterritorialization). Is it nevertheless reasonable— the objection will not fail to be made—to try a new 'mediterranization' of his work? Deleuze, Greek?—despite the fact that he never alluded to the Greeks, with the exception of a few formulas (soon abandoned) on the Platonic 'simulacrum,' few reflections on the suitor and the friend, and the more serious references to the Stoics?

This objection is in fact weighty. If myth and symbol are present inside the entire philosophical field, even in the state of traces, it is in their capacity as *totalities*. But this is precisely the concept that Deleuze rids himself of in the famous text of 'bricks that have been shattered to bits, and leftovers' of the 'totalites that are peripheral' and of the refusal, unlike Jean Grenier, to 'glue [. . .] [fragments] back together.'[14] Nevertheless, and this is also irrefutable, the fold 'has a real grip'! Aren't we really confronted, in Deleuze's case, with a 'totality made of fragments'? Of course, totality as such—'the beautiful, happy totality'—has been dead for a long time. It died with the advent of *logos*. But death takes hold of the living as soon as *logos* turns into the hero of political consensus (and brings together, despite appearances to the contrary, Plato and the Sophists)—the hero of an entente in the very heart of violence, of the birth of human justice and Right; of social contract; of a conciliatory 'return' to the unity of Spirit; of a transparent relation between the worker and his labor; of western democratic discussion. All these are ways of being together, in difference, in order to make *one*. They are also in agreement with the spirit of the myth.

Deleuze, therefore, is right to make the critique of totality. But philosophy has never given up pursuing this critique. And he is also right to resist the facility of a pre-established 'all.' No philosophy has ever succeeded in this. One could be grateful to Deleuze for having tried a new fold without Father, architect, or watchmaker.[15] The fact is that Deleuze's philosophy is perfectly coherent and consistent; it is a philosophy of the encounter, understood as the grasping and holding of fluxes inside one (plane or fold). Nothing can erase the center of this system—a constellation of heterogeneous elements bent and joined together—that forms only one gesture and one movement, that is, a bloc of united forces. As far as I am concerned, I see here all the characteristics of the symbol, including the fault, and this explains why I have put myself in the quest of Deleuze as if I were after Gradiva. I saw in him a special movement, a fold of the mind that I had already seen elsewhere—'elsewhere just like here.'

This discovery, besides being a joy, could have given me the painful security of a shelter, if I had not at the same time discovered the veritable originality of Deleuze—his opening of new pathways. Taking advantage, undoubtedly, of his reading of Bergson, he found the way to resolve the *closure of the symbol*[16] and to stop a very long evolution that the more one denies the more it persists in philosophy. He understood, perhaps not as clearly as he had wanted, that the only way to continue exploring that specificity of philosophy (with its *grand forms taking hold of us*, creating miracles in phenomenology and allowing many a seduction, thanks to Heidegger's work—think, for example, of the latter's homage to Dilthey, in *Being and Time*) consists in the association of the *actual and the virtual* in one and the same 'symbol,'—the symbol, for example, of 'the fold.'

We must then repeat that Deleuze's philosophy *is not* a philosophy of the virtual. To ignore that, in his case, there is no question of preferring the virtual to the actual is to refuse *to read* him and *not to allow him to be read*. If Deleuze found himself compelled in order to oppose a philosophy turned emphatically toward actualized forms to valorize the side of the virtual, and if he frequently speaks of forces, factory, verbs, becomings, processes, and passages, it is in order to allow people to grasp the fact that reality is a process of actualization *and* virtualization within only one (fragmented, fleeing, and open) whole. The 'smooth' cannot be conceived without the striated, or the minor without the major, or deterritorialization without the territory, or the line of flight without the system. But above all, this does not mean that these are complementary insipid claims, mobilized for the sake of consensus or of a zero sum game. Otherwise, Deleuze would have rejoined the repetitive tendency of classical philosophy. The one must *make one* and the multiple must make *multiplicities*, in the plural, in a zone of extreme vicinity and a departure toward the 'over there' of the future. There is a tragic element in Deleuze—the tragic element of life—appropriately condensed in the oxymoron that defines his thought: *heterogeneous continuity* or, as Sophocles used to say, *pantoporos aporos*. Absolute overview, utopia, *Erewhon, Aion.*

Is there *micropolitics*, in Deleuze? Certainly. From the becoming-trace of myth, he retains *the density of a trait of becoming*, giving man and every being that has become a particle force and an utopic power of change—speed, and unpredictability. From the symbol, he retains the infinite passage of the interval that re-injects the virtual inside the actual and makes rigid forms move, after indexing them on flight.

Is this a philosophically bearded Deleuze? No. Because against alienation and exploitation as forms of transcendence, against reification—these eternally recurring problems—one must know what to do: to become, as an individual or as a mass or a pack, a flight able to pierce the walls of a thought that only knows how to ossify processes and to indurate the extremes.

This is a Deleuze re-attached to the origin—suddenly both very old and very young, because he makes one rethink the entire tradition.

Notes

* Translated by Constantin V. Boundas and Crina Bondre Ardelean

1 Deleuze, G. (1994), *Difference and Repetition*, trans. P. Patton (New York: Columbia University Press), 23–4.

2 This requires, in the case of Deleuze's politics, a re-examination of his proposition, 'crowned anarchy,' which refers to Antoine Artaud's *Heliogabale* (Paris: Gallimard, 1979) and even more secretly to Max Stirner's *The Ego and Its Own*. The latter is the freest and most corrosive book ever written (the price Stirner paid for it is well known). I take this opportunity to observe that Marx's recurring joke on 'saint Bruno' and 'saint Max' (nobody laughs with it today) manifests that the one supposed to be the most 'saint' in history, the most given to a devout faith, is not the one we think he is.

3 See on this point 'Deleuze et l' utopie,' (2001), in M. Riot Sarcey, T. Bouchet, A. Picon (eds) *Dictionnaire des Utopies* (Paris: Larousse).

4 Deleuze, G. (1991), *Empiricism and Subjectivity: An Essay on Hume's Theory of Human Nature*, trans. C. V. Boundas (New York: Columbia University Press), 23, 39–40: 'Being the bond of ideas, [the fancy] moves through the universe, engendering fire dragons, winged horses, and monstrous giants. . . . Sympathy extends itself naturally into the future . . . To integrate sympathies is to make sympathy transcend its contradiction and natural partiality. . . . The moral and social problem is how to go from real sympathies which exclude one another to a real whole which would include these sympathies. The problem is how to extend sympathy.'

5 Cresson, A. and Deleuze, G. (1952), *Hume, sa vie, son oeuvre, sa philosophie* (Paris: Presses Universitaires de France), 56.

6 See my essay 'Deleuze et les possibilités de vie,' *Revue Internationale de Philosophie* 6, 241 (Sept. 2007).

7 See Kant, I., *Critique of Judgement* Par. 6, 9, 11. 21, 39 and 40; see also Larthomas J-P. (1985), *De Shaftesbury à Kant* (Lile: Thèse de Doctorat d' Etat), part 3, chap. 10; Frank, M. and Larthomas, J-P. (1994), *Sur la troisième Critique: Textes rassemblées et présentés par Dominique Janicaud* (Combas: L' Éclat); Deleuze, G. (1984), *Kant's Critical Philosophy: The Doctrine of the Faculties*, trans. H. Tomlinson and B. Habberjam, chap. 3; Renaut, A. (1999), *Kant aujourd'hui*, chap. 8.

8 Deleuze, G. (1990), *Expressionism in Philosophy: Spinoza*, trans. M. Joughin (New York: Zone Books), 312.

9 Leibniz, G. W.,'Insensible Perceptions,' in P. Remnant and J. Bennett (eds), *New Essays on Human Understanding* (Cambridge: Cambridge University Press, 1996); 'Lettre à la reine Sophie Charlotte du 8 mai, 1704,' in *Principes de la Nature et de la Grâce et autres textes* (Paris: Garnier-Flammarion, 1996), 79.

10 The following remark of Deleuze's *Negotiations*, 171 is rarely quoted: 'Unless we form a series—even an imaginary one—we will be entirely lost,' 171.

11 Deleuze, G. (1990), *Negotiations*, trans. M. Joughin (New York: Columbia University Press), 143.

12 Hénaff, M. (2001), *Le prix de la vérité* (Paris: Seuil).

13 Griaule, M. (1997), *Dieu d' eau* (Paris: Fayard).

14 Deleuze, G. and Guattari, F. (1982), *Anti-Oedipus: Capitalism and Schizophrenia*, trans. R. Hurley, M. Seem, and H. R. Lane (New York: Viking Press), 42.

15 These are, as we know, the three functions of God in Leibniz.

16 Notice what is both true and also caricatural in the title of Koyré's book (1962), Du *monde clos à l' univers infini* (Paris: Presses Universitaires de France).

Index